Light and Liberty

JEFFERSONIAN AMERICA

Jan Ellen Lewis, Peter S. Onuf, and Andrew O'Shaughnessy, Editors

Light & Liberty

Thomas Jefferson and the Power of Knowledge

EDITED BY

ROBERT M. S. MCDONALD

University of Virginia Press   Charlottesville and London

University of Virginia Press
© 2012 by the Rector and Visitors of the University of Virginia
All rights reserved
Printed in the United States of America on acid-free paper

First published 2012

1 3 5 7 9 8 6 4 2

Library of Congress Cataloging-in-Publication Data
Light and liberty : Thomas Jefferson and the power of knowledge / edited by
Robert M.S. McDonald.
   p.   cm. — (Jeffersonian America)
Includes bibliographical references and index.
ISBN 978-0-8139-3236-1 (cloth : alk. paper) — ISBN 978-0-8139-3237-8 (e-book)
   1. Jefferson, Thomas, 1743–1826—Political and social views. 2. Jefferson, Thomas, 1743–
1826—Knowledge and learning. 3. Jefferson, Thomas, 1743–1826—Influence. I. McDonald,
Robert M. S., 1970– II. Title: Thomas Jefferson and the power of knowledge.
   E332.2.L54 2012
   973.4'6092—dc23

2011022102

Light and liberty go together.

—Thomas Jefferson to Tench Coxe, 1 June 1795

Knowledge is power . . . knowledge is safety . . . knowledge is happiness.

—Thomas Jefferson to George Ticknor, 25 November 1817

Contents

FOREWORD

This volume contains revised and expanded versions of essays first delivered at a conference at the United States Military Academy at West Point on September 22 and 23, 2008, commemorating the opening of the academy's new library building, Thomas Jefferson Hall. Completed after ten years of planning and construction costs of $65 million—the first new academic building at the academy in thirty-six years—it occupies 148,000 square feet. By virtue of its location and bright lighting, the library is very prominent; the naming of the structure in honor of the third president of the United States, together with a life-size bronze statue of him on the first floor, gives renewed prominence to the historical association between the United States Military Academy and its founder, Thomas Jefferson.

Jefferson seems an unlikely progenitor of a military academy. He distrusted standing armies, preferring a citizen militia. He was acutely aware that, throughout history, military coups and army commanders posed the greatest danger to republics, and that the republic of ancient Rome by such means was brought under the tyranny of emperors. As president, Jefferson reduced the size of the army and navy, contributing to the inadequate state of defenses at the beginning of the War of 1812. His policies had an almost pacifist quality, as he sought to use means other than force in international affairs, most notoriously through the 1807 Embargo Act. He had an almost utopian belief that there could be permanent peace in a world of democratic republics united by trade.

Jefferson is rarely given much credit for his role in establishing the United States Military Academy. It is even argued that it served merely as a pretext to insinuate his own Republican supporters, displacing over time the Federalists who controlled the army. Robert McDonald, a member of the history department at West Point, and his wife, Christine, have convincingly argued otherwise, both in their essay in this volume and elsewhere. They demonstrate that Jefferson, who reviewed several proposals at the end of the Revolutionary War, was an early proponent of a military academy long before he became president. Indeed, he was initially much more interested in the concept than the more militaristic Alexander Hamilton. The need for a military academy was not self-evident. Britain did not have a military academy, other than the training provided for artillery officers at Woolwich. Jefferson wrote a detailed commentary on a proposal by Baron von Steuben, who would have been familiar with the academies in Prussia and continental Europe. Jefferson only briefly wavered in his enthusiasm when the Federalists were in power and Hamilton embraced the idea. As the McDonalds have demonstrated, Jefferson saw the military academy as a means to extend republican government into the West and "expand, explore, secure, and develop the frontier for liberty-loving Americans." Just as he later wanted the University of Virginia to have a modern curriculum, as opposed to what he regarded as an outmoded course of study at the College of William and Mary, he wanted the military academy to offer practical and useful subjects, like engineering, that would prove beneficial in developing the national infrastructure. Toward the end of his life, he affirmed that he had always regarded the military academy as "of major importance to our country."

The opening of Thomas Jefferson Hall has not only revived the institutional memory of Jefferson at West Point; it also occasioned collaboration with the Thomas Jefferson Foundation, which owns and operates Monticello, currently the only private home in the United States designated by the United Nations as a World Heritage Site. The Honorable John Charles Thomas, former justice of the Virginia Supreme Court—where he was the youngest person and the first African American to receive an appointment— and a current member of the Board of Trustees of the Thomas Jefferson Foundation, "worked quietly behind the scenes," in the words of Brigadier General Patrick Finnegan, Dean of the Academic Board at West Point, to ensure that the library was named after Thomas Jefferson. "Although Jefferson was imperfect," Thomas maintains, "he had a perfect idea that all men are created equal." When he spoke at the academy in November 2001, he had been surprised by the lack of a memorial to Jefferson. Thomas served as the driving force behind an initiative of the Thomas Jefferson Foundation to re-create Jefferson's Monticello study, which was funded by a former chairman of the foundation, Thomas A. Saunders III. Replicas of Jefferson's revolving chair, revolving table, lap desk, revolving bookstand, long chair, polygraph machine, riding boots, and side table now stand centrally located within the library. Following the formal opening ceremonies on September 24, there was a parade by the cadets, before the salute of the Thomas Jefferson Foundation's president, Dan Jordan, and its chairman, Alice Handy.

The "Light and Liberty" conference, subtitled "Thomas Jefferson and the Power of Knowledge," led to this volume and constituted yet another result of the collaboration between the United States Military Academy and Monticello. Cosponsored by the Robert H. Smith International Center for Jefferson Studies, the research and education institute of the Thomas Jefferson Foundation established in 1994 and renamed ten years later in recognition of a major gift by Mr. and Mrs. Robert H. Smith, the primary purpose of the center is to foster scholarship and disseminate knowledge about the life and times of Jefferson. Located on its own seventy-eight-acre estate opposite Monticello, the site includes the Jefferson Library, which, when it opened in 2002, became the first library dedicated to a Founding Father. The Smith International Center offers fellowships to scholars, both domestic and inter-national. It edits the retirement papers of Thomas Jefferson, which are pub-lished by Princeton University Press. It hosts conferences abroad, a visiting guest speaker program, and a regular seminar. It has archaeology and pub-lications departments. It sponsors courses for schoolteachers, continuing adult education, and educational programs for some 14,000 schoolchildren. It befittingly represents a major investment for a historic house in research and education.

It is a pleasure to acknowledge the role of Professor Robert McDonald in organizing the "Light and Liberty" conference. His research on the founding of the academy, in many ways, complements the naming of the library in giving greater ascendancy to Jefferson at West Point. As a member of the history faculty at the academy, he represents a personal link between the two institutions, having held a fellowship at the Smith International Center at Monticello, and having completed his undergraduate work at the University of Virginia. Indeed, he met his wife, and coauthor, at the Smith International Center! He and Christine were gracious hosts throughout the period of the conference. He arranged the transportation, meals, and accommodation of all the participants, the conference program, and the prior distribution of the papers to generate discussion between the speakers. He did much to ensure that the conference was widely attended by cadets, who are now much more aware of the legacy of Thomas Jefferson.

Andrew Jackson O'Shaughnessy
Saunders Director
Robert H. Smith International Center for Jefferson Studies

Acknowledgments

This volume traces its origins to a November 2007 conversation that began on the roof of Thomas Jefferson Hall, then an active construction site and now the library building at the United States Military Academy. Despite the hardhat on his head and the sheetrock stacked on the unfinished structure's unfinished floors, Colonel (Retired) Daniel Ragsdale, then West Point's vice dean for education, had the foresight to acknowledge that, all appearances aside, in less than a year Jefferson Hall would be ready for a series of events to celebrate the opening of its doors as well as the myriad means through which West Point works to educate and inspire cadets to embark on careers devoted to the defense of liberty. What better way to inaugurate the military academy's new library—named for the academy's founder—than to convene a group of scholars to consider Thomas Jefferson's multitudinous efforts to enlighten America's citizens and encourage them, in innumerable capacities, to embrace and advance his expansive vision for a free society?

Without Colonel Ragsdale's support, the September 22–23, 2008, conference from which this volume emerged would not have been possible. The enthusiastic encouragement of Brigadier General (Retired) Patrick Finnegan, then West Point's dean, and especially Colonels Lance Betros and Matthew Moten, who led the academy's Department of History during the conference's planning and execution, also proved crucial. Colonels Gian Gentile and Ty Seidule served as stalwart advocates, as did Lieutenant Colonel Gail Yoshitani, whose sincere interest in and support for the project helped to shepherd this collection toward publication. Majors Brian Dunn, Jeremy Finn, Matthew Hardman, Jeremy James, John Mini, Peter Rayls, Seanegan Sculley, William

Taylor, and Christian Teutsch, along with Frank Martini and James McNally, then a newly minted second lieutenant, proved West Point's history department to be a team of individuals no less gracious than generous. Deborah Monks, the history department's executive officer, deserves special thanks for her assistance. So do Vicky Kiernan and Patricia Higgins, who did their best to untangle frustrating thickets of government bureaucracy. Former cadets who now serve as army officers—such as Richard Houghton, Alexander Humes, Riley Lynch, Terence McElroy, Michael Monty, and Dylan Potter—impressed participants with their intelligence, hospitality, and eager assistance. West Point's alumni organization, the Association of Graduates, very generously provided the funding.

The leadership of Colonel Scott Krawczyk and Professor Elizabeth Samet, who oversaw an extensive program of events of which the conference was only one part, contributed mightily to the success of the library's opening. Caleb Cage, a West Point graduate and former American history major, and Major Greg Tomlin, then an army captain and future American history instructor, presented their Iraq War memoir, *The Gods of Diyala,* as one of the first volumes to join West Point's library in its new home. Their participation in Jefferson Hall's inaugural festivities imparted both gravity and abundant good cheer.

So did the involvement of the Thomas Jefferson Foundation, which owns and interprets Monticello. Members of Monticello's staff and Board of Trustees presented the foundation's gift to West Point—exacting replicas of Jefferson's suite of office furniture and personal effects now displayed on the library's main floor—made possible through the generosity of Thomas A. Saunders III. Monticello also helped to arrange for the dedication of Jefferson Hall the keynote address by former Virginia Supreme Court justice and Monticello trustee John Charles Thomas as well as the cosponsorship of the conference by the Robert H. Smith International Center for Jefferson Studies. The participation of the Thomas Jefferson Foundation underscored the bond between the executors of two great trusts inherited from Jefferson by the American people.

The efforts of the people associated with another fine Jeffersonian institution, the University of Virginia Press—particularly Richard Holway, Raennah Mitchell, Mark Mones, and the anonymous readers who shared careful and thoughtful critiques—proved crucial to the production of this collection of essays, which the authors dedicate to two individuals. The first, Daniel P.

Jordan, served as the president of the Thomas Jefferson Foundation for more than two decades during which its work to shed light on the world of a man described as an "apostle of liberty" gained impressive breadth and depth. Jefferson Hall's dedication, which Dan and his gracious wife, Lou, not only supported but also attended, marked the beginning of his concluding weeks at the helm of Monticello. Among the first of the contributors to this volume to suggest that it be dedicated in Dan's honor was Frank Shuffelton, a long-standing professor at the University of Rochester. His exhaustive bibliography of books and articles on Jefferson earned him renown as probably the only person to have read nearly everything ever written about America's third president. His other publications, whether on Jefferson or other topics relating to early America, earned him a reputation for penetrating insight and prudent scholarship. His generous capacity for friendship and mentorship earned him the affection of the many individuals who mourned his passing, including the coauthors, who dedicate their work to his memory.

Abbreviations

AHP	Harold C. Syrett and Jacob E. Cooke, eds. *The Papers of Alexander Hamilton.* 27 vols. New York, 1961–87.
AJL	Lester J. Cappon, ed. *The Adams-Jefferson Letters: The Complete Correspondence between Thomas Jefferson and Abigail and John Adams.* Chapel Hill, N.C., 1959.
Ford	Paul Leicester Ford, ed. *The Writings of Thomas Jefferson.* 10 vols. New York, 1892–99.
JER	*Journal of the Early Republic*
L&B	Andrew A. Lipscomb and Albert Ellery Bergh, eds. *The Writings of Thomas Jefferson.* 20 vols. Washington, D.C., 1903–4.
Lib. Cong.	Library of Congress, Washington, D.C.
TJ	Thomas Jefferson
TJP	Julian P. Boyd et al., eds. *The Papers of Thomas Jefferson.* 36 vols. to date. Princeton, N.J., 1950–.
TJP:RS	J. Jefferson Looney, ed. *The Papers of Thomas Jefferson: Retirement Series.* 6 vols. to date. Princeton, N.J., 2004–.
TJW	Merrill D. Peterson, ed. *Thomas Jefferson: Writings.* New York, 1984.
WMQ	William and Mary Quarterly

Light and Liberty

Introduction

T HOMAS JEFFERSON BELIEVED THAT "LIGHT AND LIBERTY GO TO-
gether." He affirmed that "no one more sincerely wishes the spread of
information among mankind than I do" because no one had "greater confidence in its effect towards supporting free and good government." He also
warned that "if a nation expects to be ignorant and free, in a state of civilization, it expects what never was and never will be." He understood that "even
under the best forms" of government, "those entrusted with power have, in
time, and by slow operations, perverted it into tyranny." Illuminating "the
minds of the people," he thought, constituted "the most effectual means of
preventing" such an occurrence. Societies already suffering from subjugation
needed only to "enlighten the people generally, and tyranny and oppressions
of body and mind will vanish like spirits at the dawn of day." Jefferson viewed
knowledge as the foundation of a republic of free and responsible individuals
who both understood their rights and stood ready to defend them. Throughout his career he promoted the education of his countrymen, never wavering
from his faith "that kno[w]le[d]ge is power, that kno[w]le[d]ge is safety, and
that kno[w]le[d]ge is happiness."[1]

Yet Jefferson, who voiced real optimism about the efficacy of enlightenment, nonetheless made palpable his anxiety about Americans' capacity for
the government of themselves and others. He was not alone. At the start of
the American Revolution, Alexander Hamilton dismissed "the multitude,

who have not a sufficient stock of reason and knowledge to guide them." John Adams, in 1815 surveying the wreckage of the French Revolution, asked if "the Nineteenth Century [is] to be a Contrast to the Eighteenth? Is it to extinguish all the Lights of its Predecessor?" At the time Jefferson held out hope that "altho' your prophecy has proved true so far . . . it does not preclude a better final result." Whatever and wherever the threat to liberty, the "light from our West seems to have spread and illuminated the very engines employed to extinguish it." Yet his optimism wavered. Ten years later, after the Missouri Crisis and the splintering of the Jeffersonian Republicans (and Jeffersonian republicanism) made manifest by the election of 1824, he informed another friend that he felt "left alone amidst a new generation whom we know not, and who know not us."[2]

As historian Drew McCoy has noted, "it was commonly assumed in Revolutionary America that a republican form of government was particu-larly precarious because it could succeed only in an extraordinary society of distinctively moral people." Adams, for example, contended that "there is so much Rascality, so much Venality and Corruption, so much Avarice and Ambition . . . among all Ranks and Degrees of Men even in America, that I sometimes doubt whether there is public Virtue enough to support a Re-public." At the conclusion of the Constitutional Convention, a woman re-portedly asked Benjamin Franklin whether America would have a monarchy or a republic. "A republic," he replied, but only "if you can keep it."[3]

Representative government was not an end in and of itself. It was a means to an end greater than itself. Liberty—the right of individuals to make what-ever choices and assume whatever risks they wished that did not trample on the rights of others—constituted the principal aim of government. Jefferson penned three drafts of the address that he delivered at his inauguration in March 1801. Despite all his editing, one set of lines remained largely un-changed: Although "the will of the majority is in all cases to prevail, that will, to be rightful, must be reasonable." No majority could deny with legitimacy that "the minority possess their equal rights."[4]

How best to tame the mass of the people and prevent what Alexis de Tocqueville would later describe as "the tyranny of the majority"? In the first decades following America's War for Independence, education was merely one of the answers. Instead of reading, writing, and arithmetic, many looked toward religion, which the 1780 Massachusetts constitution described as so essential to "good order and [the] preservation of civil government" that it authorized local officials to "make suitable provision . . . for the institution of the public worship of GOD, and for the support and maintenance of public protestant teachers of piety, religion and morality, in all cases where such provision shall not be made voluntarily." Jefferson considered this wrong-headed, mostly because he objected to the means through which Massachusetts sought to promote morality. Its leaders' goal, however, he shared. In Virginia, he and James Madison led a frontal assault on the church establishment that resulted in the 1786 passage of the Virginia Statute for Religious Freedom. "Almighty God hath created the mind free," Jefferson's bill proclaimed. It only made sense that "all attempts to influence it by temporal punishments, or burthens, or by civil incapacitations, tend only to beget habits of hypocrisy and meanness, and are a departure from the plan of the holy author of our religion." Citizens had less to fear from those with whom they disagreed than they did from those who would use the force of law to compel agreement. "Truth is great," he wrote, "and will prevail if left to herself."[5]

Jefferson, of course, believed that instead of an "Empire of Laws" (the America to which Adams aspired), the United States should constitute an "Empire of Liberty." Curing the nation's ethical ills required medicine from the government less than it did the strengthening of society. For him, no better citizens existed than farmers. He wrote that "those who labour in the earth are the chosen people of God" in no small part because the "corruption of morals in the mass of cultivators is a phenomenon of which no age nor nation has furnished an example." Men who worked their own land were independent, industrious, self-sufficient, disinterested, protective of their rights, and attentive to their communities. Farmers, however, needed acreage. The wishful thinking expressed in his inaugural address—that America possessed "room enough for our descendents to the thousandth & thousandth generation"—ignored the fact that America's population nearly doubled every twenty years. The purchase of the Louisiana Territory not only doubled the size of the United States but also, Jefferson understood, America's lifespan as an agrarian republic.[6]

His admiration of middling farmers resulted not only from the qualities that rendered them fit for republican citizenship but also from their republican manners. The habits and tastes of Americans, he thought, mattered greatly. In the spring of 1800, he predicted with confidence that "the great body of the people" would rebuke his Federalist opponents, whose "madness

& extravagance"—whose liveried coaches and regal levees—would serve to alienate "people through all the states" who embraced not only "republican forms, republican principles" and "religious & civil freedom" but also "economy" and "simplicity." Less than a year later, when Jefferson broke with tradition by walking to his inauguration, his prediction rang true. He set out to change the culture of American politics. Handshakes replaced courtly bows. At presidential dinners, round tables with unassigned seating displaced the rectangular tables—with "high" and "low" ends—of his predecessors. The mouths of visitors to the Executive Mansion fell open when, to their amazement, Jefferson answered his own door—at least once, reportedly, with slippers on his feet. America's political culture should reflect republican sensibilities, he thought, and not absorb the residue of an aristocratic era whose time had passed.[7]

Whether acting as a cultural exemplar, a cultivator of citizens, a liberator from oppression, or an educator of his countrymen, Jefferson felt more at ease than when serving in a position of command. As president, of course, he commanded America's military, but in his eyes the role of soldiers and sailors was not to oppress the people but to protect the people from oppression. When a French dignitary present at a military parade expressed surprise that, as commander-in-chief, he wore civilian clothes and not some sort of uniform, Jefferson explained that his attire underscored his belief that "the civil is superior to the military power." No wonder the Frenchman later reported to Napoleon that, in America, government was "neither seen [n]or felt."[8]

A government that was nearly invisible and undetectable stood as one of Jefferson's greatest aspirations. His greatest fantasy was that Americans would hardly require government at all. He saw government as inherently collective and coercive, as fundamentally hostile to individuals and their freedoms. In his eyes it should protect liberty but more often than not served as freedom's greatest threat. Especially worrisome was that "the natural progress of things is for liberty to yield, and government to gain ground." Jefferson worked to turn back the tide, to use the governments of his state and his nation to bolster Americans' capacities for individual self-government. Political power, he believed, possessed its greatest legitimacy when it empowered citizens.[9]

This volume focuses on some of Jefferson's most "Jeffersonian" contributions to the founding generation's rich discussion about the most efficacious means to bring about the most American of ends. How best to enlighten the people? How best to liberate them from the ignorance and vice that had corroded and corrupted once-great civilizations? How best to sustain the virtues and values that would perpetuate the American republic? How to do all of this while still maintaining what Jefferson described as a "wise and frugal government, which shall restrain men from injuring one another" while leaving "them otherwise free to regulate their own pursuits of industry and improvement, and . . . not take from the mouth of labor the bread it has earned"?[10]

These questions could have inspired any number of essays on any number of topics. In addition to the important themes considered within these pages, it is not difficult to imagine writers focusing on Jefferson's thoughts about the education of Native Americans or African Americans, his views on the education of women, his efforts to school his own children and grand-children, how his reformation of presidential etiquette and entertaining imparted to his countrymen a new model of republican simplicity, and the ways in which he used his presidential addresses to inform citizens of the new republic how best to behave as new republican citizens. Yet even with the inclusion of these subjects, this volume could never represent more than a partial treatment of Jefferson's larger project to turn into Jeffersonians subsequent generations of Americans. This volume, in other words, is of necessity selective. While Jefferson imposed no limits on his own influence, here we must limit our coverage of it—hopeful nonetheless that the topics selected are more broadly suggestive.

Brian Steele's essay, which constitutes the volume's first chapter, stands out as the most broad and suggestive of all. When Jefferson grappled with the daunting question of how best to equip America for responsible self-government he took solace in the belief that the United States enjoyed particular advantages that rendered its people singularly well positioned to govern themselves. Unlike the "*canaille* of Paris," who had been disabled by centuries of political and ecclesiastical oppression, the free citizens of the United States enjoyed a sound "sociological foundation" upon which to build a republic. What most limited the prospects for free government in Europe, Jefferson believed, were European people, whose opinions had been "nourished in error, and vitiated and debased . . . by ignorance, indulgence and oppression." In America, however, the people enjoyed "in ease and security the full fruits of their own industry." They were "enlisted by all their interests on the side of law and order, habituated to think for themselves, and to follow their reason as their guide." In 1786 and 1787, when news of Shays's Rebellion in central and western Massachusetts sent his peers into a panic, Jefferson felt reassured by both the willingness of the rebels to resist what they considered tyrannical measures and the good sense of others, who not only rallied under the standard of law and order to put down the uprising but also treated with mercy nearly all of its misguided participants. The people stood willing not only to defend their rights but also their representative government.[11]

Jefferson, according to Steele, ascribed to several different factors the American success story. There was the meritocratic, egalitarian nature of America's "natural aristocracy." There was the willingness of Americans to ensure that all of their fellow citizens had at least the basic tools necessary to govern themselves and contribute to the marketplace of ideas. There was also an understanding that toleration for people of different faiths and acceptance of religious diversity stood the best chance of advancing both faith and reason.

Yet the advantages enjoyed by Americans were not enough, Johann Neem maintains, to assure Jefferson that they could enjoy the happiness that they had a right to pursue. Neem is brave enough to tackle the difficult question of how Jefferson, who favored such a narrow conception of government, could on the state level advocate the forcible confiscation from the mouths of Virginians the fruits of hard-earned labors to fund a broad-based system of education. One of the primary tasks of government, after all, was to protect individuals' right to their property. When president, moreover, Jefferson's reading of the Constitution as a contract limiting federal power caused him to channel his desire for a national university, which he believed required the sanction of a constitutional amendment, through a national military academy.[12]

Neem makes a bold argument that Jefferson embraced a more expansive view of government within Virginia because he also embraced a more expansive view of individual rights. "What use was it to be born free," Neem asks, if Americans lacked the education "to make the most of freedom" and "engage in their own pursuits of happiness"? The question was especially vexing in an agricultural economy in which people counted wealth in acres and slaves more often than in dollars. Although cash economies facilitate fluid exchange and more rapid social mobility, landed ones favored the consolidation of acreage and human capital in the hands of the well-born. This held true even in America—even after the purchase of Louisiana—before the development of canals, steamboats, and railroads opened areas beyond navigable rivers to commercial agriculture. When the goal was meritocracy, Jefferson enthused, "legislators cannot invent too many devices for subdividing property."[13]

Jefferson, Neem suggests, drew a line between the fruit of one's labors and the land on which the fruit took root. While the first stood sacrosanct, the second, as Jefferson wrote, men had divided up "for the encouragement of industry." If "there are in any country, uncultivated lands and unemployed poor," then "it is clear that the laws of property have been so far extended as to violate natural right." He stopped short of applying that description to Virginia, but he had no problem repealing his state's primogeniture law, which from the earliest times had passed along to eldest sons all the property of fathers who died without having drawn up wills. (Under Jefferson's 1785 law, the land of an intestate property-holder divided equally among all his children and his wife.) This constituted a simple enough tactic; it broke up estates without curtailing property rights. But Jefferson also had no problem levying taxes on landholders in order to support his proposed system of education because, Neem suggests, an "inherited aristocracy of knowledge fundamentally threatened individual liberty." By working for broader access to education, in other words, Jefferson hoped to extend to ever more citizens the opportunities that knowledge made possible.[14]

Richard Samuelson's essay both complements and complicates Neem's interpretation. Each recognizes Jefferson's attempt to unleash a natural aristocracy capable of challenging the old order of birth and inherited wealth. Although Neem focuses on Jefferson's thoughts about the right of individuals to rise according to their merit, Samuelson concentrates on Jefferson's parallel concern for the good of society. Samuelson, moreover, cares less about Jefferson's opinions than how he formulated them—a difference, perhaps, that helps to explain how his interpretation is distinct from Neem's. Neem looks for uplift while Samuelson focuses on filtering mechanisms: A progressive system of education, Jefferson noted, would ensure that "the best geniuses will be raked from the rubbish annually." They would rise within their communities to positions of influence, leading their fellow citizens to choose men of real merit and character as representatives. This, according to Samuelson, amounted to an imperfect but nonetheless important device enabling voters, at election time, to divide "the aristoi from the pseudo-aristoi" and "the wheat from the chaff." If for Neem Jefferson's proposed system of education aimed to empower citizens to build satisfying lives, for Samuelson it aimed to enable them to choose wisely their leaders.[15]

As Samuelson is quick to point out, these interpretations are not mutually exclusive. Jefferson, in his view, had "greater hopes" than John Adams, who plays a major supporting role in his essay, "that the common man could be raised up." Education would make it possible for "ordinary Americans both to live as free and independent citizens and, at the same time, to recognize true worth and vote it into office." According to Samuelson, Jefferson envisioned these enlightened people acting not only as voters and filters but also as leaders, for when "worth and genius" had "been sought out from every condition of life" and "prepared by education for defeating the competition of wealth and birth," members of the public could safely assume "public trusts." They could not only elect their supposed superiors but also attain the level of superiority that would earn for them their fellow citizens' votes.

If the essays by Steele, Neem, and Samuelson can be said to address *why* Jefferson looked to education to more firmly tether America's ship of state, then the essays by Cameron Addis, Christine Coalwell McDonald and me, Frank Shuffelton, Craig Reynolds, and Gaye Wilson focus on *how* he hoped to enlighten his countrymen. Addis's chapter, for example, makes clear that, for Jefferson, education was not indoctrination. In a land where every institution of higher learning was merely a college, Jefferson sought to create an actual university with a curriculum that was "broad and liberal and *modern.*" In a country where colleges advanced the teachings of particular religious denominations, he instead insisted on an institution based on the more ecumenical goals of "peace, reason and morality."[16]

This, Addis points out, aimed to level the intellectual playing field and create a free marketplace for ideas, but it also invited more than its fair share of controversy. Presbyterian clergyman John Holt Rice, for example, led a populist campaign that characterized the University of Virginia as a cradle of "infidelity" because of its secular origins. Jefferson, meanwhile, described it as a school promoting principles that "all sects could agree on" based, as Addis describes them, on "a universal constellation of values." Maybe that was the problem. Institutions made no one happy when they tried to please everyone; they became so inoffensive that their apparent lack of conviction offended all. Jefferson displayed a highly uncommon capacity for open-mindedness when he encouraged his nephew to examine with skepticism the existence of God. Even in religion free enquiry should trump faith, for this was God's plan. "Your own reason," Jefferson insisted, "is the only oracle given you by heaven." Who else would have given such advice?[17]

The freewheeling spirit of open-minded inquiry at Jefferson's university was not without limit, nor did it always yield the desired results. Political realities forced Jefferson to compromise his vision at the same time that cultural changes—ones, Addis points out, that "the free religious market that he helped to create" both reflected and reinforced—complicated the attainment of his goals. It is true that Jefferson's university, which featured as its most prominent building a library and not a chapel, taught classics, philosophy, and chemistry to future religious leaders such as Baptist James B. Taylor, who later planted the roots of the University of Richmond. Yet it is also true that religious leaders co-opted Jefferson's university. An Episcopal minister, S. H. Tyng, in 1840 found great success at a university that he believed had been established in "direct and designed hostility to Christianity." The students to whom he preached stood out as the "most attentive and interested" audience of his career.

Not all seemed so angelic. In marked contrast to the visions of both Jefferson and his detractors stood University of Virginia students who exemplified habits neither scholarly nor pious. In particular, there were the drunkards who hurled bottles of urine through their professors' windows and sank a corpse from the medical school in the pond that served as the water supply. There was even Jefferson's great-great-grandnephew, whom the university expelled for his work as the ringleader of student disturbances.

At the United States Military Academy, Jefferson's other school, things went more according to plan—especially if Jefferson intended to create an institution that would educate and train future army officers to chart, conquer, and open up for settlement the American West. As Christine Coalwell McDonald and I explain, this was the outcome of Jefferson's efforts in behalf of West Point. Scholars have made much of the apparent paradox that Jefferson first opposed and then championed a national school for the training of military officers. In the 1790s, when Alexander Hamilton called for the establishment of such an academy, Jefferson argued that the Constitution gave the national government no such power. Yet only weeks after his inauguration Jefferson directed Henry Dearborn, his secretary of war, to set plans in motion to establish a military academy at West Point. Given what we know about

Jefferson's understanding of the Constitution, it seems likely that his earlier opposition reflected not a sincere belief that an academy would violate the national government's charter but instead a sincere fear that a Hamiltonian academy would undermine the nation's character.[18]

At the heart of Jefferson's feud with Hamilton were their differing visions for the future of America. Hamilton wanted the United States to grow into a commercial empire not unlike Great Britain. Jefferson, meanwhile, envisioned an "empire of liberty" the likes of which the world had never seen. He looked not east with a plan to imitate but west toward the vast expanse of land on which he hoped independent-minded Americans would create an egalitarian society of self-governing individuals. In this campaign West Point and its graduates played a pivotal role.

Jefferson, who affirmed late in life that he had always considered West Point to be of "major importance to our country," never declared specifically what he hoped the institution would achieve. In recent years, scholars have done their best to connect the dots to suggest either that Jefferson aimed to use West Point to republicanize the army or, in a manner consistent with the Constitution, use the national government to promote education.[19] Christine McDonald and I find persuasive both of these interpretations, especially since each served Jefferson's larger vision for a transcontinental republic united by informed consent. This, we propose, amounted to Jefferson's ultimate ambition for the institution. Certainly the early military academy possessed a decidedly western character. The curriculum, the research interests of the faculty, and the geographical composition of the student body—all of which took shape not only with Jefferson's blessing but also as a result of his input—suggest that he viewed West Point as means to shape a westward-looking army prepared to expand the frontiers of a nation eager to turn its back on the wars, corruption, and ignorance of aristocratic Europe.

Yet Jefferson had no desire for Americans to turn their backs on Europe altogether. Instead, as Frank Shuffelton's essay points out, Jefferson served as a conduit of information for "an extended body of friends and associates" hailing from throughout "the transatlantic world." Since published works, together with letters, served as his primary medium of intellectual exchange, Shuffelton describes him as the Enlightenment's "colporteur"—a term in vogue at the time for itinerant retailers of books. As Shuffelton demonstrates, the label fits, for wherever the peripatetic bibliophile found himself—Paris, Philadelphia, Monticello, or elsewhere—he displayed not only a "canine appetite" for acquiring books but also an assiduous desire to loan them out, recommend their purchase to others, and summarize their findings in missives addressed to correspondents in both Europe and America.[20]

If Jefferson hoped to use West Point to help establish a republican "empire of liberty," then through his network of literary associates he helped to establish a republic of letters. As in nearly all of his educational endeavors, he aimed not only to advance knowledge but also to buttress a broad political agenda. As Shuffelton maintains, Jefferson's "Enlightenment colportage . . . was ultimately an act of patriotism that would be no simple matter of one-way traffic across the Atlantic." Instead, it served as "a mutually enriching process," for "Jefferson was interested in importing the latest European thinking to America" no less than he was "interested in exporting American knowledge to Europe."

He was not, however, indiscriminate in his interests. Jefferson worked more as a filter than a funnel, directing toward friends texts reflecting his somewhat idealized conception of the world and how it should be. Through his many correspondents, he indulged most fully his desire for a community where reason was king and slavery existed not as a physical condition but instead as a state of ignorance best battled by the propagation of truth. This is not to say that Jefferson and his epistolary network ignored the real-world problems of corruption and coercion; it is that the means of exchange provided Jefferson with greater opportunities to frame debates, define his terms, and choose his battles. Through his *Notes on the State of Virginia* and other projects, he labored to correct Europeans' misperceptions about America, insisting "on the progressive quality of American life, on the general improvement of conditions for ordinary people." As Shuffelton points out, "his observations, concerned with getting right the details of present-day America, also conveyed a strong sense of what America might become, of its true character as a land that would make good on its promising beginnings." His partisanship toward America led him oftentimes to see Europe's glass half empty—to maintain that immersion in European society could lead astray all but the most "fully-formed" American republicans—but he believed nonetheless that books from France, England, and Italy had much to teach his new nation's inhabitants. By making available to his countrymen the most edifying productions of European science and literature, he enabled them to enjoy the best of both worlds. Young Americans could bask in the salubrious moral climate of their own society while reading, for example, *Don Quixote* and other European novels presenting instructive examples of good and bad behavior "to fix . . . the principles and practices of virtue."

Jefferson worked to provide Americans with uplifting models not only through literature but also through architecture. As Craig Reynolds suggests, he viewed the built environment as an important component of the sociology of liberty. Here also he trained his eye across the Atlantic for works worthy of emulation, and here again his tastes were selective. He spurned as unenlightened Europe's gothic structures, which aimed to intimidate and dumbfound, as well as that continent's versions of the "rude, misshapen piles" of brick and mortar that marred the streets of Williamsburg. Instead, he favored buildings that presented examples of natural proportion, symmetry, and timelessness. His design for the Virginia State Capitol drew inspiration from the Maison Carrée at Nîmes, the University of Virginia's Rotunda echoed Rome's Pantheon, and at Monticello he borrowed design elements from the Imperial Baths of Diocletian. The only practicable way to cultivate Americans' appreciation for the "beautiful art" of architecture, Jefferson informed Madison, was to present them with worthy "models for . . . study and imitation."[21]

Yet Jefferson aimed to shape more than his countrymen's tastes. By seeking to transform the architectural environment of his state and, by extension, the entire nation, Jefferson sought to provide fellow citizens with a new context within which to conceptualize relations between individuals and their governments. Reynolds posits that Jefferson sought to create "for the populace a tangible representation of the abstract Enlightenment principles that formed the basis of American liberty." To achieve this end he designed not only buildings of great prominence but also provided a plan for courthouses. "Seen and used most frequently by common citizens," Jefferson's prescriptions for courthouse design may have had the most widespread influence of all of his efforts—at least during the first half of the nineteenth century, when most were built, and before his designs for Monticello, the University of Virginia, and the Virginia State Capitol gained international critical acclaim. Given that Jefferson appears to have drawn only one generic design for a courthouse, the dozens of public buildings that resulted—which Reynolds demonstrates "served as monuments to openness and transparency, justice and just proportions, and the egalitarian belief that easily-accessible and inexpensive materials could contribute to the construction of buildings both solid and . . . built for the ages"—apparently resulted from not only the appeal of Jefferson's plan but also a masterfully leveraged campaign to disseminate it.

As Reynolds points out, Jefferson's design combined an interior arrangement long customary in Virginia courthouses with a radically new exterior. Instead of a bell tower, Jefferson's courthouse featured a pediment supported by four two-story columns. Instead of wood clapboards, his plan called for red brick. Generous provision of windows to let in light and air, together with an exterior portico that functioned both as an outdoor room and inviting entrance, emphasized transparency and accessibility. The scheme, Reynolds writes, amounted to "light and liberty expressed in masonry form." Just as Jefferson hoped that his university would send forth scholars to spread useful knowledge, craftsmen responsible for its construction continued their careers by applying to new projects expertise gained under its founder's tutelage. One of them, Dabney Cosby, probably helped to build three county courthouses and in the process influenced other craftsmen who participated in the construction of many more. All of these buildings conformed to the essential elements of Jefferson's original plan.

Gaye Wilson's essay, "Recording History," also highlights Jefferson's efforts to educate Americans by providing them with a model that he considered worthy of emulation. In this instance, however, he was the model. In 1821, when the faculty and cadets at the United States Military Academy commissioned Thomas Sully to complete a full-length portrait of their institution's founder, the artist spent over a week at Monticello. There he completed a head-and-shoulders portrait and sketched studies for the final version that he delivered to West Point in 1822. Undoubtedly the two men, whose interests overlapped, enjoyed conversations on a wide range of topics. Wilson provides plenty of evidence suggesting that one of them was Jefferson's vision for how Sully should depict him. Certainly Sully's final rendering, which presented Jefferson as an exemplar of republican simplicity, reflected how Jefferson imagined and portrayed himself.

Whatever the influence of Sully's subject, Wilson's sensitive and exhaustive account of the portrait makes clear that the Philadelphia artist served no less effectively than Dabney Cosby as a purveyor of Jeffersonian sensibilities. Unlike Sully's initial study for the full-length portrait, which pictured Jefferson grasping a sheaf of papers while perched above a crowd, the simplified painting delivered to West Point suggests restraint and self-effacement more than the stoking of democratic passion. In this final version Jefferson stands alone holding a single scroll. The cut of his plain black suit—a symbol of the common man—dates to the years of his presidency. His fur-lined coat, quite possibly the one he obtained from Thaddeus Kosciuszko, linked him with the Polish republican whose services to the United States included the design of fortifications at West Point during the American Revolution. Even his footwear, which featured simple laces rather than aristocratic buckles, scored points for republicanism. Sully painted a beam of light illuminating first Jefferson's face, then the document in his hand, and finally the base of a column towering next to him. As Wilson demonstrates, the distinctive marble column situates Jefferson neither at Monticello, nor the Executive Mansion, nor in the Senate where, during the administration of John Adams, he presided. Instead, the column anchors Jefferson in the original chamber of the House of Representatives, the people's assembly. What an appropriate way to portray a man of the Enlightenment, an individual who conceived important documents illuminating important principles that, in important ways, liberated so many Americans.

Taken together, the essays contained in this volume add context and detail to what we know about Jefferson's efforts to enlighten fellow citizens. They break new ground regarding his motivations for encouraging the dissemination of information as well as the means that he employed to achieve his goals. They do not, however, supplant the efforts of Jennings Wagoner, the doyen of scholars on Jefferson and education, to provide a definitive overview of Jefferson's institutional efforts to propagate knowledge. They also provide no competition for Philip Alexander Bruce's magisterial history of the University of Virginia, Cameron Addis's impressive study of the university's founding and early decades, or recent efforts to examine the origins of Jefferson's military academy at West Point. They do not even constitute an answer to James Gilreath's 1999 *Thomas Jefferson and the Education of a Citizen,* a large and diffuse collection of diverse essays that examine not only Jefferson's efforts to educate voters but also his views on slavery, women, relations with Native Americans, and other topics not closely related to the enlightenment of men formally included within the political process.[22]

As Joyce Appleby points out in this volume's afterword, the limitations of

Jefferson's vision still matter and his views on race, slavery, and gender continue to merit careful consideration. Yet this study aims less to point out what he did not do or did not think than what he actually accomplished or contemplated. The cumulative effect of the essays in this volume is to highlight the fact that Jefferson worked to propagate knowledge in different ways to serve different but related purposes, all of which connected to his vision for a fairer, freer, more democratic America populated by citizens more capable of individual self-government.

As several of the essays suggest, however, Jefferson sought to achieve these Jeffersonian goals by employing Jeffersonian tactics. Although his ends were luminescent, shadows often obscured his means. Never comfortable with direct confrontation and power politics, Jefferson felt more at ease when engaging in the soft diplomacy of dinner parties with carefully managed guest lists and artfully written personal letters that asked leading questions and offered false confidences. "Take things always by the smooth handle," he advised on more than one occasion. When the situation called for hostility, he preferred to work through others. In 1793, for example, he called upon Madison to write newspaper essays taking Hamilton to task: "For god's sake, my dear Sir, take up your pen, select the most striking heresies, and cut him to pieces in the face of the public." Reinforcing this picture of an indirect, manipulative Jefferson are the final five chapters in this volume, which hint that, if Jefferson really believed that "tyranny and oppressions of body and mind will vanish like spirits at the dawn of day," as he told P. S. Du Pont de Nemours, when efforts took effect to "enlighten the people generally," then he also understood that targeted campaigns, designed to educate specific people in specific ways, promised an even greater potential to have an impact.[23]

If these essays suggest an irony, it is that Jefferson struggled mightily to construct an America so Jeffersonian that it could get on just fine without him. This was why he campaigned for the expansion of educational opportunity, established the University of Virginia as an institution liberated from ecclesiastical prejudices, created the United States Military Academy to liberate the nation from a European future, served as a switchboard for knowledge passing between correspondents on either side of the Atlantic, and presented to his countrymen sturdy models of republican restraint. "*The earth,*" he told Madison, "*belongs . . . to the living,*" but even after he passed from it, he took care to ensure that his ideals lived on.[24]

At some point during his final year, he wrote out instructions for his tombstone and epitaph, a monument that to his spirit would be "the most gratifying." For the grave he prescribed "a plain die or cube . . . surmounted by an Obelisk" bearing "the following inscription, & not a word more":

Here was buried

Thomas Jefferson

Author of the Declaration of American Independence

of the Statute of Virginia for religious freedom

& Father of the University of Virginia.

He affirmed that "by these, as testimonials that I have lived, I wish most to be remembered."[25] He might also have listed his posts as legislator, governor, minister to France, secretary of state, vice-president, and president of the United States, but he understood that his fame rested on his reputation as a liberator of body, soul, and mind. His real greatness, he wanted posterity to understand, came not from the power that men had given to him, but from the power that he had given to men.

While the text of the epitaph evoked his lifelong struggle for liberty, the obelisk on which he wanted it inscribed—a literal subtext—denoted light. Herodotus's *History,* frequently recommended by Jefferson to others, associates obelisks with the sun. So does the elder Pliny's *Natural History,* which he kept in his library. It describes the obelisk as a form developed by the ancient Egyptians, symbolizing "the Sun's rays" and oftentimes bearing hieroglyphic accounts "of natural science according to the theories of the Egyptian sages." Jefferson also owned a copy of Vivant Denon's *Travels in Upper and Lower Egypt,* which suggests that rulers of the region's lost civilization used obelisks as signposts "to make certain things known to their subjects for their common good."[26]

How fitting that the monument marking Jefferson's final resting place reinforced his lifelong contention that education led to liberation. Light *did* lead to liberty, both by empowering individuals and strengthening the social fabric. It could emanate from institutions of learning, refract from one person to another, or reflect from works of philosophy, literature, architecture, or art. It could shine through the collective efforts of citizens working together or through their governments or as a result of the singular actions of one self-governing individual.

Notes

1. TJ to Tench Coxe, 1 June 1795, *TJP*, 28:373; TJ to Hugh L. White and others, 6 May 1810, *TJW*, 1222; TJ to Charles Yancey, 6 January 1816, Ford, 10:4; TJ, A Bill for the More General Diffusion of Knowledge, [1778], *TJP*, 2:526; TJ to P. S. Du Pont de Nemours, 24 April 1816, *TJW*, 1387; TJ to George Ticknor, 25 November 1817, Ford, 10:96.

2. Alexander Hamilton to John Jay, 26 November 1775, *AHP*, 1:176–77; John Adams to TJ, 13 November 1815, *AJL*, 456; TJ to Adams, 11 January 1816, ibid., 459; TJ to Francis A. van der Kemp, 11 January 1825, TJ Papers, Lib. Cong.

3. Drew R. McCoy, *The Elusive Republic: Political Economy in Jeffersonian America* (Chapel Hill, N.C., 1980), 5; John Adams to Mercy Warren, 8 January 1776, in *Warren-Adams Letters, Being Chiefly a Correspondence among John Adams, and John Warren, 1743–1814*, 2 vols., ed. Worthington Chauncey Ford (Boston, 1917–25), 1:202; Benjamin Franklin, quoted in "Papers of Dr. James McHenry on the Federal Convention of 1787," *American Historical Review* 11 (1906): 618.

4. TJ, First Inaugural Address, 4 March 1801, *TJP*, 33:139, 144, 149.

5. Massachusetts Constitution, 2 March 1780, in *The Founders' Constitution*, ed. Philip B. Kurland and Ralph Lerner (Indianapolis, Ind., 1987), 1:12; TJ, A Bill for Establishing Religious Freedom, [1779–86], *TJP*, 2:545–46.

6. TJ, *Notes on the State of Virginia*, ed. William Peden (Chapel Hill, N.C., 1954), 164–65; TJ, First Inaugural Address, 4 March 1801, *TJP*, 33:145.

7. TJ to Edward Livingston, 30 April 1800, *TJP*, 31:546–47; Joyce Appleby, "Thomas Jefferson and the Psychology of Democracy," in *The Revolution of 1800: Democracy, Race, and the New Republic*, ed. James Horn, Jan Ellen Lewis, and Peter S. Onuf (Charlottesville, Va., 2002), 155–71. See also Robert R. Davis Jr., "Pell-Mell: Jeffersonian Etiquette and Protocol," *The Historian* 43 (1981): 509–29.

8. Margaret Bayard Smith, *The First Forty Years of Washington Society*, ed. Gaillard Hunt (New York, 1906), 397.

9. TJ to Edward Carrington, 27 May 1788, *TJP*, 13:208–9.

10. TJ, First Inaugural Address, 4 March 1801, ibid., 33:150.

11. TJ to William Johnson, 12 June 1823, L&B, 15:441–42.

12. See David N. Mayer, " 'Necessary and Proper': West Point and Jefferson's Constitutionalism," in *Thomas Jefferson's Military Academy: Founding West Point*, ed. Robert M. S. McDonald (Charlottesville, Va., 2004), 67–68; Jennings L. Wagoner Jr. and Christine Coalwell McDonald, "Mr. Jefferson's Academy: An Educational Interpretation," in ibid., 118–53.

13. TJ to James Madison, 28 October 1785, *TJP*, 8:682.

14. Ibid.; Holly Brewer, "Entailing Aristocracy in Colonial Virginia: 'Ancient Feudal Restraints' and Revolutionary Reform," *WMQ* (1997): 315.

15. TJ, *Notes on the State of Virginia*, in *TJW*, 272; TJ to John Adams, 28 October 1813, *AJL*, 388.

16. TJ to Joseph Priestley, 18 January 1800, *TJP*, 31:320.

17. TJ to Peter Carr, 10 August 1787, ibid., 12:15–17.

18. Mayer, "Necessary and Proper," 54–76.

19. TJ to Jared Mansfield, 13 February 1821, TJ Papers, Lib. Cong.; Theodore J. Crackel, "The Founding of West Point: Jefferson and the Politics of Security," *Armed Forces & Society* 7 (Summer 1981): 529–43; Wagoner and McDonald, "Mr. Jefferson's Academy," 118–53.

20. TJ to John Adams, 17 May 1818, *AJL*, 524.

21. TJ to Madison, 20 September 1785, *TJP*, 8:535.

22. See Jennings L. Wagoner Jr., *Jefferson and Education* (Charlottesville, Va., 2004); Philip Alexander Bruce, *History of the University of Virginia, 1819–1919*, 5 vols. (New York, 1922); Cameron Addis, *Jefferson's Vision for Education, 1760–1845* (New York, 2003); Theodore J. Crackel, *Mr. Jefferson's Army: Political and Social Reform of the Military Establishment, 1801–1809* (New York, 1987), esp. ch. 3; Theodore J. Crackel, *West Point: A Bicentennial History* (Lawrence, Kan., 2002), esp. chs. 2–3; McDonald, ed., *Thomas Jefferson's Military Academy;* James Gilreath, ed., *Thomas Jefferson and the Education of a Citizen* (Washington, D.C., 1999).

23. Merry Ellen Scofield, "The Fatigues of His Table: The Politics of Presidential Dining during the Jefferson Administration," *JER* 26 (2006): 449–69; Andrew S. Trees, *The Founding Fathers and the Politics of Character* (Princeton, N.J., 2004), 13–43; TJ to Thomas Jefferson Smith, 21 February 1825, *TJW*, 1500; TJ to Charles Clay (enclosure to Paul Clay), 12 July 1817, Ford, 10:93; TJ to Madison, 7 July 1793, *TJP*, 26:444; TJ to P. S. Du Pont de Nemours, 24 April 1816, *TJW*, 1387.

24. TJ to Madison, 6 September 1789, *TJP*, 15:392.

25. Jefferson, Epitaph, [1826], *TJW*, 706.

26. Herodotus, *The History of Herodotus*, trans. George Rawlinson, 4 vols. (London, 1858), 2:183; Pliny, *Natural History*, trans. H. Rackham and D. E. Eicholz, 10 vols. (Cambridge, Mass., 1947–62), 10:51, 57; Vivant Denon, *Travels in Upper and Lower Egypt, During the Campaigns of General Bonaparte*, trans. (London, 1802), Appendix No. 2, n.p. According to E. Millicent Sowerby, Jefferson owned the edition of Denon's *Travels* cited above; he owned Herodotus's *History* in a Greek and Latin text (Herodotus, *Herodoti Halicarnassensis Historia* [Glasgow, 1761]) and Pliny's *Natural History* in Latin and French (Caius Plinius Secundus, *Histoire Naturelle de Pline Traduite en François, avec le Texte Latin rétabli d'après les meilleures leçons manuscrites*, 12 vols. [Paris, 1771–82] and C. Plinii Secundi, *Naturalis Historiae*, 3 vols. [Rotterdam, 1668–69]); see Sowerby, comp., *Catalogue of the Library of Thomas Jefferson*, 5 vols. (Washington, D.C., 1952–59), 4:153, 1:7–8, 458–59.

"The Yeomanry of the United States Are Not the *Canaille* of Paris"

Thomas Jefferson, American Exceptionalism, and the "Spirit" of Democracy

BRIAN STEELE

T HE SOURCE OF MUCH OF OUR PRESENT AMBIVALENCE ABOUT JEFFER-
son is rooted in the awkward tension between our sense that he was not
inclusive enough to qualify as what most of us today would be willing to call a
"democrat," on the one hand, and, on the other, that he was, nevertheless, too
naïve about the ability of ordinary white men to make wise decisions in a
deliberative democracy to offer us anything useful in the way of a political
theory. There are so many compelling and well-understood reasons to challenge Jefferson's long-standing association in the American imagination with
our more expansive concept of "democracy" that it seems gratuitous to revisit
them here. Jefferson's complicity with slavery, his mostly unchecked racism,
his hostility to women's participation in high politics, and his embrace of a
more traditional conception of elite leadership than any later American politics would allow all provide a number of asterisks next to Jefferson's name in
the record book of our democracy.[1]

Yet Jefferson's name belongs in that book, and not just for the usually
agreed-upon reasons: that his "magical" words belie his lifestyle and provide
a rhetorical touchstone toward which all movements to make American
democracy more inclusive have nodded.[2] What ultimately makes Jefferson a
"democrat" in his day—and ours—is his willingness to trust the political
and moral instincts of the American public, and, by theoretical extension,

the democratic element in any properly constituted political community—
however unfortunately circumscribed by race and gender—in a way that few
political theorists before or since have done. By the late eighteenth century,
government had long been considered "too important a matter to be entrusted to the people."[3] Yet Jefferson shared little of the distrust of the "democracy" that had long characterized political theory and statesmanship.[4] As
he told William Johnson in 1823—and he never seemed to tire of repeating
it—the main difference between him (and his party) and the Federalists was
his willingness to trust the judgment of ordinary citizens. "The cherishment
of the people," he wrote, "was our principle, the fear and distrust of them,
that of the other party."[5] As John Adams once told him, and as generations
of Americans have confirmed, the "foundation" of Jefferson's "Unbounded
Popularity" was his "steady defence of democratical Principles."[6]

Adams meant Jefferson no compliment. Throughout their justly fabled
correspondence, Adams suggested—and some historians have echoed him—
that Jefferson was naïve and idealistic, at best, and blessedly ignorant or
utopian, at worst. But Adams misunderstood Jefferson. Jefferson's embrace
of the people may have inspired the world—and he hoped it would.[7] But, as
in multiple other areas, Jefferson's commitment to universal enlightenment
principles in this instance coexisted with a belief that only the American
people were ready for self-government. In other words, there was, he believed, a sociological foundation for his optimism about Americans and not
merely an idealistic one. "Popular taste," as Joyce Appleby has so nicely put it,
may have been "the final arbiter for Jefferson," but the taste he valued was one
that demanded a certain cultivation—a cultivation that he believed only
Americans had experienced.[8] It was not just any popular taste that Jefferson
considered authoritative, then, but one alert, deeply informed, and shaped by
an unhindered moral sense; *and* one that reached certain enlightened conclusions. What is perhaps most striking about Jefferson's democratic instincts is
how intimately linked they were with a faith in the *peculiar* ability of a
particular people—the American people—to arrive at truth and govern themselves. What distinguished Jefferson and the Republicans, he insisted, was
their belief "that men, enjoying in ease and security the full fruits of their
own industry, enlisted by all their interests on the side of law and order,
habituated to think for themselves, and to follow their reason as their guide,
would be more easily and safely governed, than with minds nourished in

error, and vitiated and debased, as in Europe, by ignorance, indigence and oppression."[9] This late statement is consistent with what Jefferson suggested throughout his lifelong correspondence and public career: only Americans seemed to be a public sufficiently enlightened to trust. In short, this is yet another case in which Jefferson's nationalism speaks a universal or cosmopolitan language, which, in turn, has long misdirected our attention to the universal *claims* rather than to the nationalist assumptions on which such claims rested.

Jefferson is long remembered as a champion of international democracy, and his faith in the God-given capacity of human beings to live in society and govern themselves is undeniable.[10] To be sure, Jefferson saw the American Revolution as an example to the rest of the world, and hoped that the "ball of liberty" would continue to "roll 'round the globe." But democracy was not as easy as all that.[11] Liberty would come only to "the enlightened part" of the globe, for "light & liberty," Jefferson told Tench Coxe, "go together."[12] The corollary of this point is that without "light" there can be no "liberty." In other words, it is impossible to speak meaningfully of liberty in the absence of capacity for enjoying it. (For a fuller exploration of this theme, see Johann Neem's essay in this collection.) As Jefferson noted in 1805, "the people are the only safe depositories of their own liberty," but those people "are not safe unless enlightened to a certain degree." Even American liberty would be "a short-lived possession unless the mass of the people could be informed to a certain degree."[13]

Fortunately, Jefferson believed, the American people were sufficiently enlightened to preserve their own liberty. America remained, Jefferson told the citizens of Washington, D.C., in 1809, "the sole depository of the sacred fire of freedom and self government."[14] Other nations would "be lighted up" only when and "if" they "shall ever become susceptible to its benign influence." Self-government was the human ideal, but its spread was limited to the capacity of various national communities to handle it. American democracy did not come ready-made for export.

So Jefferson's assertions about America's capacity for self-government partook of and contributed to a larger discourse about American identity and exceptionalism.[15] Jefferson's optimism about democracy was rooted in his sense that the American people possessed an exceptional "spirit" that would both resist tyranny and preserve law and order, as well as a "public opinion" that could be trusted to give energy and direction to government. Jefferson was such an enthusiastic democrat, in other words, largely because he was an American nationalist.

Much has been made of Jefferson's support of the French Revolution. But Jefferson's enthusiasm for that event was late and short-lived.[16] Prior to 1789, he repeatedly insisted that the French were not ready for self-government; they would do best to settle for a benevolent constitutional monarchy until they were exercised in the habits of self-government. And the convulsions that ended in Terror and, eventually, military dictatorship only served to confirm his initial warnings and to disappoint deeply the enthusiasm he did experience after 1789.[17] As for the Spanish American republics, which Jefferson welcomed in theory, he never once imagined that they would end in anything other than military despotisms. The problem in France and Spanish America, as Jefferson explained again and again, was that the people there simply did not yet have the capacity for self-government. This was not a judgment about any *natural* inferiority. There was nothing inherent in the people that disqualified them for democracy. The opposite is true. Culture, unique historical circumstances, environmental characteristics, but especially, multiple generations of despotic government and the power of the Catholic Church over the minds of the people, had taken human beings created by God for freedom and self-government and rendered them incapable of running their own affairs. It was sad, but true. Spanish Americans would gain independence from Spain, and Jefferson wished them well, but he was under no illusions about the possibility for self-government once Spain had fled the hemisphere. "History," he told Baron von Humboldt, "furnishes no example of a priest-ridden people maintaining a free civil government. This marks the lowest grade of ignorance, of which their civil as well as religious leaders will always avail themselves for their own purposes." In Spanish America, in other words, an elite class of priests and aristocrats had for so long held a monopoly over social, cultural, and financial capital, that the people had been rendered incapable of engaging in democratic politics.

As a result, the Spanish American republics "must end in military despotisms," Jefferson believed. "The different castes of their inhabitants, their mutual hatreds and jealousies, their profound ignorance and bigotry," he feared, "will be played off by cunning leaders, and each be made the instrument of enslaving the others."[18] Since the people of Latin America had been "habituated from their infancy to passive submission of body and mind to their kings and priests," their lethargy and submissive spirit rendered them unqualified "to think and provide for themselves." This naturally made them "instruments . . . in the hands of" despots.[19] The South Americans certainly had the same *right* to self-government that all people possessed by nature, and all Americans should cheer on their effort. "But the question is not what we wish," Jefferson insisted, "but what is practicable."[20] The real trouble would not be throwing off external tyranny. For the people of Spanish America, the most "dangerous enemy is within their own breasts."[21] The "ignorance & bigotry of the mass" led Jefferson to "doubt their capacity to understand and to support a free government."[22] On the contrary, such "ignorance and superstition" would "chain their minds and bodies under religious and military despotism." He worried that "the degrading ignorance into which their priests and kings have sunk them, has disqualified them from the maintenance or even knowledge of their rights." A move straight from such despotism to self-government was unthinkable. Much better, Jefferson argued again and again, for these people to "obtain freedom by degrees only; because that would by degrees bring on light and information, and qualify them to take charge of themselves understandingly."[23] So, "as their sincere friend and brother," he urged not revolution and republicanism but "an accommodation with the mother country . . . until they shall be sufficiently trained by education and habits of freedom to walk safely by themselves." Only then, Jefferson said, would they be prepared "for complete independence."[24]

This was exactly the advice Jefferson had offered the French reformers with whom he was associated in the 1780s. The French people wanted liberty, but they lacked the light necessary to maintaining it, so the best for which they could hope was a constitutional monarchy. As he told Madison in 1788, "the misfortune" of the French people was "that they are not yet ripe for receiving the blessings to which they are entitled. I doubt, for instance, whether the body of the nation, if they could be consulted, would accept of a Habeas corpus law, if offered them by the king. If the Etats generaux, when they assemble, do not aim at too much, they may begin a good constitution . . . If they push at much more, all may fail."[25] The French, like the South Americans, had the same rights as other peoples to self-government and liberty. Jefferson's concern was that neither of them had the necessary character, manners, and spirit to maintain those blessings. Such acquisition demanded time and a steady "amelioration of the condition of the people" until they were "capable of more." Jefferson assumed that "more than a generation will be requisite" for such a task. Liberty would not avail what he called "an unprepared people."[26]

Looking back years later, Jefferson believed his initial instincts had been right. The French had sought more than they were capable of handling and the results had been tragic. Having lived through Robespierre and Bonaparte, the French people were now, in 1815, back to their "ante-revolutionary condition . . . nearly where [they] were at the *Jeu de paume* on the 20th of June 1789."[27] The point, Jefferson told Du Pont, was that "the excellence of every government is it's adaptation to the state of those to be governed by it." In other words, the worth of a government can be judged by how adequately it matches the propensities of its people. Americans, Jefferson noted, were "constitutionally & conscientiously Democrats," so they could handle the maximum amount of liberty. Until other national peoples met this standard, their rightful share of liberty would need to be tempered by more heavy-handed government than Jefferson usually advocated.[28] If "an unprepared people" acquired freedom "by mere force or accident" (instead of through long "habituation" and "growth in the progress of reason"), then they would immediately pervert their freedom into "a tyranny still, of the many, the few, or the one."[29] What he considered proper for both France and Latin America was hardly "the best possible government," Jefferson admitted, only "the best" such degraded peoples could "bear."[30]

Americans, by contrast, had "sucked in the principles of liberty as it were with their mother's milk."[31] American republicanism was located "not in our constitution," but "in the spirit of our people." And this American spirit, Jefferson asserted in a remarkable statement, "would oblige even a despot to govern us republicanly."[32] The character of the American people, in other words, would force even tyrants to abide by republican principles if they ever hoped to govern Americans.

In an earlier iteration of this view, Jefferson told William Carmichael, American minister to Spain, during a war scare in 1790, that Spain would never be able to control America's western citizens. These "could be quiet but a short time under a government so repugnant to their feelings." Even if the Spanish managed to control the American West for a time, these Americans "would communicate a spirit of Independence to those with whom they should be mixed"—the contagion of the American "spirit," in other words, would infect even the conquerors of American physical space.[33]

In Jefferson's thought, the nature of the regime and the character of its citizens were mutually constitutive and reinforcing; American republicanism was the natural fit for a people who had long enjoyed self-government. The American people, Jefferson asserted over and again, would not long suffer a government that did not ascend from their will; nor could they abide a government inconsistent with their republican character, precisely because, as Jefferson put it, "our countrymen" had been "impressed from their cradle" with the "habit of self government" and the principles of republicanism "so that with them it is *almost innate.*"[34]

The French Revolution had failed, by contrast, Jefferson came to believe, because it depended largely on "the mobs of the cities," a people "debased by ignorance, poverty and vice." Such people simply "could not be restrained to rational action."[35] But in America, he asserted, "the proper spirit of the people" would shape the behavior of even an "absolute Monarch" as long as "our present character remains, of order, industry and love of peace."[36]

Public spirit for Jefferson essentially connoted the *engagement* of the American people. And engagement seemed to mean two things, primarily. One, that Americans were alert and informed enough to recognize, and courageous enough to resist, tyranny when it appeared in whatever guise. Two, that Americans were devoted to law and order and to the preservation of their union and system of government. These two facets of public spirit seem in tension: one is the "spirit of resistance" to government while the other is a devotion to law and obedience to constituted authority. But they are complementary in Jefferson's thought.

Jefferson's confidence in the American people was rooted in his sense that they were exceptional. "Never was a finer canvas presented to work on than our countrymen" he effused to John Adams in 1796 in a letter in which he spelled out some of the characteristics that rendered Americans uniquely able to govern themselves. "All" Americans, he said, were "engaged in agriculture or the pursuits of honest industry, independent in their circumstances, enlightened as to their rights, and firm in their habits of order and obedience to the laws." The lesson was clear: "If ever the morals of a people could be made the basis of their own government, it is our case."[37] In America, he told Adams years later, "every one may have land to labor for himself if he chuses; or, preferring the exercise of any other industry, may exact for it such compensation as not only to afford a comfortable subsistence, but wherewith to provide for a cessation from labor in old age." It followed, Jefferson noted, that "every one, by his property, or by his satisfactory situation, is interested in the support of law and order. And such men may safely and advantageously reserve to themselves a wholsome controul over their public affairs, and a degree of freedom, which in the hands of the Canaille of the cities of Europe, would be instantly perverted to the demolition and destruction of every thing public and private. The history of the last 25 years of France," Jefferson asserted, "and of the last 40 years in America, nay of it's last 200 years, proves the truth of both parts of this observation."[38]

Here, and elsewhere, Jefferson made several striking claims about the United States. First is his claim of its unique prosperity. Because of the "immensity of land" in the United States, Americans were "a people at their ease," in possession of a "lovely equality" in which most families, by and large, were not artificially burdened with poverty, and where the agricultural labor of men was sustaining and even profitable.[39] America was essentially a classless society, Jefferson told Thomas Cooper, with "no paupers" and very few rich.[40] All Americans worked and all maintained a comfortable competence. This generalized prosperity created a kind of rough equality that freed people to achieve their natural human potential and to indulge their independence, following their moral sense unclouded by artificial hierarchies or crushing dependence. Two hundred years' experience with this kind of freedom rendered Americans familiar with the habits of self-government and comfortable, as well as safe, with their liberty. In short, American circumstances had forged a people safe with the franchise and with a degree of liberty unknown in the history of the world: "men susceptible of happiness, educated in the love of order, habituated to self-government, and valuing its blessings above all price."[41]

All of these characteristics were easy to contrast with those of Europe. Since Europeans were "not at their ease," Jefferson argued, they lived degraded lives.[42] Every man in Europe, Jefferson argued, was "either the hammer or the anvil."[43] European aristocracy created artificial hierarchies that stifled human potential and condemned the mass of society to ignorance and poverty, leaving people without a true stake in society or any public spirit that might preserve republican government.

The claims Jefferson made about America were not original or unique to him, although he articulated them as well as or better than anyone else ever did. America's association with prosperity, mild government fostering private pursuits of betterment and happiness, and remarkable fluidity and comparative social mobility—all of which, the narrative went, cultivated a unique character in the American people—had been part of the European conception of America from the time it first entered the "Old World's" consciousness.[44]

Adam Smith himself gave his seal of approval to this view, praising the American farmer "who cultivates his own land, and derives his necessary subsistence from the labour of his own family." Such a yeoman, Smith reported, considered himself "really a master, and independent of all the world"— precisely the kind of condition Jefferson believed fostered the unique American spirit. In contrast, as Smith noted in a familiar passage from the *Wealth of Nations,* the laborer in Europe, where land was scarce and the division of labor had advanced to a much more considerable extent, spent his "whole life . . . performing a few simple operations," and consequently, had "no occasion to exert his understanding or to exercise his invention in finding out expedients for removing difficulties which never occur." Such a laborer "naturally loses, therefore, the habit of such exertion, and generally becomes as stupid and ignorant as it is possible for a human creature to become." Perhaps most damning here, from Jefferson's perspective, was that such a worker was soon rendered "altogether incapable of judging . . . the great and extensive interests of his country; and unless very particular pains have been taken to render him otherwise, he is equally incapable of defending his country in war."[45] It was excellence in precisely these public virtues that Jefferson believed characterized Americans.

To be sure, Jefferson continued to hold out hope that liberty would eventually spread around the globe. But Jefferson seemed compelled by observation to consider America the only living example of the kind of society he craved for the rest of the world. The American example to the world was the only example that gave him hope that all men would one day "burst the chains under which monkish ignorance and superstition had persuaded them to bind themselves, and to assume the blessings and security of self-government."[46] "Opinion is power," he told Adams earlier, "and that opinion will come. Even France will yet attain representative government." But he did not expect to see this happen during his own lifetime, and he predicted that "rivers of blood may yet flow" before the realization of his vision.[47] The contrast between these real but distant hopes for the world and his confident assertions about the present character of the United States is striking.

For now, government had to be tailored to fit the character of its people. As Jefferson told William Lee, "every people have their own particular habits, ways of thinking, manners, etc., which have grown up with them from their infancy, are become a part of their nature, and to which the regulations which are to make them happy must be accommodated." Unfortunately, Jefferson said, "no member of a foreign country can have a sufficient sympathy with these. The institutions of Lycurgeus, for example would not have suited Athens nor those of Solon Lacedaemon."[48] If the question was whether to "mould our citizens to the law, or the law to our citizens," Jefferson largely came down on the side of the latter. In any case, he told John Quincy Adams, American lawmakers could not neglect the "peculiar character" of the American citizenry.[49]

Accordingly, one of Jefferson's principal critiques of the Federalists in the 1790s was that they were attempting to force upon Americans a style of government ready-made for the European societies he described, but ill suited for the American people. Part of the reason the Federalists governed with a heavy hand, hoping, Jefferson imagined, to consolidate power in the central state and create a more authoritarian system of government for America, was that they did not understand "the difference between the rabble who were used as instruments" for the French revolutionaries, "and the steady & rational character of the American people, in which [they] had not sufficient confidence." The Federalists, "like the rest of mankind," were justifiably "disgusted with atrocities of the French revolution" but, unlike the Republicans, they forgot about the unique spirit of the American people.[50] The Federalists had to be resisted, Jefferson thought, precisely because they were not sufficiently well attuned to what was special about the American people.

Early in his political career, Hamilton had suggested to John Jay what he believed all history to that point had confirmed: "when the minds of [the people] are loosened from their attachment to ancient establishments and courses, they seem to grow giddy and are apt more or less to run into anarchy."[51] Hamilton carried this view to his grave. But everything in Jefferson's analysis of the American people suggested that Hamilton and the Federalists were wrong. Americans, unlike the French proletariat, indeed, unlike most peoples of history, had proven themselves capable of casting off tyranny *while* resisting the impulse to licentiousness that had damned the French Revolution. The Federalist program failed to recognize this and was, thus, an inappropriate political agenda for the American republic. Accordingly, Jefferson characterized his own election to the presidency in 1800 as "the resistance which our republic has opposed to a course of operation *for which it was not destined."* His victory, he wrote, had proven "a strength of body which affords the most flattering presages of duration. . . . The character which our fellow citizens have displayed on this occasion gives us every thing to hope for the permanence of our government."[52]

Jefferson's critique, then, turned Federalist campaign literature on its head. Castigating Jefferson's program as "Laputian" and inattentive to experience, Federalists warned against the dangers of experimentation in politics.[53] But, for Jefferson, it was the Federalists who had been ignoring American experience and had rooted their politics in a theory based upon the experiences of other peoples. As a political program for Americans, then, the Federalist agenda—rather than the Jeffersonian—was incongruent with reality. No useful positive lessons for Americans, in fact, could be drawn from the experiences of the peoples of history. Seeking precedents for proper governance from ancient Rome, "where the government was of a heavy-handed unfeeling aristocracy, over a people ferocious, and rendered desperate by poverty and wretchedness," would be folly and "misapplied . . . to a people, mild in their dispositions, patient under their trial, united for the public liberty, and affectionate to their leaders."[54]

The Federalists, Jefferson argued, had worked "to recover . . . in practice the powers which the nation had refused"—setting themselves up as "authorities independent of [the people's] will," working to "maintain their privileged orders in splendor and idleness, to fascinate the eyes of the people, and excite in them an humble adoration and submission, as to an order of superior beings." The Federalists attempted this move to reestablish in America "the doctrines of Europe" precisely because they extrapolated from the universal human experience to that point in history without taking into account the unique experience of the United States.[55] And the American *nation,* Jefferson argued, rejected their politics precisely because that very experience, he believed, had prepared them for new and greater possibilities than political theorists of the past could reasonably expect from other peoples.

If the ancients offered little in the way of guidance, neither did the contemporary experiences of other peoples. In light of Federalist propaganda associating Jefferson with the madness of the French Revolution, it is worth remembering that Jefferson worried lest the American people linked their own experience too closely to the trajectory of the French republic. It remained crucial for Jefferson—"very material," as he put it—that the American people ("our countrymen") remain "sensible that their own character & situation are materially different from the French." Americans should "be made" to understand, he wrote, "that whatever may be the fate of republicanism" in France, "we are able to preserve it inviolate here."[56]

The most salient difference between Jefferson and the Federalists, by Jefferson's own reckoning, was not his "utopianism" about worldwide democracy and revolution so lampooned in Federalist campaign literature. It was his sense that Americans had, in fact, shrugged off the fetters that had for so long bound the majority of the world's peoples—of necessity—to governments of hierarchy, deference, and force. In their attempt to govern such a people with the tools that had served rulers of the European past, Federalists were simply out of date and out of touch with American realities.

Jefferson's Americans, then, maintained an alert "spirit of resistance" to tyranny that was uncharacteristic of the lethargic, ignorant, poverty-stricken masses in other nations. The American habit of "order and obedience to the laws" constituted the corollary to this spirit.[57] The paradox is more apparent than real. For Jefferson, these were different manifestations of a single spirit. American "love of liberty," its "steady character," was manifested in both the spirit of resistance to tyranny and its complement, "obedience to law, and support of the public authorities." In both, Jefferson recognized "a sure guaranty of the permanence of our republic."[58] The American government would be, Jefferson argued, "a model for the protection of man in a state of freedom and order." Neither was dispensable or, in his view, necessarily excluded the other.[59]

Throughout the Revolutionary era, good Whigs recognized that tyranny was not the only threat to liberty; licentiousness—liberty's "other"—also remained a very real likelihood in governments responsive to the people.[60] Because the two existed along a continuum, the founders, Jefferson among them, were never unconcerned about the potential threat licentiousness posed to republican government. Most put a premium on the ability "to discriminate the spirit of liberty from that of licentiousness," as George Washington put it.[61] Much of Jefferson's criticism of European efforts to overthrow tyranny, justifiable though they may be, revolved around his sense that Europeans were not yet capable of stopping at the mean between the vice of degradation on the one hand and the excess of licentiousness on the other. Even European immigrants to America, he worried, would "bring with them the principles of the governments they leave, imbibed in their early youth." And, "if able to throw them off, it will be in exchange for an unbounded licentiousness, passing, as is usual, from one extreme to another. It would be a miracle were they to stop precisely at the point of temperate liberty."[62] And, indeed, "freedom" handed to the proletariat of Europe, Jefferson warned, "would be instantly perverted to the demolition and destruction of every thing public and private."[63] Jefferson grew to be so enthusiastic about the possibilities for the maintenance of liberty in the American Republic, then, precisely because, he believed, the dualistic American spirit he identified had equipped the American people to maintain liberty without allowing it to run—as it had in most other republics of history—into unlimited indulgence, anarchy, and, ultimately tyranny.

Jefferson first became infatuated with this phenomenon during Shays's Rebellion. To a degree largely unremarked in the scholarly literature, Jefferson's confidence about the American experiment began with Shays—not his commitment to self-government, which he believed to be a natural God-given human right, but his sense that America's political experiment would succeed. Prior to this time, especially in his *Notes on the State of Virginia,* Jefferson had expressed anxiety about the ability of Americans to maintain their republics. In the section on "manufactures," Jefferson noted that it was the "manners and spirit of a people which preserve a republic in vigor."[64] But in the previous two sections, Jefferson had suggested that the "spirit of the people" might not be "an infallible, a permanent reliance." In fact, the "spirit of the times may alter, will alter. Our rulers will become corrupt, our people careless." After the Revolution, Jefferson expected things to go "down hill." "Human nature," Jefferson asserted, "is the same on every side of the Atlantic." American political leaders might soon become enamored with the trappings of power. The people, he feared, would soon "forget themselves, but in the sole faculty of making money, and will never think of uniting to effect a due respect for their rights."[65]

And if it was, in fact, the "manners and spirit of a people which preserve a republic in vigor," the next section of the *Notes* was even more frightening. It does not seem an accident that Jefferson chose the query about American "manners" to address slavery in Virginia. Much can be and has been written on this short but deeply emotional passage, but what seems most striking about it in this context is how clearly Jefferson suggests that slavery more or less undermined everything he considered exceptional and superior about America. Slavery fostered and cultivated a hereditary aristocracy with its attendant habits of tyranny, undermining rights, morals, industry, and love of country.[66] Read together, these sections of the *Notes* form a depressing kind of picture of the future of the United States—particularly in terms of developing a public spirit sufficient to maintain republican government and rights. Here, accordingly, Jefferson placed a good deal of hope in institutions to check a declining character in the public and its leaders. Because the spirit manifested during the Revolution might be ephemeral, and since manners (of Virginians, anyway) were already suspect because of the presence of slavery, institutional checks and balances seemed a proper remedy. "Better to keep the wolf out of the fold, than to trust to drawing his teeth and talons after he shall have entered." Surely "the time to guard against corruption and tyranny," he averred, "is before they shall have gotten hold on us."[67] Combined with his concerns about the Virginia Constitution and his fears that it had laid the groundwork for legislative despotism, these sections of the *Notes* suggest an anxiety about American character that historians typically do not associate with Jefferson.[68]

Jefferson's ordinarily effusive optimism about the American future struggled, during these years, then, with a collective post-Revolutionary fear that Americans lacked the virtue required for the maintenance of self-government.[69] But Shays's Rebellion—which only confirmed such fears for so many American leaders—perversely appears to have done something extraordinary for Jefferson's confidence. Even as it drove most American leaders toward institutional checks on the public, the rebellion in western Massachusetts infused Jefferson, by contrast, with a new confidence in the *character* of the American people and partially checked the resort to institutions he had encouraged in the *Notes*. Jefferson never lost his commitment to checks and balances or his concern that power was corrupting. But he did come to embrace—to a degree that John Adams and many later historians found problematic—a sense that the spirit of the public would prove itself an efficacious, if not entirely sufficient, check on both tyranny from above and anarchy from below. That such a public spirit had, in Jefferson's view, been cultivated and sustained by institutions uniquely appropriate to the United

States suggests that the distinction scholars have posited between those favoring institutional checks on public wickedness and those trusting public virtue to sustain a republic may be too starkly drawn. Jefferson believed in institutions, but gradually gained a confidence that those very institutions might cultivate a public character that could be somewhat self-sustaining. So, in Jefferson's view, institutions and character were mutually reinforcing, precisely why he spent a good deal of energy investing the laws of Virginia with practices that would continue to shape republican character.

This insight first became prominent in his thought in the aftermath of Shays. John Jay's letter informing him of the turbulence in Massachusetts "really affected me," he said, largely because Jay suggested that concerns about anarchy were leading people to look to more authoritarian structures to maintain order: the "rational and well-intentioned," and "more sober part of the people," Jay wrote, in their quest for "for Peace and Security," might even consider monarchy.[70] But a disarming letter from John Adams quickly restored his faith. From then on, Jefferson seemed unconcerned, even nonchalant about Shays's Rebellion, telling some alarmed correspondents not to worry, that "a little rebellion now and then" was a good thing: "I like to see the people awake and alert."[71] He was now "persuaded," he wrote, "that the good sense of the people will always be found to be the best army."[72]

Shays's Rebellion ultimately taught Jefferson two lessons. The first was that the American people were not lethargic but could be counted upon to sense and resist tyranny in their government should such arise. The second was that the American people could be counted upon to defend their governments when unlawful threats to them appeared. This only seems paradoxical or contradictory. Jefferson believed the spirit of the rebels was to be cherished, even when it was dead wrong, precisely because it would compel government honesty and justice. But what was really great about the Shays story was that the common sense of the people eventually intervened to *defuse* the rebellion. The ultimate outcome of Shays's uprising, in fact, was "confidence in the firmness of our governments" because of the "interposition of the people themselves *on the side of government*."[73] Shays's Rebellion was ultimately pacified in large part, Jefferson believed, because of the "discretion which the malcontents still preserved"—itself a telling sign of the nature of American public spirit. But similarly "tumultuous meetings" in Connecticut and New Hampshire ended because "the body of the people rose in support of government and obliged the malcontents to go to their homes."[74]

Jefferson's endorsement of the people's attention to public affairs, on both sides of the issue—the public spirit of the rebels (misinformed though it was) *and* the public spirit of those who supported law and order—is a nice window into Jefferson's conception of the dual nature of the American spirit.

Shays's Rebellion gave Jefferson "no uneasiness" for a variety of reasons: from the vantage point of despotic Europe, a bit of resistance to authority looked positively refreshing to him.[75] And the reports he had generally assured him that the "rebellion" was a misconceived (though somewhat justifiable) expression of discontent, rather than a full-scale assault on the constituted institutions of society.[76] "No injury was done . . . in a single instance to the person or property of any one." The rebellion lasted, he said, less than twenty-four hours and ended largely because the "rebels" had enough public spirit to back off in the face of majority rejection of their proposals.[77] In Europe, much more "ferocious" insurrections occurred every few years; in Turkey, they "are the events of every day." "Compare" these bloody rebellions, he challenged Madison, with "the order, the moderation and the almost self extinguishment of ours."[78]

One of the idiosyncrasies that ultimately separated Jefferson from his famous contemporaries among the revolutionary "brotherhood" was not, as is commonly supposed, a lack of commitment to strong government and order but a willingness to trust the capacity of the American people to preserve such order without running headlong into anarchy. What distinguished Jefferson from either Hamilton or Adams in this regard was that he, like Adams (and unlike Hamilton), valued and hoped for the engagement of the people. But, unlike Adams, Jefferson believed that the American people were uniquely capable of engagement (checking tyranny) *while* preserving order and good government. This helps to explain his initial response to the Constitution. The Philadelphia Convention, he told Adams's son-in-law William Smith, had been "too much impressed by the insurrection of Massachusetts: and in the spur of the moment they are setting up a kite to keep the hen-yard in order."[79] This statement has often been misunderstood to signal Jefferson's opposition to a national state, on the one hand, and his celebration of rebellion, on the other. And, of course, in the same letter, Jefferson exclaimed to Smith: "God forbid we should ever be 20 years without such a rebellion." But the key word here is *such*. Shays's Rebellion, as Jefferson told Smith, was clearly misconceived. Even so, Jefferson felt encouraged that the people rose up to defend against what they *believed* to be a threat to their liberty.

But Jefferson also thought that the rebellion had been quelled by popular defense of government and order once the people understood the truth about their situation. In other words, the spirit of resistance he so "cherish[ed]" had also diffused the rebellion and should not, he believed, become an excuse for setting up an unnecessary check on popular spirit which was, after all, quite capable of righting itself given adequate and accurate information. The context of Jefferson's letter to Smith—and what sets up his famous "endorsement" of Shays's Rebellion—is his concern about "lies" in the European press "about our being in anarchy." Jefferson wrote Smith to dispel these distortions, registering his astonishment that even Americans could have come to believe them. The only disturbance he could see was Shays's, and history had not produced any other "instance of rebellion so honourably conducted." What kind of rebellion was Shays's? One manifesting the "spirit of resistance," to be sure, but one conducted more or less decently and in order—one that quickly dispersed upon the majority's rejection of its goals.

This is what Jefferson found so remarkable about the whole thing. Theorists like Adams would continue to wrestle with complex schemes—checks and balances, executive authority, and the cultivation of a hereditary aristocracy—to harness the spirit of the people without unleashing its dangerous potential for anarchy. For Jefferson, by contrast, the search was largely over by 1787. The American people had proven themselves capable of resisting tyranny without running headlong into unnecessary licentiousness or insurrection. What Shays seemed to teach Jefferson was that the American public was not indefinitely malleable by demagoguery; that it would not be building a house on sand to rest the state's foundations in the national will—at least in America where the people were independent, informed, and alert. Jefferson's excitement about this extraordinary fact is palpable. This could very well be the political discovery of the ages: a people whose very character allowed them to harness all the positive good embodied in popular vigilance while, at the same time, checking its tendency (throughout history) to run amok to the very destruction of popular government and the reestablishment of despotic states. Unlike "governments of force," which included even "most . . . republics," American governments, Jefferson seemed to suggest, could be "mild in their punishment of rebellions," not "discourag[ing] them too much"—precisely because there was ultimately little to fear from such a people (at least for "honest republican governors"). In America, popular vigilance—even when it "produced" individual incidents that were "absolutely unjustifiable"— actually could be encouraged as a healing "medicine necessary for the sound health of government" or a "storm" cleansing the atmosphere, rather than suppressed out of fear of its potential for destruction. For now, this seemed largely peculiar to the American situation, which is another reason why Jefferson continued to hold up the American example as not necessarily an easily emulated model but a beacon of hope for what *might* one day become possible for all peoples.[80]

In this context, Jefferson's embrace of the "natural aristocracy" of virtue and talent—what he called "the most precious gift of nature for the instruction, the trusts, and government of society"—was not the blind faith that Adams and others imagined. He knew as well as Adams that the natural aristocracy was capable of quickly turning into a pack of wolves. But based on his experience with the American people, he expected that they would see such a move well before it happened and check its progress. The American people, he asserted, were uniquely capable of recognizing this aristocracy and electing it to public office. In fact, in his most famous letter on the subject, Jefferson told Adams that the very definition of a good government was one in which the people were rendered capable of recognizing and electing the natural aristocracy.[81] This may seem cynical—or we may be cynical, rather, about the way "public opinion" generally seemed to magically coincide with Jefferson's own, but what is truly remarkable about his argument to Adams is that for the first time in human history the "democracy" had become so trustworthy that its opinion embraced the most advanced views of the "aristocracy" and granted an enthusiastic consent to the implementation of the ideas of the most progressive philosophers, scientists, and officeholders. In this way, Jefferson balanced his more traditional commitment to enlightened leadership with his fear of power and his embrace of popular engagement in politics. The American people—even common people who did not necessarily have the wherewithal or intellectual capacity to run national affairs— did, Jefferson argued, have the sense to distinguish statesmen from demagogues and to evaluate wisely the performance of elected officials. They also possessed the courage to stand against them when those officials went astray. But Jefferson was not just a Pollyanna—optimistic in the face of all evidence to the contrary. He believed these things about the *American* people in a way that he could not muster for others because of his sociological appraisal of the American experience. His exceptionalism was hardly a leap into the utopian dark.

We tend to forget the context in which Jefferson made such claims for the American democracy. Since the best governments were, of necessity, shaped to fit the peculiar character of the people of a nation, most governments in history had been governments of force or corruption.[82] Self-government of all varieties had long been associated with anarchy and descent into tyranny. Pure democracies, as Madison noted in the tenth *Federalist*, "have ever been spectacles of turbulence and contention; have ever been found incompatible with personal security or the rights of property; and have in general been as short in their lives, as they have been violent in their deaths."[83] Madison argued that a compound federal republic was the solution or "cure" for these problems inherent in direct democracy. Jefferson also tended to agree with Madison throughout his life about the impracticability of pure democracy for the United States since such governments were of necessity "restrained to very narrow limits of space and population" not much larger than "a New England township." But he tended also to not make much of the distinction between a representative republic (the term he favored) and a democracy. In other words, he disengaged democracy from its traditionally narrow definition and asserted that the American republic could more safely incorporate "the direct action of the citizens" without fear of anarchy precisely because the character of the American people and its experiment with representative democracy had "rendered useless almost everything written before on the structure of government."[84]

The United States had the "strongest Government on earth," he said, precisely because the American citizen, "at the call of the law, would fly to the standard of the law, and would meet invasions of the public order as his own personal concern."[85] In notes he took for his first inaugural address, Jefferson hoped that "the distinctive mark of an American" would be that "in cases of commotion he enlists himself under no man's banner, enquires for no man's name but repairs to the standard of the laws."[86] Alexis de Tocqueville later echoed Jefferson, noting that "each individual" in America had "a personal interest in seeing to it that everyone obeys the law." Since everyone ("apart from slaves, servants, and paupers") is allowed to vote, an attack on the laws must "either change the nation's opinion or trample upon its will." In America, Tocqueville posited, "the common man has an exalted idea of political rights because he has such rights."[87] Or, as Jefferson colorfully asserted, "where every man . . . feels that he is a participator in the government of affairs . . . he will let the heart be torn out of his body sooner than his power be wrested from him by a Caesar or a Bonaparte."[88] When the law is the people's handiwork, the people will obey it and rise to defend it.

This is precisely the way Jefferson later explained the collapse of Aaron Burr's conspiracy before it could really do any damage. The very moment Jefferson "apprised our citizens that there were traitors among them, and what was their object, they rose upon them wherever they lurked, and crushed by their own strength what would have produced the march of armies and civil war in any other country. The government which can wield the arm of the people must be the strongest possible." The lesson of the Burr Conspiracy, Jefferson argued, was "that we are a people capable of self-government, and worthy of it."[89] The episode called to mind Shays's Rebellion, except that this time Jefferson could only sympathize with one of the sides. "The suppression of the late conspiracy by the hand of the people, uplifted to destroy it whenever it reared its head," made clear, he thought, the people's "fitness for self-government, and the power of a nation, of which every individual feels that his own will is a part of the public authority."[90]

The same people, presumably, could resist government tyranny while, at the same time, remaining committed to a properly constituted government. This is one reason Jefferson counseled patience to fellow Republicans sickened by Federalist measures in the 1790s. Federalist behavior might energize some Republicans to actual "insurrection," but "nothing," Jefferson warned, "could be so fatal." Perhaps glancing back at Shays's Rebellion, he warned that this was "not the kind of opposition the American people will permit." Outright rebellion at such a time "would check the progress of the public opinion and rally them round the government," a government perverted to Federalist goals. Based on his reading of earlier episodes in American history, Jefferson remained willing to wait out the good sense of the people. As Jefferson said of Shays's Rebellion, the people "may be led astray for a moment, but will soon correct themselves."[91] This was Jefferson's consistent mantra throughout the 1790s as well. Patience would be rewarded, for the people would rally, the "reign of witches" would pass, and the republic would be saved.[92]

This narrative depicting a spontaneous rallying of the American citizenry left out a good deal of politicking. Nevertheless, Jefferson believed that his election proved once again both a spirit of resistance to tyranny and a "love of order and obedience to the laws."[93] The election's outcome served as Jefferson's evidence that he had been right: the American people really *were* enlightened after all; they really were able to sort truth from fiction and separate the natural aristocratic "wheat" from the Federalist "chaff."[94] Near the end of his life, Jefferson remembered how the Federalist desire for monarchy had been, as he put it, "completely foiled by the universal spirit of the nation."[95] It was this spirit that Jefferson had counted on to preserve the republic, and when it finally happened, he could barely contain his enthusiasm. "We can no longer say there is nothing new under the sun," he gushed to Joseph Priestley shortly after his victory. "For this whole chapter in the history of man is new. The great extent of our Republic is new. Its sparse habitation is new. The mighty wave of public opinion which has rolled over it is new." The Federalists, including President Adams himself, had nearly brought down the curtain on the American enlightenment, Jefferson suggested, pretending "to praise and encourage education," but only "the education of our ancestors," rejecting "all advances in science" and proclaiming that we could never "go beyond" those ancestors "in real science."[96] This Federalist endorsement of the past as the repository of all wisdom, Jefferson had earlier predicted to Priestley, was "not an idea which this country will endure."[97] And, indeed, the election seemed to fulfill the prophecy: the people had "recovered from delusion" with "order & good sense."[98]

Many years after the fact, John Adams ran across this letter to Priestley when it was published—to Jefferson's embarrassment—in a memoir which Adams was reading.[99] He demanded that Jefferson explain himself, playfully mocking Jefferson's effusive encomium to the "mighty wave of public opinion." "Oh! Mr. Jefferson! What a Wave of public Opinion has rolled over the Universe? . . . What 'a wave' has rolled over Christendom for 1500 years? What a Wave has rolled over France for 1500 Years supporting in Power and Glory the Dinasty of Bourbon? What a Wave supported the House of Austria? What a Wave has supported the Dinasty of Mahomet, for 1200 Years? . . . What a Wave has the French Revolution spread?"[100] Adams is as hilarious as he is loveable in this correspondence, but he misunderstood Jefferson's point. Jefferson did not trust the "mighty wave of public opinion" which swept over France during the Terror, or any of the other waves Adams described. He trusted the public opinion of a particular people, enlightened and uniquely suited for democratic governance. What was new "under the sun" about the election of 1800 was not that a population rose up to affect world affairs, nor even that a government had elicited popular support, but that this American people proved itself so capable of distinguishing what was suited to the governance of a free people from what was more appropriate for the rule of European peasants (unfair as such a characterization of Adams's thought such an assertion might be).

Jefferson's enthusiasm about what he later called the "Revolution of 1800" was all the greater precisely because that election confirmed what he had long claimed about the American people. For the first time in human history, Jefferson believed, the democracy had defended its rights and upheld liberty without giving in to the unbridled passion that had always doomed republics in the past. This confirmation of what Jefferson had discovered about the American people during Shays's Rebellion rendered Jefferson "much better satisfied now of [the Republic's] stability than I was before it was tried."[101]

As with Shays, "the most pleasing novelty" of the election, Jefferson had told Priestley, was that the "mighty wave" had "so quickly subsid[ed] over such an extent of surface to it's true level again." Once again, in other words, an aroused people had rejected "delusion" not with terror but with an "order & good sense" that "augurs well for the duration of our Republic." The Republic would last precisely because the entire episode had manifested— once again—a "strength of character in our nation" which no other political theorists in history had been able to count upon.[102]

In short, as Jefferson put it to Lafayette, "the yeomanry of the United States are not the canaille of Paris." They were "very different materials" from the rabble of European cities. The "cement of this Union is in the heart-blood of every American" and there was no other government on earth "established on so immovable a basis."[103]

Jefferson began with the universal and natural rights of man, but because, as he put it, the "habits of the governed determine in a great degree what is practicable," these "*same original principles,* modified *in practice* according to the different habits of different nations, present governments of very different aspects."[104] This goes some distance toward reconciling Jefferson's universalism (and his grounding of rights and political freedoms in nature) with his American exceptionalism (rooted, as it was, in history) and renders apparent only the tension between his Enlightenment embrace of endless progress and his awareness of the historicity of institutions and human experience.

Jefferson's America was no "exception" to the laws of nature and of nations that governed other peoples; his "American exceptionalism" (if indeed that is the most accurate phrase with which to describe his position) indicates exclusivity and, for Jefferson, a kind of superiority, but only relative to the progress of other peoples to that point in time, not fixed and exclusive for all time.[105] America itself was not guaranteed its unique position in the absence of the particular historical and social conditions that made it possible. American "self-preservation" would last, Jefferson said, only "till a change of circumstances shall take place."[106] And his program of reform, described in many of the following chapters, suggests his appreciation of the ways in which those circumstances demanded active perpetuation. The source of his hope was not the inevitability of endless progress but rather the historical moment in which America happened to find itself and his sense that Americans could and would continue to sustain its promise.[107]

His appraisal of American conditions animated Jefferson's conviction that America was "destined" to remain "a barrier against the returns of ignorance and barbarism" throughout the world. "Old Europe," he told Adams, "will have to lean on our shoulders, and to hobble along by our side, under the monkish trammels of priests and kings, as she can. What a Colossus shall we be when the Southern continent comes up to our mark! What a stand will it secure as a ralliance for the reason and freedom of the globe."[108]

In 1816, Jefferson sent John Taylor a fragment from a poem that nicely encapsulated some of his own views about the stabilizing potential of the American spirit:

> What constitutes a State?
> Not high-raised battlements, or labor'd mound,
> Thick wall, or moated gate;
> Not cities proud, with spires and turrets crown'd;
> No: men, high-minded men;
> Men, who their duties know;
> But know their rights; and knowing, dare maintain.
> These constitute a State.

Things would continue to go well with America, he told Taylor, "while our present character remains."[109] It was precisely this character that Jefferson believed exceptional about Americans, which is why his much-lauded championing of democracy, at least during his own day, tended to stop at the borders of the United States. Other peoples could have American democracy when, and only when, they became more like Americans; and Americans could remain the world's hope for the future only as long as they maintained its remarkable character and the conditions that had cultivated it.

Notes

1. Conor Cruise O'Brien, "Thomas Jefferson: Radical and Racist," *Atlantic Monthly* 278 (October 1996): 53–74. For reflections on Jefferson's declining modern reputation among professional historians, see Peter S. Onuf, "The Scholars' Jefferson," *WMQ* 50 (1993): 671–99; and Francis Cogliano, *Thomas Jefferson: Reputation and Legacy* (Charlottesville, Va., 2006).

2. See Joseph J. Ellis, *American Sphinx: The Character of Thomas Jefferson* (New York, 1997), 10; Joyce Appleby, "Jefferson and his Complex Legacy," in *Jeffersonian Legacies*, ed. Peter S. Onuf (Charlottesville, Va., 1993), 1–16; Sean Wilentz, "American Historians vs. American Founding Fathers: The Details of Greatness," in *New Republic* (March 29, 2004).

3. J. R. Pole, *The Gift of Government: Political Responsibility from the English Restoration to American Independence* (Athens, Ga., 1983), xi.

4. Traditionally used (often negatively) by political thinkers to describe direct citizen participation in government, the word *democracy* over time lost much of this original meaning and became more closely associated with representative republics that were responsive to popular majorities made up of a universally enfranchised citizenry. For important reflections on the meanings of the word in the late eighteenth century, see R. R. Palmer, "Notes on the Use of the Word 'Democracy' 1789–1799," *Political Science Quarterly* 68 (June 1953): 203–26. For a critique of the imprecision with which the term has been used to describe the governments of early America, see J. R. Pole, "Historians and the Problem of Early American Democracy," *American Historical Review* 67 (April 1962): 626–46. For a brilliant discussion of the confused uses of this term in contemporary political discourse, see Fahreed Zakaria, "The Rise of Illiberal Democracy," *Foreign Affairs* (November/December 1997). For a helpful discussion of the difficulties of evaluating early American government and institutions in terms of current democratic discourse, see Alan Gibson, *Understanding the Founding: The Crucial Questions* (Lawrence, Kans., 2007), 46–90. For one central aspect of the modern definition of democracy, see Alexander Keyssar, *The Right to Vote: The Contested History of Democracy in the United States* (New York, 2000).

5. TJ to Judge William Johnson, 12 June 1823, L&B, 15:442.

6. John Adams to TJ, 13 July 1813, *AJL*, 356.

7. TJ to John Dickinson, 6 March 1801, *TJW*, 1084–85.

8. Joyce Appleby, "Commercial Farming and the 'Agrarian Myth' in the Early Republic," *Journal of American History* 68 (March 1982): 833–49.

9. TJ to William Johnson, 12 June 1823, L&B, 15:441–42; TJ to William Green Munford, 18 June 1799, *TJW*, 1064–65.

10. See, for example, TJ to John Adams, 14 October 1816, *AJL*, 492.

11. See, for example, TJ to John Melish, 13 January 1813, L&B, 13:212; and TJ to Du Pont, 24 April 1816, in *Correspondence between Thomas Jefferson and Pierre Samuel Du Pont de Nemours, 1798–1817*, ed. Dumas Malone (Boston, 1930), 182.

12. TJ to Tench Coxe, 1 June 1795, in *The Works of Thomas Jefferson*, 12 vols., ed. Paul Leicester Ford (New York, 1904–5), 8:183, hereafter cited as "Federal Edition."

13. TJ to Littleton Waller Tazewell, 5 January 1805, *TJW*, 1149.

14. TJ to the Citizens of Washington, 4 March 1809, L&B, 16:347.

15. In an enormous literature on American "exceptionalism," see, by way of introduction: Michael Kammen, "The Problem of American Exceptionalism: A Reconsideration," *American Quarterly* 45 (March 1993): 1–43; Ian Tyrrell, "American Exceptionalism in an Age of International History," *American Historical Review* 96 (October 1991): 1031–55; Michael McGerr, "The Price of the 'New Transnational History,'" *American Historical Review* 96 (October 1991): 1056–67; Laurence Veysey, "The Autonomy of American History Reconsidered," *American Quarterly* 31 (Autumn 1979): 455–77; and Byron E. Shafer, ed., *Is America Different? A New Look at American Exceptionalism* (New York, 1991).

16. Despite his brief, and undeniable, enthusiasm in the early 1790s, Jefferson later made a conscious effort to disassociate himself from the most egregious excesses of the French Revolution, associating himself with Lafayette and other moderates in his memoirs. For this insight, see Robert M. S. McDonald, "Thomas Jefferson and Historical Self-Construction: The Earth Belongs to the Living?" *The Historian* 61 (1999): 295. For sober assessments of Jefferson's French Revolution, see R. R. Palmer, "The Dubious Democrat: Thomas Jefferson in Bourbon France," *Political Science Quarterly* 72 (September 1957): 388–404; and Lawrence S. Kaplan, *Jefferson and France: An Essay on Politics and Political Ideas* (New Haven, Conn., 1967), 27–30, 33–35. These treatments should be read in light of the fact that for Jefferson, as Nicholas Onuf and Peter Onuf have rightly noted, "the important thing about the French Revolution was that it vindicated the principle of national self-determination," a principle Jefferson never relinquished. See Onuf and Onuf, *Nations, Markets, and War: Modern History and the American Civil War* (Charlottesville, Va., 2006), 231. For a more traditional reading of Jefferson and the French Revolution, see Gordon S. Wood, *Empire of Liberty: A History of the Early Republic, 1789–1815* (New York, 2009), 179–81. A more judicious assessment is in Stanley Elkins and Eric McKitrick, *Age of Federalism* (New York, 1993), 314–17 and 336–54.

17. Jefferson later acknowledged to John Adams that Adams's "prophecies" about the likely outcome of the French Revolution "proved truer than mine." See TJ to Adams, 11 January 1816, *AJL*, 459.

18. TJ to Baron Alexander Von Humboldt, 6 December 1813, L&B, 14:21. For his part, John Adams agreed with Jefferson that "a free government and the Roman Catholick religion can never exist together in any nation or Country, and consequently . . . all projects for reconciling them in old Spain or new are Eutopian, Platonick and chimerical." Adams to TJ, 3 February 1821, *AJL*, 571. Also see Adams to TJ, 19 May 1821, ibid., 573; and Adams to TJ, 15 August 1823, ibid., 595. Jefferson and Adams egged each other on in this conviction: see TJ to Adams, 4 September 1823, ibid., 596.

19. TJ to Adams, 4 September 1823, ibid., 596.

20. TJ to Lafayette, 14 May 1817, L&B, 15:117.

21. TJ to John Adams, 17 May 1818, *AJL*, 524.

22. TJ to Du Pont de Nemours, 24 April 1816, in Malone, ed., *Correspondence between Jefferson and Du Pont*, 186.

23. TJ to John Adams, 17 May 1818, *AJL*, 524.

24. TJ to Lafayette, 14 May 1817, L&B, 15:117; TJ to John Adams, 22 January 1821, *AJL*, 570.

25. TJ to Madison, 18 November 1788, *TJP*, 12:188–89. On this sentiment, also see TJ to John Jay, 19 November 1788, ibid., 212–13.

26. TJ to Lafayette, 14 February 1815, L&B, 14:245–46.

27. TJ to Du Pont de Nemours, 28 February 1815, and 15 April 1811, in *Correspondence between Jefferson and Du Pont*, ed. Malone, 151, 132. For the same sentiment, see TJ to Lafayette, 14 February 1815, L&B, 14:245–46.

28. TJ to Du Pont de Nemours, 24 April 1816, in *Correspondence between Jefferson and Du Pont*, ed. Malone, 181.

29. TJ to Lafayette, 14 February 1815, L&B, 14:245–46.

30. TJ to Du Pont de Nemours, 24 April 1816, in *Correspondence between Jefferson and Du Pont*, ed. Malone, 187.

31. TJ to Richard Price, 7 August 1785, *TJP*, 8:357.

32. TJ to Samuel Kercheval, 12 July 1816, L&B, 15:35.

33. Jefferson to William Carmichael, 2 August 1790, *TJP*, 17:114. These quotations come from Jefferson's *Outline of Policy on the Mississippi Question*, which he enclosed in the letter.

34. TJ to John Breckenridge, 29 January 1800, *TJP*, 31:344, emphasis added.

35. TJ to John Adams, 28 October 1813, *AJL*, 391.

36. TJ to John Taylor, 28 May 1816, L&B, 15:22.

37. TJ to John Adams, 28 February 1796, *AJL*, 260.

38. TJ to John Adams, 28 October 1813, ibid., 391.

39. TJ, *Notes on the State of Virginia*, ed. William Peden (Chapel Hill, 1954), 164; TJ to Maria Cosway, 12 October 1786, *TJP*, 10:448. This theme of unusually widespread prosperity is as old as the idea of America and remains a prominent component in contemporary American exceptionalism. See Jack P. Greene, *The Intellectual Construction of America: Exceptionalism and Identity from 1492 to 1800* (Chapel Hill, N.C., 1993); and David M. Potter, *People of Plenty: Economic Abundance and the American Character* (Chicago, 1954).

40. TJ to Thomas Cooper, 10 September 1814, L&B, 14:182. Also see TJ, *Notes*, ed. Peden, 133.

41. TJ, First Annual Message, 8 December 1801, *TJW*, 503.

42. "Notes of a Tour through Holland and the Rhine Valley," *TJP*, 13:27–28; 36, n. 29, emphasis added.

43. TJ to Charles Bellini, 30 September 1785, *TJP*, 8:568.

44. Greene, *Intellectual Construction of America*.

45. Adam Smith, *The Wealth of Nations*, in *The Essential Adam Smith*, ed. Robert L. Heilbroner (New York, 1986), 250–51, 302.

46. TJ to Roger C. Weightman, 24 June 1826, *TJW*, 1517.

47. TJ to John Adams, 11 January 1816, *AJL*, 460.

48. TJ to William Lee, 16 January 1817, L&B, 15:100–101.

49. TJ to John Quincy Adams, 1 November 1817, L&B, 15:145.

50. TJ, The "Anas," "Explanations of the 3. volumes bound in marble paper," [1818], in Federal Edition, 1:183.

51. Hamilton to John Jay, 26 November 1775, AHP, 1:176–77.

52. TJ to James Warren, 21 March 1801, *TJP*, 33:398–99, emphasis added.

53. See Linda Kerber, *Federalists in Dissent: Imagery and Ideology in Jeffersonian America* (Ithaca, N.Y., 1970), esp. 1–22.

54. TJ, *Notes*, ed. Peden, 129.

55. TJ to Justice William Johnson, 12 June 1823, *TJW*, 1470.

56. TJ to John Breckinridge, 29 January 1800, *TJP*, 31:344–45.

57. TJ to John Adams, 28 February 1786, ibid., 28:618.

58. TJ, Eighth Annual Message, 8 November 1808, *TJW*, 549.

59. TJ to Thaddeus Kosciusko, 21 February 1799, L&B, 10:115.

60. See John Phillip Reid, *The Concept of Liberty in the Age of the American Revolution* (Chicago, 1988), esp. 32–37.

61. George Washington, First Annual Message to Congress, 8 January 1790, in *The Papers of George Washington, Presidential Series*, 15 vols. to date, ed. W. W. Abbot et al. (Charlottesville, Va., 1987–), 4:545.

62. TJ, *Notes*, ed. Peden, 84–85.

63. TJ to Adams, 28 October 1813, *AJL*, 391.

64. TJ, *Notes*, ed. Peden, 165.

65. Ibid., 161, 121.

66. Also see Madison, "Notes for the *National Gazette* Essays" [ca. 19 December 1791–3 March 1792], in *The Papers of James Madison, Congressional Series*, 17 vols., ed. William T. Hutchinson et al. (Chicago and Charlottesville, Va., 1962–91), 14:163–64.

67. TJ, *Notes*, ed. Peden, 121.

68. Ibid., 120.

69. See Gordon S. Wood, *The Creation of the American Republic* (Chapel Hill, N.C., 1969), 97–114; Richard L. Bushman, *The Refinement of America: Persons, Houses, Cities* (New York, 1992), 186–203.

70. John Jay to TJ, 27 October 1786, *TJP*, 10:488–89.

71. TJ to Abigail Adams, 22 February 1787, ibid., 11:174; TJ to Abigail Adams, 21 December 1786, ibid., 10:621.

72. TJ to Edward Carrington, 16 January 1787, ibid., 11:49.

73. Ibid., emphasis added. Jefferson never endorsed the "motives" or methods of the insurgents. These, he admitted, were "founded in ignorance," and "produced acts absolutely unjustifiable." TJ to William Stephens Smith, 13 November 1787, ibid., 12:356; TJ to Madison, 30 January 1787, ibid., 11:92.

74. TJ to William Carmichael, 26 December 1786, ibid., 10:633.

75. TJ to James Madison, 30 January 1787, ibid., 93.

76. See, for example, John Adams to TJ, 30 November 1786, ibid., 10:557.

77. TJ to William Carmichael, 26 December 1786, ibid., 633.

78. TJ to Madison, 20 December 1787, ibid., 12:442.

79. TJ to Smith, 13 November 1787, ibid., 12:355–57.

80. TJ to Madison, January 30, 1787, in *Republic of Letters*, ed. Smith, 2:461.

81. TJ to Adams; also see TJ to Walter Jones, 2 January 1814, L&B, 14:47; and TJ to Du Pont de Nemours, 24 April 1816, in *Correspondence between Jefferson and Du Pont*, ed. Malone, 182.

82. TJ to Adams, 28 February 1796, *AJL*, 259–60.

83. Madison, "Ten," in *The Federalist*, ed. J. R. Pole, (Indianapolis, 2005), 52.

84. TJ to John Taylor, 28 May 1816, L&B, 15:19–22; TJ to Isaac Tiffany, 26 August 1816, ibid., 15:66; Palmer, "Notes on the Use of the Word 'Democracy,'" 212.

85. TJ, First Inaugural Address, 4 March 1801, *TJW*, 493. As Paul A. Rahe has noted, even Antifederalists distanced themselves from Shays; see Rahe, *Republics Ancient and Modern*, 698, 1100, n. 44. What makes Jefferson unusual here is not his bloodlust for "rebellion," but his equanimity in the face of danger to public order from the democracy.

86. Notes for First Inaugural Address, in Federal Edition, ed. Ford, 9:193.

87. Tocqueville, *Democracy in America*, trans. Arthur Goldhammer (New York, 2004), 273–77.

88. TJ to Joseph C. Cabell, 2 February 1816, L&B, 14:422.

89. TJ to Isaac Weaver, 7 June 1807, ibid., 11:220–21.

90. TJ to the Representatives of the people of New Jersey in their Legislature, 10 December 1807, ibid., 16:295.

91. TJ to Edward Carrington, 16 January 1787, *TJP*, 11:49.

92. See, among others, TJ to John Taylor, 1 June 1798, L&B, 10:44–47; TJ to James Lewis Jr., 9 May 1798, ibid., 37; TJ to Elbridge Gerry, 26 January 1799, ibid., 80–83; TJ to Thaddeus Kosciusko, 21 February 1799, ibid., 115–16; TJ to Robert R. Livingston, 28 February 1799, ibid., 118–19; TJ to Thomas Lomax, 12 March 1799, *TJP*, 31:77–78; TJ to William Green Munford, 18 June 1799, *TJW*, 1065; TJ to Priestley, January 27, 1800, L&B, 10:148; TJ to Thomas Mann Randolph, 2 February 1800, ibid., 151; TJ to Rush, 23 September 1800, *TJP*, 32:167–68; TJ to John Dickinson, 6 March 1801, ibid., 33:196; TJ to James Warren, 21 March 1801, ibid., 398.

93. TJ to Benjamin Waring, 23 March 1801, L&B, 10:235.

94. TJ to John Adams, 28 October 1813, *AJL*, 388.

95. TJ to Judge William Johnson, 12 June 1823, L&B, 15:443.

96. TJ to Priestley, 21 March 1801, *TJW*, 1086.

97. TJ to Priestley, 27 January 1800, L&B, 10:148.

98. TJ to Priestley, 21 March 1801, *TJW*, 1086.

99. See Adams to TJ, 29 May 1813, 10 June 1813, and TJ's response on 15 June in *AJL*, 325–27, 331–33, along with the editorial note on p. 288.

100. Adams to TJ, 14 June 1813, ibid., 330.

101. TJ to Joseph Priestley, 21 March 1801, *TJW*, 1085–86. Also see a similar expression in TJ to John Tyler, 28 June 1804, L&B, 11:33.

102. TJ to Priestley, 21 March 1801, *TJW*, 1086.

103. TJ to Lafayette, 14 February 1815, L&B, 14:252.

104. TJ to P. S. Du Pont de Nemours, 18 January 1802, *TJW*, 1101.

105. See the important reflections on the nature of this problem in Daniel Rodgers, "Exceptionalism," in *Imagined Histories: American Historians Interpret the Past*, ed. Anthony Molho and Gordon S. Wood (Princeton, N.J., 1998), 21–40, esp. 22–23; Carl N. Degler, "In Pursuit of an American History," *American Historical Review* 92 (February 1987): 1–12; and Eric Foner, "Why Is There no Socialism in the United States?" *History Workshop Journal* 17 (1984): 57–80.

106. TJ to Priestley, 21 March 1801, *TJW*, 1086.

107. See Johann Neem, "The Early Republic: Thomas Jefferson's Philosophy of History and the Future of American Christianity," in *Prophesies of Godlessness: Predictions of America's Imminent Secularization, from the Puritans to the Present Day*, ed. Charles Mathewes and Christopher McKnight Nichols (New York, 2008), 35–52, esp., 41–42; and Maurizio Valsania, " 'Our Original Barbarism': Man vs. Nature in Thomas Jefferson's Moral Experience," *Journal of the History of Ideas* 65 (2004): 627–45.

108. TJ to Adams, 1 August 1816, *AJL*, 484–85.

109. TJ to John Taylor, 28 May 1816, L&B, 15:21. The poem is Sir William Jones, "An Ode in Imitation of Alcaeus" (1781). Compare the original poem by Alcaeus of Mytilene translated and explicated in Rahe, *Republics Ancient and Modern*, 30.

"To Diffuse Knowledge More Generally through the Mass of the People"

Thomas Jefferson on Individual Freedom and the Distribution of Knowledge

JOHANN N. NEEM

> Books constitute capital. A library book lasts as long as a house, for hundreds of years. It is not then an article of consumption but fairly of capital, and often in the case of professional men, setting out in life it is their only capital.
> —Thomas Jefferson to James Madison, 16 September 1821

THOMAS JEFFERSON IS FAMOUS FOR STATING IN THE DECLARATION OF Independence that it was "self-evident . . . that all men are created equal . . . with certain unalienable Rights." But rights were only Jefferson's starting point. Jefferson believed that Americans would also need the tools necessary to take advantage of their newfound freedom. What use was it to be born free if citizens could not use their freedom to promote "life, liberty, and the pursuit of happiness"? Despite often being invoked simply as an advocate of rights and limited government, Jefferson strongly supported an active state that would widely distribute knowledge, enabling each American to make the most of freedom.

Certainly Jefferson opposed the centralizing and what he believed were the elitist tendencies of the rival Federalist party. Yet this did not mean that Jefferson concluded that individual freedom and active government were inherently at odds. What mattered to Jefferson was whether public policy enhanced or limited individual freedom. In the case of public education, Jefferson believed it served liberty's cause by developing the moral and intellectual capabilities of Americans, capabilities that were necessary for them to be active republican citizens and to pursue happiness in their private affairs.

The capability approach to freedom has been articulated recently by economist Amartya Sen and philosopher Martha Nussbaum. Freedom amounts to more than simply being allowed to do a thing. What matters equally is whether one has access to the resources necessary actually to be able to do it. Sen argues, and Jefferson would have agreed, that the goal of government in a free society must be "the expansion of the 'capabilities' of persons to lead the lives they value—and have reason to value."[1] In other words, a free society is composed of individuals who have both the right and the capability to use their freedom to live a life of their choosing. To Jefferson, public education was vital to enhancing the capability of the new republic's citizens to enjoy the freedoms their rights protected.

To understand what Jefferson hoped education would do for American children, it is important to have a sense of his conception of human nature.[2] Jefferson believed that Old World education, and its replication in some New England colleges, corrupted young Americans' true moral nature. Instead of being taught to rely on their own inner resources, traditional education made children slaves to their priestly educators. In contrast, Jefferson's educational program was premised on his understanding of human nature from Epicurus, Jesus, and Scottish moral sense philosophy. Jefferson hoped that education would enable citizens to engage in their own pursuits of happiness. This required an education that cultivated those faculties of human nature vital to pursuing happiness. But what did it mean to be happy? As Jean Yarbrough argues, it is hard to know what Jefferson thought about happiness when he wrote the Declaration of Independence. We must instead look to his later letters, when he reflected on his ideas during the contemplative years of his retirement.[3]

In 1819 Jefferson wrote that he considered himself to be "an Epicurean." Epicurus's philosophy, Jefferson believed, contained "everything rational in moral philosophy, which Greece and Rome have left us." From Epicurus, Jefferson learned two things. The first was that happiness was premised on an innate human desire to seek pleasure. But Epicurus did not equate pleasure with following one's immediate desires, Jefferson wrote. Instead, one must look to the long run and accept momentary challenges, and even pain, if it produces a "greater pleasure." A happy person, therefore, must have the rational capability to make choices that will produce the most happiness in the long run, and the mental discipline to put aside immediate pleasure in order to engage in "well-regulated indulgences." This, Jefferson concluded, means that a truly happy person would be a virtuous one. Virtue is not based on some abstract category; it is put to the test of "utility." In Jefferson's eyes, the virtues that most successfully promoted happiness were prudence, temperance, fortitude, and justice.[4]

The second major lesson Epicurus taught Jefferson, and one that would shape his own understanding of Jesus's teachings, was to avoid what he considered to be unnecessary metaphysical explanation. Epicurus argued that to fear death and the gods was irrational. Since death is the absence of being, it should not be something living beings must fear nor to which they should look forward. And since the gods are presumably capable of taking care of themselves, their concerns are not humanity's concerns.[5] As Jefferson wrote to John Adams in 1820, existence is proven through the senses: "I feel: therefore I exist." God endowed matter with powers or faculties detectable through scientific research. To move beyond an awareness of these faculties to talk about such metaphysical conceptions as the soul is "to talk of *nothings.*" Instead, Jefferson urged Adams to focus on what human nature is and what human beings do rather than on the mystical sources behind it all. "Rejecting all organs of information therefore but my senses," he wrote, "I rid myself of Pyrrhonisms with which an indulgence in speculations hyperphysical and antiphysical so uselessly occupy and disquiet the mind."[6] To Jefferson, one need not look into the soul, but instead examine what constitutes human nature based on our own experience of it.

Influenced by reading Scottish moral sense philosophy—including Lord Kames, whom he considered "one of the ablest" moral philosophers—Jefferson argued that the two most important faculties to cultivate for promoting human happiness are reason and the moral sense.[7] Reason was necessary to guide people to their greatest happiness, and to enable them to question authority. But the moral sense, a fundamental aspect of human nature, fitted human beings to live in society, where they could benefit from the comforts civilization provides.[8] To Jefferson, the moral sense was an innate attribute of human nature. When God created human beings, he fitted them for their social lives. "The Creator would indeed have been a bungling artist, had he intended man for a social animal, without planting in him social dispositions," Jefferson wrote in 1814.[9] Daniel Walker Howe argues that to Jefferson the moral sense was a rational capability.[10] Although Jefferson never developed a formal theory about the moral sense, his writings suggest that he believed it closer to a prerational emotive faculty that provides each person a natural foundation for morality and interpreting others' actions. He referred to the moral sense as a "a moral instinct . . . which prompts us irresistibly to feel and to succor" the "distresses" of others.[11] This conception of the moral sense is closer to Francis Hutcheson's—it is an irresistible response that individuals have to others' actions and an irresistible instinctual guide to their own. Writing about Native Americans, Jefferson argued in *Notes on the State of Virginia* that, despite living in primitive political societies, their "moral sense of right and wrong," which he likened not to reason but to "the sense of taste and feeling," guided their actions.[12] As early as 1771, Jefferson referred to humanity's natural ability to rejoice at benevolent actions and recoil from cruel ones as an "emotion."[13]

What role did this emotive moral sense play? It ensured that human beings fulfilled their duties to each other—and more important, that human nature was structured so as to make one's fulfillment of that duty pleasurable. Some might argue that this turns benevolence into selfishness, but Jefferson thought otherwise. Relying on his materialist Epicurean conception of human nature, Jefferson responded that since "the moral sense, or conscience, is as much a part of man as his leg or arm," it was a fact of our original design, and the pleasure we took from benevolent action was neither selfish nor anything else. It was simply part of being human.[14]

But, of course, Jefferson understood that human nature is complex, that human beings are capable of selfish, passionate behavior as well as rational, benevolent action.[15] The moral sense, like reason, therefore required cultivation. "Encourage all your virtuous dispositions, and exercise them whenever an opportunity arises," he encouraged his nephew, Peter Carr, "being assured that they gain strength by exercise, as a limb of the body does, and that exercise will make them habitual."[16] Since the moral sense could be strengthened, education provided the basis for morality. "The want or imperfection of the moral sense in some men, like the want or imperfection of the senses of sight and hearing in others, is no proof that it is a general characteristic of the species," he maintained. "When it is wanting, we endeavor to supply the defect by education, by appeals to reason and calculation, by presenting the being so unhappily conformed, other motives to do good and to eschew evil, such as the love, or the hatred, or rejection of those among whom he lives, and whose society is necessary to his happiness and even existence."[17] Those who had a weaker moral sense than others proved the reality of natural deviation from the norm. It might be corrected by appealing to reason and interest, and, Jefferson believed, by schools that would help young children strengthen their own moral sense.

Jefferson read the teachings of Jesus through both Epicurus and Scottish moral sense theory. In a remarkable 1820 letter, he implied that he likened the Federalist party to ancient Jews and argued that Jesus, like Jefferson's Republican party, liberated the temple (America) and restored its true foundation—the innate goodness of humanity. Jews, like Federalists, followed the teachings of Moses, "a being of terrific character, cruel, vindictive, capricious, and unjust." Jesus, on the other hand, understood and advocated "the best qualities of the human head and heart." Whereas Moses "instilled in his people the most anti-social spirit," Jesus "preached philanthropy and universal charity and benevolence."[18] Jesus thus taught humans about their true nature, their capability to engage in moral action. In doing so, Jesus illuminated the ways in which the keepers of the temple—the priests and the politicians—had corrupted human nature to serve their own needs. Restoring to humans their true nature—from which, as Joyce Appleby argues, Jefferson believed we had long been alienated—would allow the moral sense to reign once more, along with the rational individual pursuit of happiness.[19]

Near the end of his life, perhaps influenced by early Romanticism, Jefferson suggested that every human being's pursuit of happiness was unique. Even if human nature is simply matter endowed with certain faculties, it was possible, Jefferson averred in 1814, that "her creation is of individuals." He wrote that "no two animals are exactly alike; no two plants, nor even two leaves or blades of grass; no two crystallizations." One might therefore conclude that "no two particles of matter are of exact resemblance." The result was an "infinitude of units or individuals." We must classify these units or individuals into broad categories based on their "resemblance," but we must always remember that generalizations are our imposition on nature's diversity.[20]

This letter, however suggestive of the future of American liberalism during the 1830s and 1840s, does not reflect the majority of Jefferson's writing. Instead, like other Enlightenment thinkers, he tended to universalize human nature, focusing on what human beings shared in common rather than on those attributes that distinguished one from the other. Nonetheless, Jefferson's letter suggests that he understood that the universal pursuit of happiness might require different people to pursue different paths. Education must prepare them to find their own way.

Jefferson hoped for a society in which all citizens could engage in the pursuit of their private happiness, knowing also that the moral sense ensured that one's private pursuits would not conflict with one's social duties.[21] But all this requires citizens who can and will engage in the pursuit of happiness. However natural Jefferson may have imagined these citizens, he recognized that the qualities of democratic humanity had to be cultivated. On the one hand, the shackles of the past had to be removed. For generations, people had been born into dependence in a world marked by inequality. People had to learn to think of themselves as equal to each other, and to learn how to engage in their own pursuits of happiness. They needed to throw off the psychology of dependence and learn to think as democrats.[22] But they also needed the *capability* to engage in their own pursuits of happiness, and this required access to education.

Jefferson believed that Americans, like Europeans, had long been denied the right and the capability to engage in their own pursuit of happiness. One reason was that knowledge, a prerequisite both to making rational decisions about one's own life and to sustaining republican government, had too long been in a few hands. In Europe, and still in New England with its established churches, access to knowledge was, according to Jefferson, determined by an aristocracy of wealth and religion. In other words, cultural capital was owned by the few and denied to the many. Education's job was to distribute widely cultural capital—knowledge and skills—to all.

Jefferson understood implicitly Pierre Bourdieu's argument that capital comes in three forms—economic, cultural, and social—and that each reinforces the other. Economic capital is generally defined as money and wealth. Cultural capital, on the other hand, involves access to knowledge—to education—which one might use either to earn wealth or to reinforce one's status in society relative to others. Social capital has to do with one's social status, and the benefits and privileges that status brings. Nobles in the Old World transformed their control over economic and cultural capital into social capital; they then used their social status to reinforce their hold over wealth and education. Jefferson hoped to destroy this close alliance between capital and power. He believed that by ensuring the wide distribution of cultural capital—education—he could prevent the emergence of a few families with high social capital while also ensuring each citizen the capability to participate to their full potential in society. The state had to guarantee each citizen access to cultural capital, to education, if each citizen was to have a fair opportunity to make something of himself.[23]

Jefferson believed that a world dominated by an inherited aristocracy of knowledge fundamentally threatened individual liberty. First, such an arrangement threatened popular self-government by denying people the knowledge and skills they would need as citizens. Second, it denied human beings access to the resources necessary to pursue their own happiness. Jefferson condemned Old World societies for sustaining aristocracies while denying ordinary people an opportunity to nourish their own human potential. Instead, Jefferson urged, in a series of letters exchanged late in life with his good friend and former political rival John Adams, the replacement of an inherited "artificial aristocracy" with a republican "natural aristocracy." Jefferson hoped that cultural capital, as well as economic and social capital, would no longer be the inherited domain of a few powerful families, but instead would be distributed anew each generation.

In their latter years, Jefferson and Adams renewed their friendship, which had been damaged by the partisan conflicts of the 1790s. As Adams touchingly told Jefferson, "You and I ought not to die, before We have explained ourselves to each other."[24] One of the more famous exchanges to emerge from their renewed friendship concerned the question of aristocracy. Adams suggested that, despite what they might wish, true equality is impossible in an imperfect world. Unfortunately, Adams wrote, "Beauty Wealth, Birth" always won out against "Genius and Virtues." A well-constructed government must both take advantage of the talents of a society's aristocracy while limiting its dangers.[25] Jefferson agreed with Adams that there existed a "natural aristocracy among men," but that is where their agreement ended.[26]

Jefferson, unlike Adams, distinguished between a society's natural and its artificial aristocracy. Artificial aristocracies, he wrote, are "founded on wealth and birth, without either virtue or talents." Elites who inherited economic and social capital dominated society regardless of their actual merit. In contrast, a society's natural aristocracy, which Jefferson considered "the most precious gift for the instruction, the trusts, and government of society," was made up of those with the most "virtue and talents." These men could emerge from any part of society so long as they had access to the resources they needed to improve themselves. Jefferson therefore urged that Americans do all they could to limit the inheritance of both wealth and cultural capital, which was the basis of elites' social capital. Voters must be permitted to choose the best men for office regardless of their birth. But voters would need to be educated in order "to select the veritable aristoi, for the trusts of government, to the exclusion of the Pseudalists," or the artificial aristocracy.[27]

Jefferson feared both the landed aristocracy that made up Europe's noble class and the wealth and privileges inherited by the established church and its clergy. Members of the established clergy used their positions to retain cultural authority—they were what Christopher Grasso has called a "speaking aristocracy"—in order to promote their ideas and interests. In Jefferson's eyes, the established clergy, like any other artificial aristocracy, used its legal position to gain privileged access to the public sphere and cultural capital.[28] As Jefferson wrote to a friend soon after his election to the presidency, "I have sworn on the altar of god, eternal hostility against every form of tyranny over the mind of man."[29] He saw the election of 1800 as being between the true advocates of human happiness (his Republican party) and the Federalist apostles of "bigotry in Politics & Religion," who would "bring back the times of Vandalism, when ignorance put everything into the hands of power & priestcraft."[30] Through their control of cultural capital, New England's Federalists had "hood-winked" American citizens "from their principles." Jefferson's election was proof that the people had seen through the Federalist clergy's lies.[31]

Perhaps the most pressing danger posed by the established clergy was that it denied Americans (and Europeans) knowledge of Jesus's true teaching, and thus one major source of private and public happiness. Since Jesus's death, priests had corrupted Jesus's teaching with invented doctrines. The established church's domination of Christian teaching had long prevented people from learning of the source of happiness and its basis in human nature. Jefferson, on the other hand, hoped to strip Christianity "of the rags in which they [the ministers of the established churches] have enveloped it" and restore Christianity's "original purity and simplicity."[32] The established church had masked the radical simplicity of Jesus's message and Americans needed to recover it from the "rubbish in which it is buried."[33] The Bible, he believed, was written by humans and suffered from human errors. In 1823 Jefferson wrote confidently that "the day will come when the mystical generation of Jesus, by the supreme being as his father in the womb of a virgin will be classed with the fable of the generation of Minerva in the brain of Jupiter. But we may hope that the dawn of reason and freedom of thought in these United

States will do away with all this artificial scaffolding, and restore us to the primitive and genuine doctrines of this the most venerated reformer of human errors."[34] Intellectual progress depended therefore on what Jefferson called a "wall of separation" between church and state.[35] Ministers of established churches relied on the state's power to reinforce their own cultural authority while limiting the freedom of expression and the public use of reason. Separating church from state would strip the clergy of its artificial power and ensure that reason was free to fight lies.

Destroying the artificial aristocracies of wealth and religion required, Jefferson believed, more than destroying the elite's inherited control over cultural capital. It would require undermining its control of wealth, or economic capital. Jefferson's most vivid exploration of this question came in a 1785 letter he wrote to James Madison reflecting on his observations during a walk in Fontainebleau, France. Jefferson was struck by the "unequal division of property which occasions the numberless instances of wretchedness which I had observed in this country and is to be observed all over Europe." Land, the most important form of economic capital in agricultural societies, was concentrated among an elite few who, he observed, "employ the flower of the country as servants." Ordinary people, denied the fruits of their own labor, had little opportunity to engage in their own pursuits of happiness. Jefferson urged instead the wide distribution of capital. "Legislators cannot invent too many devices for subdividing property," he argued. He advocated the abolition of primogeniture and a progressive land tax to limit elites' incentive to accumulate more land than they could productively use. There also came a point at which inequality was no longer justifiable: "Whenever there are in any country uncultivated lands and unemployed poor, it is clear that the laws of property have been so far extended as to violate natural right." Property, as Jefferson learned from John Locke, grew out of mixing one's labor with the land. Aristocrats had more land than they could use productively, while others were denied wrongly the ability to gain access to the land that they needed. To Jefferson, "the earth is given as a common stock for man to labor and live on. If for the encouragement of industry we allow it to be appropriated, we must take care that other employment be provided to those excluded from the appropriation. If we do not, the fundamental right to labor the earth returns to the unemployed."[36]

Even as he concluded that one could have too much land, he did not seek absolute equality because he believed that both property and its limits were premised on the natural right to gain the legitimate fruits of one's labor. On the one hand, one could not take from a living person what he earned by the sweat of his brow. On the other hand, no one has a right to more than he has earned or can use so long as there are others who are in need, as Jefferson made clear to Madison. Regardless of any present inequalities, however, Jefferson was adamant that "the law of nature" mandated redistributing economic capital between generations.[37]

Two tools sustained the artificial aristocracy's control over economic capital. The first, entails, enabled elites and such institutions as endowed charities and the established church to lock up their land beyond the public's reach forever, maintaining an elite minority's control over society's resources. The second, primogeniture, ensured that landed property was passed whole from one generation to the next, allowing families to consolidate and expand wealth across time. Jefferson concluded that both entails and primogeniture sustained inequality and limited the ability of members of the present generation to make the full use of their individual liberty. He believed "'that the earth belongs in usufruct to the living;' that the dead have neither powers nor rights over it. The portion occupied by an individual ceases to be his when himself ceases to be, and reverts to the society."[38] Only those currently living could lay claim to the land and its bounty, to capital. The idea that one generation could bind the next would enable the dead to limit the freedom of the living. The living have a natural right, Jefferson argued, to the property of those no longer living.

Breaking up inherited aristocracies—whether they were formed by individual families or by the established church—was only the first step, however. Once the keepers of knowledge were denied a virtual monopoly in cultural capital, the people themselves would have to gain access to it. It was here that formal, public education becomes important to Jefferson.

Education's purpose in a republic, Jefferson argued in *Notes on the State of Virginia*, was "to diffuse knowledge more generally through the mass of the people."[39] Richard D. Brown notes that, to Jefferson and other founders, "being informed was a key ingredient of hegemony, just as ignorance sustained the submissiveness of ordinary people."[40] Concentrations of capital produce concentrations of power, Jefferson believed, whether that capital took the form of land or education. Without access to cultural capital, American citizens would be denied the tools and knowledge they needed to govern themselves and to engage in the private pursuit of happiness. A liberal society must therefore provide citizens with access to the capital they need to become flourishing, free individuals.

From the perspective of the republic, Jefferson was clear, the best guarantee against tyranny was an educated citizenry. Of all the goals Jefferson had for public education, "none is more important, none more legitimate, than that of rendering the people the safe, as they are the ultimate, guardians of their own liberty."[41] It is no accident, then, that Jefferson's proposed bill was "for the more general diffusion of knowledge."[42] American leaders, Jefferson argued, must arise from the people themselves "without regard to wealth, birth or other accidental condition or circumstance." Yet most citizens lacked the means to attend school and ready themselves for civic leadership even if "nature hath fitly formed and disposed [them] to become useful instruments for the public."[43] Aristocracies of knowledge, like aristocracies of wealth, sustained their political power by controlling access to capital. In a republic, leaders should be chosen based on their qualities, not their birth. By making education widely available, by diffusing cultural capital broadly, both ordinary citizens and future leaders would be made fit to protect their liberties.[44]

One reason to think about the wide distribution of knowledge in terms of capital is that, to Jefferson, knowledge was progressive. As Henry May writes, Enlightenment thinkers "were sure they lived in a new age. For them, Enlightenment was an unsparing sunrise, revealing the wickedness and folly of ancient ideas and institutions, illuminating also the fundamental goodness of man."[45] Jefferson would have agreed. But if knowledge is progressive and if discoveries about the natural and human worlds are usually made by the most educated elites, each generation must ensure the broad distribution of every increase in cultural capital or else the initial allotment of knowledge would be made meaningless.

Jefferson did not believe that the progress of knowledge was a necessary component of history. Unlike his contemporary Condorcet, Jefferson's classical republican learning made him constantly fearful that the Enlightenment might be corrupted. He considered the 1790s—which he dubbed the "reign of witches"—to be proof positive that if elites controlled cultural capital and limited the freedom of reason to counter error, human progress might be thwarted.[46] Jefferson saw in the Federalists' Sedition Act proof that elites hoped to limit the people's enlightenment, their access to true knowledge, by muzzling critics of the government and the emerging opposition press. Jefferson and his Republican allies had refused to be silenced, however, and his election to the presidency proved that "the band is removed, and now they [the people] see for themselves."[47] In his 1801 inaugural address, Jefferson noted that freedom requires constant vigilance. No natural law will ensure progress. America's liberation from the tyranny of kings and priests was not inevitable but required "the wisdom of our sages and blood of our heroes." In the 1790s Americans had strayed from the true path to progress. If it ever happened again, Jefferson urged his fellow Americans to "retrace our steps and to regain the road which alone leads to peace, liberty, and safety."[48]

The true path requires reason to be free to combat error and ignorance and to enlighten the people. In *Notes on the State of Virginia*, Jefferson wrote that "reason and free enquiry are the only effectual agents against error." He noted that "reason and experiment [in the sciences] have been indulged, and error has fled before them. It is error alone which needs the support of government. Truth can stand by itself."[49] If reason was permitted free reign in civil society's public sphere, as well as in America's schools, myths would constantly give way to truth. Over time, our knowledge of the natural and human worlds would increase. He therefore condemned those who espoused the "Gothic idea that we are to look backwards, instead of forwards for the improvement of the human mind."[50] When Jefferson examined the past, he saw the progress made by scientific research. He considered it "cowardly" to believe that "the human mind is incapable of further advances," adding that this false belief is the doctrine of "despots."[51] Despots in church and state need to control access to knowledge in order to sustain the lies that keep them in power. In a republic, however, the freedom to reason ensured that truth would gain ground over time as reason emerged victorious in successive battles against inherited prejudice and error.

If knowledge is progressive, each generation would produce more cultural capital than the one before, and thus it was imperative that this knowledge be made available to all people. The future would be bright if each generation added "their own acquisitions and discoveries" to the knowledge it had inherited and then handed "the mass down for successive and constant accumulation." This could not fail to "advance the knowledge and well-being of mankind."[52]

It is for this reason that Jefferson concluded that copyrights and patents on ideas were against nature—for ideas belong to the world, not to individuals. In an 1813 letter he connected the importance of breaking up inherited economic capital to cultural capital. He argued that, since the earth belongs to the living and since the dead cannot claim property rights over it, "it would be curious, then, if an idea, the fugitive fermentation of an individual brain, could, of natural right, be claimed in exclusive and stable property." An idea by its very nature cannot be exclusively possessed from "the moment it is divulged." Moreover, "no one possess the less, because every other possesses the whole of it." Unlike the theft of physical property, taking an idea robs no one of its possession. "Inventions then cannot, in nature, be a subject of property," Jefferson believed. Certainly, government might grant inventors exclusive rights for a limited period in order to encourage scientific progress. But Jefferson was not convinced that this was necessary. Such monopolies over knowledge, Jefferson wrote, "produce more embarrassment than advantage to society." Scientific progress is limited by allowing ideas to be owned exclusively. If happiness depends on the progress of science and the arts, Jefferson suggested, cultural capital ought not to be owned exclusively over generations, and of natural right cannot be.[53]

Since Jefferson supported the wide diffusion of knowledge in order to promote public and private happiness, it follows that Jefferson would have recognized that, as knowledge advances, so too must the subjects schools teach. Students require access to the most up-to-date cultural capital their teachers can provide. Otherwise, they would grow up in ignorance, subject to the superior knowledge of the elite. Education in a republic therefore would be different than "the education of our ancestors" because it would embrace the knowledge gained by reason.[54] American educational institutions must not be tied down by the past but must instead push knowledge forward, and provide that knowledge to republican citizens. As Virginia's governor in the midst of revolution, Jefferson had hoped to remove all theology professors from his alma mater, believing that they promoted ignorance over truth. "Science is progressive," Jefferson argued in 1805, and "what was useful two centuries ago is now become useless, e.g. one half of the professorships of W[illia]m & Mary."[55] When Jefferson shifted his concern to founding the new University of Virginia, he proclaimed that it would be a secular institution committed to teaching the natural and human sciences. Ethics would replace theology. In his 1818 report of the commissioners supervising the establishment of the university, he condemned the view "that to secure ourselves where we are, we must tread with awful reverence in the footsteps of our fathers."[56] If knowledge is progressive, then educational institutions must also be progressive. This means that what they teach must change as knowledge increases. In other words, every generation's cultural capital must be distributed to the students of the rising generation.

What should schools teach? Jefferson's conception of human nature suggests a belief that schools must impart to all citizens the knowledge and skills they needed to pursue happiness and be competent, active republican citizens. Education's purpose was to overcome what Sen calls a "capabilities deprivation," the situation when the existence of a right is not accompanied by the ability to take advantage of it. On similar grounds, but thinking purely about the civic aspect of education rather than the private pursuit of happiness, Richard D. Brown has argued that Jefferson and other American leaders believed that an informed citizenry capable of fulfilling its public duties required the state to promote actively the means of gaining information, including schools and other institutions that promote knowledge.[57]

In his "Bill for the More General Diffusion of Knowledge" (1778), Jefferson proposed a tiered public system. The bill, which never passed in its proposed form, had several aspects. First, it mandated every county to elect annually three aldermen. On the first Monday in October, the aldermen would meet and divide their counties into "hundreds," or small wards, each containing sufficient children for a school while remaining small enough so that "all children within each hundred may daily attend the school." The electors in every hundred would then meet on the third Monday of October to decide where to build a school house, or to repair an existing one. Every boy and girl in the county would attend the ward elementary school "gratis," at the public expense, so that they would learn "reading, writing, and common arithmetick." Jefferson proposed that aldermen appoint an overseer for every ten or so ward schools who would, in turn, appoint a teacher, visit the school regularly, and make curricular decisions.[58]

Above the ward elementary schools would be a series of public grammar schools to educate the brightest boys in Greek and Latin. In these schools, tuition would be required, but every September each overseer of the ward elementary schools would appoint the best male pupil under his supervision "whose parents are too poor to give them farther education." These especially bright and promising boys would go on to grammar school at public expense. As a result, even as schooling became more privileged, a few boys would be able to continue forward regardless of their parents' economic condition. The best pupil from every district would then go on to the College of William and Mary "to be educated, boarded, and clothed, three years" at public expense.[59]

The most important aspect of Jefferson's plan was the ward elementary school. It was not only the most inclusive but, to Jefferson, it provided every white Virginian the education she or he would need to pursue her or his own life and livelihood and, for males, to take part in the selection of lawmakers. These schools were to be the bedrock of the republic and the foundation for each individual's pursuit of happiness. Their curricula therefore must aim to promote both private and public welfare. Elementary ward schools would encourage people's innate moral and intellectual capabilities—their moral sense and reason—as well as provide the basic cultural literacy required for each person to fulfill his or her civic roles. Education thus enabled individuals to locate and to pursue their happiness and to be citizens.

Jefferson proposed that elementary schools teach those subjects that are necessary for all people. He understood that only a few would go on to become political leaders, and those people would require a more advanced education at later stages, culminating in college. But for ordinary boys and girls—those destined to become farmers and their wives—a broad, general liberal education was necessary "proportioned to the condition and pursuits of his life."[60] General elementary education must impart what an individual needed to know to function as a citizen, namely "to judge for himself what will secure or endanger his freedom."[61] But education is more than civic; for those not destined to become political leaders, it must "qualify them for [both] their pursuits and duties."[62] In 1818, as Jefferson set out to establish the University of Virginia, he reflected on the nature of education in Virginia more generally, and distinguished between the objects of elementary education and the cultivation of future leaders at the secondary and collegiate level. Primary education, Jefferson wrote, must

- "give to every citizen the information he needs for the transaction of his own business;
- "enable him to calculate for himself, and to express and preserve his ideas, his contracts and accounts, in writing;
- "improve, by reading, his morals and faculties;
- "understand his duties to his neighbors and country, and to discharge with competence the function confided to him by either;
- "know his rights; to exercise with order and justice those he retains;

to choose with discretion the fiduciary of those he delegates; and to notice their conduct with diligence, with candor, and judgment;

- "And, in general, to observe with intelligence and faithfulness all the social relations under which he shall be placed."[63]

This list, it is clear, seeks to enhance a person's intellectual and moral capabilities. First, every person must be able to "improve . . . his morals and faculties," or his moral sense and reason. This would require a curriculum that provided opportunities to understand the principles of morality and to practice them. In addition, every white Virginian must learn to think and to analyze material—to use one's reason properly. To be educated as "men and citizens," Jefferson continued in his report, students must "be taught reading, writing and numerical arithmetic, the elements of mensuration, (useful in so many callings,) and the outlines of geography and history."[64] In other words, students must not only learn the skills they need to think, write, and enumerate relevant to their future occupations, but they also need some cultural literacy, especially an understanding of history.[65] History, Jefferson believed, would teach people lessons they could apply to the present, none more important than how to look for clues that one's leaders are seeking to undermine republican liberty.[66] Graduates of Jefferson's proposed elementary schools would thus have understood and honed the principles of morality by strengthening their innate moral sense, gained reasoning skills, and studied the specific subjects that would enable them to pursue their private goals while being fitted for their duties as republican citizens.

Jefferson did not assume that all students were equally gifted. He believed that society should be governed by a natural aristocracy of "virtue and talents."[67] He assumed that his education program would reward those students who displayed the greatest potential by offering them higher levels of education at public expense. As he colorfully put it, his program would ensure that "the best geniusses will be raked from the rubbish annually."[68] For those students continuing to higher education, the importance of cultural literacy increased. These students would become leaders. They needed more than basic literacy and skills and more than a rudimentary understanding of a few subjects. Instead, they had to be immersed in all the major subjects in order to gain a broad understanding of how the natural and human worlds work—the knowledge they would use when they took on leadership positions. This class of students would not only be taught how to think and to use their moral sense but also language, ancient and modern history, mathematics, physics, chemistry, anatomy, medical theory, zoology, botany, mineralogy, philosophy, ethics, the law of nature and nations, and the principles of government and political economy.[69] Once this broad liberal education was complete, Jefferson recognized that students from poorer backgrounds might wish to receive professional training in order to earn a living. While wealthy students would retire "with a sufficient stock of knowledge, to improve themselves," others would go on to be educated in arts, architecture, military science, theology, law, medicine, or some other professional pursuit. These men would be part of the natural aristocracy, but they would also use their education to move up in the world by earning a better living than their backgrounds would have otherwise allowed. More important, their professional education would give them the financial base to engage in politics.[70]

Religious education, Jefferson believed, was ill suited for young children, in large part because it was often taught on authority at a time when children's minds had not yet learned how to reason. True freedom of conscience required that students be taught to reason first, and only then should they be exposed to religious traditions. He argued against "putting the Bible and Testament into the hands of children, at an age when their judgments are not sufficiently matured for religious enquiries."[71] In other words, freedom of conscience may have been a natural right but it was not a natural capability. It was instead premised on having the capability to use one's reason to analyze faith traditions and make one's own judgments about their value and truthfulness.

In sum, Jefferson's proposed curriculum for all white Virginians included the cultivation of human nature's innate moral sense and reason, combined with vocational training and the knowledge of history and ethics necessary to take part in public life. To engage in the pursuit of happiness as Jefferson (via Epicurus, Jesus, and the Scots) defined it, was to be able to choose the path that provided the most moderate, rational pleasure in the long run, while encouraging the pleasure that came from exercising one's moral sense. To be a republican citizen required not just literacy but knowledge of the past. Whether one was being prepared to engage in the private or the public realm, schools must foster each Virginian's moral and intellectual capabilities.

Central to Jefferson's education program was the local ward republic. In 1824, anticipating a Virginia state constitutional convention, Jefferson urged his fellow citizens to "adopt the subdivision of our counties into wards" of "an average of six miles square each." Each ward would be responsible for its own elementary school, militia company, poor, roads, police, and jurors, and have an elected justice of the peace and constable. In fact, Jefferson saw each ward as "a small republic within itself" through which "every man in the State would thus become an acting member of the common government."[72]

The ward republic was a way for Jefferson to ensure two things. First, local control over schools guaranteed that cultural capital would be in the hands of the people rather than elites. Second, the ward republic also provided sites of civic education in which adult citizens would manage their own affairs. Both perspectives were emphasized by Jefferson in an 1816 letter to Joseph Cabell, his friend and collaborator on the University of Virginia. Cabell had suggested that Virginians might support Jefferson's new university if it could be disconnected from the ward elementary schools. Jefferson responded that if "it is intended that the State government shall take this business into its own hands, and provide schools for every county, then by all means strike out this provision of our bill." Jefferson was certain that schools should remain under local control. Parents were the best suited to oversee their children's education. What would be next, Jefferson wondered. Should the state take over "the management of all our farms, our mills, and merchants' stores"? No, Jefferson responded. Just as small-producer capitalism ensured a free market not subject to monopoly control, so local schools ensured the wide distribution of control over society's cultural capital. Liberty is preserved, Jefferson averred, by "dividing and subdividing these republics . . . until it ends in the administration of every man's farm by himself." Power should shift upward only when an individual or a community proved incompetent to accomplish a goal.[73]

But, Jefferson continued, more was at stake than educating children. The ward republic also served as a means for adult civic education through participation.[74] As he wrote Cabell:

> When every man is a sharer in the direction of his ward-republic, or of some of the higher ones, and feels that he is a participator in the government of affairs, not merely at an election day in the year, but every day; when there shall not be a man in the State who will not be a member of some of its councils, great or small, he will let the heart be torn out of his body sooner than his power be wrested from him by a Caesar or a Bonaparte.[75]

In another letter, Jefferson wrote that "by making every citizen an acting member of the government, and in the offices nearest and most interesting to him, [the ward] will attach him by the strongest feelings to the independence of his country, and its republican constitution." Dividing Virginia into wards would allow citizens to participate in their own self-government, generating both civic skills and patriotic attachment.[76]

The ward republic thus ensured that access to knowledge was retained by the people rather than restricted by an aristocratic elite. It also allowed adults, by participating in managing schools, to practice the skills of republican citizenship while gaining a broader commitment to the common good of the communities in which they lived. In short, ward elementary schools overseen by participatory ward republics cultivated the civic capabilities of both children and adults.

No group in Jefferson's America suffered from a capabilities deprivation more than enslaved African Americans. Jefferson believed that education would help them improve their capabilities. Yet he was unable to overcome his own racism. Even as he expressed support for improving African Americans' capabilities, he refused to admit that access to cultural (and economic) capital would produce racial equality.

Jefferson opposed slavery. His commitment to natural rights and to the moral equality of all human beings—given expression in the Declaration of Independence—was unyielding. He believed that slavery was against natural law. Despite his antislavery principles, however, Jefferson in *Notes on the State of Virginia* put forth "the conjecture, that nature has been less bountiful" to black people "in the endowments of the head" than those of the heart (or moral sense). After enumerating myriad reasons why whiteness is preferable to blackness, Jefferson concluded that when black people were compared "by their faculties of memory they are equal to the whites; in reason much inferior, as I think one could scarcely be found capable of tracing and comprehending the investigations of Euclid; and that in imagination they are dull, tasteless, and anomalous."[77] As James Oakes writes, Jefferson's racism convinced him that even if blacks overcame their capabilities deprivation they would never equal white Americans.[78]

To Jefferson, black racial inferiority was not to deny that enslaved people suffered a capabilities deprivation but rather that, even when their capabilities were improved, their intellectual capability would be less than that of white Americans. In 1785 he suggested that, while he had "supposed [in *Notes*] the black man, in his present state" not equal, without further knowledge "it would be hazardous to affirm, that, equally cultivated for a few generations, he would not become so."[79] Perhaps blacks, like whites, if given the proper access to economic and cultural capital—land and education—could rise to equal levels of achievement. When Jefferson received a copy of the black mathematician Benjamin Banneker's almanac, he sent Banneker a letter. "No body wishes more than I do," he wrote, "to see such proofs as you exhibit, that nature has given to our black brethren, talents equal to those of the other colors of men, and that the appearance of a want of them is owing merely to the degraded condition of their existence, both in Africa & America. I can add with truth," he continued, "that no body wishes more ardently to see a good system commenced for raising the condition both of their body & mind to what it ought to be, as fast as the imbecility of their present existence, and other circumstances which cannot be neglected, will admit."[80] (It is not clear whether the "other circumstances" refer to the condition of slavery or to blacks' supposed natural inferiority.) At least some of blacks' inferiority, Jefferson believed, stemmed from a capabilities deprivation that could be amended by access to cultural capital.

But blacks would never be equal in intellect to whites, Jefferson assumed. When sent a book by the Bishop Henri Gregoire containing samples of the "Literature of the Negroes," Jefferson wrote Gregoire that "no person living wishes more sincerely than I do, to see a complete refutation of the doubts I myself have entertained and expressed on the grade of understanding allotted to them by nature, and to find that in this respect they are on a par with ourselves."[81] Even so, he confided to Joel Barlow that Gregoire's "credulity has made him gather up every short story he could find of men of color, (without distinguishing whether black, or of what degree of mixture)." Immediately one senses his effort to prove that any black intellectual ability must be connected to the introduction of white blood. Jefferson not only concluded that the entire collection failed to surpass the successes of the mathematician Banneker but also cast doubt on Banneker's own success absent "aid from [the white Quaker Andrew] Ellicott, who was his neighbor and friend."[82] Jefferson seemed simply unwilling to believe that blacks, if given access to the same cultural and other forms of capital, would become equal to whites.

In contrast, Jefferson believed that Native Americans might become full citizens if they embraced American agricultural practices. He believed their capabilities deprivation to be the result of cultural and not biological factors. They chose to live according to their own cultural traditions rather than embracing the superior ways of the more modern United States. By distributing to them knowledge of American ways—a form of cultural capital—they could be integrated into the American nation until, as he told them, they would "form one people with us, and we shall all be Americans; you will mix with us by marriage, your blood will run in our veins, and will spread with us over this great island."[83] Jefferson maintained in 1802 that "we consider ourselves as of the same family; we wish to live with them as one people." Even so, he was equally clear that any peaceful resolution of tensions with Native Americans would require their embrace of American culture: "We shall, with great pleasure, see your people become disposed to cultivate the earth, to raise herds of the useful animals, and to spin and weave, for their food and clothing." The result, Jefferson believed, would be more food and comfort for Native Americans.[84]

By embracing American practices, Native Americans, who shared the same intellectual potential as white Americans, would become more economically productive, and would thus have a better return on their labor. In other words, if American cultural knowledge were distributed to Native Americans, their economic and other potential would be turned into actual capabilities. Jefferson's capability-building approach to freedom, when seen from the Native Americans' perspective, thus raises many of the issues about development theory and modernization more generally—that it is considered by many to be culturally insensitive and to privilege one form of modern life over others.[85] Jefferson was aware of cultural difference, but he did not believe that all cultures were equally capable of producing individual freedom or enhancing the capabilities of their members (see Brian Steele's essay in this volume).

When it came to white women, Jefferson simultaneously believed that women were intellectually and morally equal to men and that women's sphere was in the home.[86] Republican women, like republican men, must have the tools to live up to their natural potential. Although Jefferson rarely spoke about female education, he was deeply involved in educating his daughter Martha for her future role. He believed that Martha's capabilities must be improved in order to promote the well-being of her future husband and children. He considered natural the sexual division of labor and thus believed that he was helping Martha to achieve her freedom just as his educational program prepared men for their future lives. Women would thus have their capabilities improved in order to enable their own happiness, which Jefferson assumed meant to promote their families' well-being. As many scholars have noted, "republican motherhood" simultaneously promoted the cultivation of female capabilities and placed women in service to men.[87]

Jefferson was a man both of his time and ahead of his time. While he shared many of the prejudices of the past, he believed that the American future promised new freedom for humanity—freedom premised on the development of Americans' individual capabilities. To achieve this end, Jefferson concluded, gross inequalities in access to cultural capital based on inherited wealth or status must be leveled. If freedom depended on citizens participating in their own government, citizens must have access to cultural capital if they were to be capable of undertaking their duties with competence. If education was concentrated among the few, it would forge an artificial aristocracy like any other form of capital. But if education was widely diffused, each person would be given the knowledge and skills necessary for being not just virtuous but also culturally literate participants in democratic public life. Given Jefferson's belief in the progressive nature of knowledge, each generation must ensure that the knowledge gained at the top—among society's intellectual elite—was distributed to ordinary people. As with property, the goal remained to ensure that cultural capital was not concentrated among the few. Access to land was necessary to participate in free markets; access to education was necessary to participate in democratic free government.

Education, however, would also aid Americans' own private pursuits of happiness. In a free society, Jefferson believed, ordinary people would have opportunities to promote their private affairs—from choosing their career to reading their favorite books—that never had been available heretofore in world history. If happiness, to Jefferson, involved the use of one's rational faculties to embrace pleasure and to avoid pain, and, as he hinted in one letter, this may be different for every person, and if happiness also involved the pleasures gained from benevolence, education must prepare every citizen to be able to find his or her way to happiness. In sum, self-making requires access to the resources—the cultural capital—to make one's self. By ensuring the wide distribution of knowledge to every generation, public education would give every citizen the capability to find and to pursue his or her own happiness while also ensuring that he or she has the capability to be an informed and engaged citizen.

Notes

This essay is dedicated to Prof. William Larkin Duren Jr. (1905–2008), Dean of the University of Virginia's College of Arts and Sciences from 1955 to 1962. His life was committed to making good Jefferson's promise, and extending it to all Americans regardless of race or gender.

1. Amartya Sen, *Development as Freedom* (New York, 1999), 18. See also Sen, "Equality of What?" The Tanner Lecture on Human Values (Stanford University, 22 May 1979); Martha C. Nussbaum, *Women and Human Development: The Capabilities Approach* (New York, 2000); Nussbaum, "Aristotelian Social Democracy," in *Liberalism and the Good*, ed. R. Bruce Douglass et al. (New York, 1990), 203–52; Nussbaum, "Capabilities as Fundamental Entitlements: Sen and Social Justice," *Feminist Economics* 9, nos. 2–3 (2003): 33–59; Nussbaum, "Constitutions and Capabilities: 'Perception' against Lofty Formalism," *Harvard Law Review* 121, no. 4 (2007): 4–97. For a discussion of the role of the state in promoting individual freedom, historically and sociologically, see Paul Starr, *Freedom's Power: The True Force of Liberalism* (New York, 2007). For an intriguing constitutional perspective, see John Denvir, *Democracy's Constitution: Claiming the Privileges of American Citizenship* (Champaign, Ill., 2001).

2. My understanding of Jefferson's conception of human nature relies on Jean Yarbrough, *American Virtues: Thomas Jefferson on the Character of a Free People* (Lawrence, Kans., 1998); Lorraine Smith Pangle and Thomas Pangle, *The Learning of Liberty: The Educational Ideas of the American Founders* (Lawrence, Kans., 1993), 250–64; Richard K. Matthews, *Radical Politics of Thomas Jefferson: A Revisionist View* (Lawrence, Kans., 1984); Joyce O. Appleby, *Capitalism and a New Social Order: The Republican Vision of the 1790s* (New York, 1984); Yehoshua Arieli, *Individualism and Nationalism in American Ideology* (Cambridge, Mass., 1964).

3. Yarbrough, *American Virtues*, 14–15.

4. TJ to William Short, 31 October 1819, *TJW*, 1430–32.

5. Ibid. On Epicurus, see Epicurus, *The Epicurus Reader: Selected Writings and Testimonia*, ed. Brad Inwood and L. P. Gerson (Indianapolis, 1994); Jacques Brunschwig and David Sedley, "Hellenistic Philosophy," in *The Cambridge Companion to Greek and Roman Philosophy* (Cambridge, U.K., 2003), 151–83, esp. 155–63; David Konstan, "Epicurus," in *The Stanford Encyclopedia of Philosophy* (2005), ed. Edward N. Zalta, http://plato.stanford.edu/entries/epicurus/.

6. TJ to John Adams, 15 August 1820, *TJW*, 1440–45. TJ also claimed that his materialist philosophy rested on his reading of Locke, Tracy, and Dugald Stewart. See also TJ to the Rev. Isaac Story, 5 December 1801, in *Works of Thomas Jefferson*, 12 vols., ed. Paul Leicester Ford (New York, 1904–5), 9:319–21, hereafter cited as "Federal Edition"; TJ to Mathew Carey, 11 November 1816, ibid., 12:41–42.

7. TJ to Thomas Law, 13 June 1814, *TJW*, 1338.

8. On faculty psychology in American thought, see Daniel Walker Howe, *Making the American Self: Jonathan Edwards to Abraham Lincoln* (Cambridge, Mass., 1997). The strongest argument for Jefferson's invocation of reason is Henry Steele Commager, *Jefferson, Nationalism, and the Enlightenment* (New York, 1975). The counterpart for the moral sense is Garry Wills,

Inventing America: Jefferson's Declaration of Independence (Garden City, N.Y., 1978). See also Yarbrough, *American Virtues;* Arieli, *Individualism and Nationalism,* chs. 6–8. For a discussion of the ways in which the emphasis on reason may have limited access to the public sphere, see Holly Brewer, "Beyond Education: Thomas Jefferson's 'Republican' Revision of the Laws Regarding Children," in *Thomas Jefferson and the Education of a Citizen,* ed. James Gilreath (Washington, D.C., 1999), 48–62.

9. TJ to Thomas Law, 13 June 1814, *TJW,* 1335–39.

10. Howe, *Making the American Self,* 66–77.

11. TJ to Law, 13 June 1814, *TJW,* 1337.

12. TJ, *Notes on the State of Virginia,* Query 11, *TJW,* 220.

13. TJ to Robert Skipwith, 3 August 1771, ibid., 741. See also TJ to Peter Carr, 10 August 1787, ibid., 900–905.

14. TJ to Carr, 10 August 1787, ibid., 901–2; TJ to Law, 13 June 1814, ibid., 1335–39.

15. On this point see Maurizio Valsania, " 'Our Original Barbarism': Man vs. Nature in Thomas Jefferson's Moral Experience," *Journal of the History of Ideas* 64 (2004): 627–45.

16. TJ to Carr, 19 August 1785, *TJW,* 814–18.

17. TJ to Law, 13 June 1814, ibid., 1335–39.

18. TJ to William Short, 4 August 1820, ibid., 1435–40.

19. Joyce O. Appleby, "What Is Still American in the Political Philosophy of Thomas Jefferson?" *WMQ* 39 (1982): 287–309, and *Capitalism and a New Social Order.*

20. TJ to Dr. John Manners, 22 February 1814, *TJW,* 1329–30. See also TJ to Charles Thomson, 29 January 1817, Federal Edition, ed. Ford, 12:52–53.

21. As Jefferson wrote in the Danbury Address (TJ to Messrs. Nehemiah Dodge and Others, a Committee of the Danbury Baptist Association, in the State of Connecticut, 1 January 1802, *TJW,* 510), humanity's "natural sentiments," a.k.a. the moral sense, ensure that "he has no natural right in opposition to his social duties."

22. Joyce O. Appleby, "Thomas Jefferson and the Psychology of Democracy," in *The Revolution of 1800: Democracy, Race, and the New Republic,* ed. James Horn, Jan Lewis, and Peter S. Onuf (Charlottesville, Va., 2002), 155–72.

23. Pierre Bourdieu, "The Forms of Capital" in *Handbook of Theory and Research for the Sociology of Education,* ed. John G. Richardson (New York and Westport, Conn., 1986), 241–58. See also Richard D. Brown, "Bulwark of Revolutionary Liberty: Thomas Jefferson's and John Adams's Programs for an Informed Citizenry," in *Thomas Jefferson and the Education of a Citizen,* ed. Gilreath, 91–102.

24. John Adams to TJ, 15 July 1813, in *AJL,* 357–58.

25. Adams to TJ, 2 September 1813, ibid., 370–72. See also Adams to TJ, 15 November 1813, ibid., 397–402.

26. TJ to Adams, 28 October 1813, ibid., 387–92.

27. Ibid.

28. I have developed this theme in more detail in two essays. See Johann N. Neem, "Thomas Jefferson's Philosophy of History and the Future of American Christianity," in *Prophesies of Godlessness: Predictions of America's Imminent Secularization, from the Puritans to the Present Day,* ed. Charles T. Mathewes and Christopher McKnight Nichols (New York, 2008), 35–52; "Beyond the Wall: Reinterpreting Jefferson's Danbury Address," *JER* 27 (2007): 139–54. See also Richard Samuelson, "Jefferson and Religion: Private Belief, Public Policy," in *The Cambridge Companion to Thomas Jefferson,* ed. Frank Shuffelton (Cambridge, U.K., 2009), 143–54.

On the idea of a speaking aristocracy, see Christopher Grasso, *A Speaking Aristocracy: Transforming Public Discourse in Eighteenth-Century Connecticut* (Chapel Hill, N.C., 1999).

29. TJ to Benjamin Rush, 23 September 1800, *TJW,* 1080–82.

30. TJ to Dr. Joseph Priestley, 21 March 1801, ibid., 1085–87.

31. TJ to John Dickinson, 6 March 1801, ibid., 1084–85.

32. TJ to Moses Robinson, 23 March 1801, ibid., 1087–88.

33. TJ to William Short, 31 October 1819, ibid., 1431.

34. TJ to Robinson, 23 March 1801, ibid., 1087–88; TJ to Short, 31 October 1819, ibid., 1431; TJ to Adams, 11 April 1823, ibid., 1469.

35. TJ to Messrs. Nehemiah Dodge and Others, a Committee of the Danbury Baptist Association, in the State of Connecticut, 1 January 1802, ibid., 510.

36. TJ to James Madison, 28 October 1785, ibid., 840–43. My understanding of Jeffersonian political economy depends on James L. Huston, *Securing the Fruits of Labor: The American Concept of Wealth Distribution, 1765–1900* (Baton Rouge, La., 1998). See also Peter S. Onuf, *The Mind of Thomas Jefferson* (Charlottesville, Va., 2007), 110–17; Michael Hardt, "Jefferson and Democracy," *American Quarterly* 59 (2007): 41–78; David N. Mayer, *The Constitutional Thought of Thomas Jefferson* (Charlottesville, Va., 1994), 302–8; Claudio Katz, "Thomas Jefferson's Liberal Anticapitalism," *American Journal of Political Science* 47 (January 2003): 1–17; Appleby, *Capitalism and a New Social Order;* Drew McCoy, *The Elusive Republic: Political Economy in Jeffersonian America* (Chapel Hill, N.C., 1980).

37. On these points see TJ to Joseph Milligan, 6 April 1816, in L&B, 14:466. I thank Joyce Appleby for bringing this letter to my attention.

38. TJ to James Madison, 6 September 1789, *TJW,* 959. See also TJ to John Wayles Eppes, 24 June 1813, ibid., 1280–86; TJ to Samuel Kercheval, 12 July 1816, ibid., 1395–1403.

39. TJ, *Notes,* Query 14, *TJW,* 271–72.

40. Richard D. Brown, *The Strength of a People: The Idea of an Informed Citizenry in America* (Chapel Hill, N.C., 1996), 47.

41. TJ, *Notes,* Query 14, *TJW,* 274.

42. TJ, "A Bill for the More General Diffusion of Knowledge," ibid., 365–73.

43. Ibid., 365.

44. According to Jefferson, "education would have raised the mass of the people to the high ground of moral respectability necessary to their own safety, and to orderly government; and would have compleated the great object of qualifying them to select the veritable aristoi, for the trusts of government, to the exclusion of the Pseudalists . . ." See TJ to Adams, 28 October 1813, *AJL,* 387–92.

45. Henry May, *The Enlightenment in America* (New York, 1976), 153.

46. TJ to John Taylor, 4 June 1798, *TJW,* 1048–51, at 1050. This paragraph is taken from Neem, "Thomas Jefferson's Philosophy of History."

47. TJ to John Dickinson, 6 March 1801, *TJW,* 1084–85.

48. TJ, "First Inaugural Address," 4 March 1801, ibid., 493–96. See Peter S. Onuf, *Jefferson's Empire: The Language of American Nationhood* (Charlottesville, Va., 2000), 80–108.

49. TJ, *Notes,* in *TJW,* 284–85. See also TJ, "A Bill for Establishing Religious Freedom," ibid., 346–48; TJ to Moses Robinson, 23 March 1801, ibid., 1087–88.

50. TJ to Dr. Joseph Priestley, 27 January 1800, ibid., 1072–74, at 1073.

51. TJ to William Green Mumford, 18 June 1799, ibid., 1063–66, at 1065. See also TJ to Adams, 15 June 1813, *AJL,* 331–33.

52. TJ, "Report of the Commissioners for the University of Virginia," 5 August 1818, *TJW*, 457–73, at 461–62.

53. TJ to Isaac McPherson, 13 August 1813, ibid., 1286–1295, at 1291–92. As secretary of state, Jefferson and other Cabinet members were responsible for overseeing patent applications and making determinations about their novelty, as provided for in a 1790 federal statute. Jefferson found this to be onerous and helped reform the patent application system in 1793 to reduce the secretary's role to a merely clerical one and to place the burden of proof on challengers in federal court. In doing so, he made it easier to receive a patent, violating his own principles, as he noted in the above quoted 1813 letter. For discussion of Jefferson and patents and the context for his 1813 letter, see Merrill D. Peterson, *Thomas Jefferson and the New Nation: A Biography* (New York, 1970), 450, 589–90, 937–38. See also B. Zorina Khan, "Property Rights and Patent Litigation in Early Nineteenth-Century America," *Journal of Economic History* 55 (March 1995): 58–97.

54. TJ to Joseph Priestley, 21 March 1801, *TJW*, 1085–87.

55. TJ to Littleton Waller Tazewell, 5 January 1805, ibid., 1149–53, at 1150. See also TJ to Adams, 28 October 1813, *AJL*, 387–92.

56. "Report of the Commissioners for the University of Virginia," 5 August 1818, *TJW*, 457–73. For a discussion of the University of Virginia's curriculum, see Cameron Addis, *Jefferson's Vision for Education, 1760–1845* (New York, 2003).

57. Sen, *Development as Freedom*; Brown, *The Strength of a People*, 74–84.

58. "A Bill for the More General Diffusion of Knowledge," *TJW*, 365–73.

59. Ibid.

60. TJ to Peter Carr, 7 September 1814, *TJW*, 1347–48.

61. TJ to John Tyler, 26 May 1810, ibid., 1225–27. For a discussion of Jefferson's curriculum, see Pangle and Pangle, *Learning of Liberty*, 114–24; Jennings L. Wagoner Jr., " 'That Knowledge Most Useful to Us': Thomas Jefferson's Conception of Utility in the Education of Republican Citizens," in *Thomas Jefferson and the Education of a Citizen*, ed. Gilreath, 115–33.

62. TJ to Carr, 7 September 1814, *TJW*, 1347–48.

63. TJ, "Report of the Commissioners for the University of Virginia," 4 August 1818, ibid., 457–73, at 459. Bullets inserted.

64. Ibid., 459.

65. On the idea of cultural literacy see E. D. Hirsch, *Cultural Literacy: What Every American Needs to Know* (Boston, 1987). See also Stephen Prothero's discussion of the same concept in relation to religious knowledge, *Religious Literacy: What Every American Needs to Know—and Doesn't* (San Francisco, 2007). In one of the many ironies of scholarship, Hirsch—who is considered a conservative educator by many progressive educators—provides a Jeffersonian model to redistribute what Bourdieu called cultural capital. See, for example, Douglas L. Wilson, "Jefferson and Literacy," in *Thomas Jefferson and the Education of a Citizen*, ed. Gilreath, 79–90.

66. On the role of history, see Pangle and Pangle, *Learning of Liberty*, 114–18. According to Jefferson, "History by apprising them of the past will enable them to judge of the future; it will avail them of the experience of other times and other nations; it will qualify them as judges of the actions and designs of men; it will enable them to know ambition under every disguise it may assume; and knowing it, to defeat its views. In every government on earth is some trace of human weakness, some germ of corruption and degeneracy, which cunning will discover, and wickedness insensibly open, cultivate, and improve." TJ, *Notes*, Query 14, *TJW*, 274. See also "Bill for the More General Diffusion of Knowledge," Section 1, ibid., 365.

67. TJ to Adams, 28 October 1813, AJL, 388.

68. TJ, *Notes*, Query 14, *TJW*, 272.

69. TJ to Carr, 7 September 1814, ibid., 1351.

70. Ibid., 1350–52. See also TJ's "Report of the Commissioners for the University of Virginia," 5 August 1818, ibid., 457–73, at 459.

71. TJ, *Notes*, Query 14, ibid., 273–74.

72. TJ to John Cartwright, 5 June 1824, ibid., 1490–96, at 1492–93.

73. TJ to Joseph Cabell, 2 February 1816, ibid., 1377–81.

74. On the importance of the ward republic as civic schools for adult citizens, see Matthews, *Radical Politics*, 83–87; Garrett Ward Sheldon, *The Political Philosophy of Thomas Jefferson* (Baltimore, 1991), 67–72; Onuf, *Mind of Thomas Jefferson*, 173–76; Suzanne W. Morse, "Ward Republics: The Wisest Invention for Self-Government," in *Thomas Jefferson and the Education of a Citizen*, ed. Gilreath, 264–77.

75. TJ to Joseph Cabell, 2 February 1816, *TJW*, 1377–81. See also TJ, *Autobiography*, *TJW*, 74–75.

76. TJ to Samuel Kercheval, July 12, 1816, ibid., 1395–1403, at 1399. See also TJ to John Cartwright, June 5, 1824, ibid., 1490–96, at 1492–93.

77. TJ, *Notes*, Query 14, comments on slavery, ibid., 264–70. For a discussion of the trans-Atlantic intellectual context in which Jefferson made his conclusions, see Michael O'Brien, *Conjectures of Order: Intellectual Life and the American South*, 2 vols. (Chapel Hill, N.C., 2004), 1:215–37. See also Winthrop Jordan's classic examination, *White over Black: American Attitudes toward the Negro, 1550–1812* (New York, 1968), 429–81.

78. James Oakes, "Why Slaves Can't Read: The Political Significance of Jefferson's Racism," in *Thomas Jefferson and the Education of a Citizen*, ed. Gilreath, 177–92. See also Peter S. Onuf, "'To Declare Them a Free and Independent People': Race, Slavery, and National Identity in Jefferson's Thought," *JER* 18 (1998): 1–46.

79. TJ to Chastellux, June 7, 1785, *TJW*, 799–802, at 801. See also TJ to Edward Coles, 25 August 25, 1814, ibid., 1343–46.

80. TJ to Benjamin Banneker, 30 August 1791, ibid., 982–83.

81. TJ to Henri Gregoire, 25 February 1809, ibid., 1202.

82. TJ to Joel Barlow, 8 October 1809, Federal Edition, ed. Ford, 11:120–24. On this episode see also Addis, *Jefferson's Vision*, 12. In an 1814 letter, Jefferson argued that while blacks' current degraded condition may be due to generations of deprivation, and that one might hope that in time blacks' capabilities would improve, their "amalgamation" with whites now would lead to "a degradation to which no lover of his country, no lover of excellence in the human character can innocently consent." See TJ to Coles, 25 August 1814, *TJW*, 1343–46. See also TJ to William Short, 18 January 1826, Federal Edition, ed. Ford, 12:434.

83. TJ to Capt. Hendrick, the Delawares, Mohicans, and Munries, 21 December 1808, L&B, 16:452.

84. TJ to the Brothers Miamis, Powtewatamies, and Weeauks, 7 January 1802, L&B, 16:390–91. See also TJ to Brothers Miamis and Delawares, 8 January 1803, ibid., 396–400; TJ, Confidential Message on Expedition to the Pacific (to the Senate and House of Representatives), 18 January 1803, Federal Edition, ed. Ford, 9:421–34; TJ to Chiefs of the Chickasaw Nation, Minghey, Mataha, and Tishohotana, 7 March 1805, L&B, 16:410–12; TJ to the Wolf and people of the Mandar nation, 30 December 1806, ibid., 412–17; TJ to the Chiefs of the Ottawas, Chippewas, Powtewatamies, Wyandots, and Senecas of Sandusky, 22 April 1808, ibid., 428–32; TJ to Little Turtle, Chief of the Miamis, 21 December 1808, ibid., 440–43; TJ to Captain Hendrick, the Delawares, Mohicans, and Munries, 21 December 1808, ibid., 450–54.

85. On modernization and development, see Karen Orren and Stephen Skowronek, *The Search for American Political Development* (New York, 2004).

86. My discussion of Jefferson's understanding of female education is drawn from Brian Steele, "Thomas Jefferson's Gender Frontier," *Journal of American History* 95 (2008): 17–42; Peter S. Onuf and Leonard J. Sadosky, *Jeffersonian America* (Malden, Mass. and Oxford, 2002), 82–102; Jan Lewis, " 'The Blessings of Domestic Society': Thomas Jefferson's Family and the Transformation of American Politics," in *Jeffersonian Legacies*, ed. Peter S. Onuf (Charlottesville, Va., 1993), 109–46.

87. Mary Kelley, *Learning to Stand and Speak: Women, Education, and Public Life in America's Republic* (Chapel Hill, N.C., 2006); Jan Lewis, "The Republican Wife: Virtue and Seduction in the Early Republic," *WMQ* 44 (1987): 689–721; Ruth H. Bloch, "The Gendered Meanings of Virtue in Revolutionary America," in *Rethinking the Political: Gender, Resistance, and the State,* ed. Barbara Laslett, Johanna Brenner, and Yesim Arat (Chicago, 1981), 11–32; Linda Kerber, *Women of the Republic: Intellect and Ideology in Revolutionary America* (Chapel Hill, N.C., 1980); Nancy F. Cott, *The Bonds of Womanhood: "Woman's Sphere" in New England, 1780–1835* (New Haven, 1977).

Consistent in Creation

Thomas Jefferson, Natural Aristocracy, and the Problem of Knowledge

RICHARD A. SAMUELSON

I N OCTOBER 1813, THOMAS JEFFERSON WROTE JOHN ADAMS A LONG LET-
ter on the subject of natural aristocracy. Jefferson reasoned that aristocrats
were part of the order of nature, for "it would have been inconsistent in
creation to have formed man for the social state, and not to have provided
virtue and wisdom enough to manage the concerns of society." That belief
had important implications for government. "May we not even say," Jefferson
wrote Adams, "that the form of government is best which provides the most
effectually for a pure selection of these natural aristoi into the offices of
government?" How might that be done? Elections: "*I* think the best remedy is
exactly that provided by all our constitutions, to leave to the citizens the free
election and separation of the aristoi from the pseudo-aristoi, of the wheat
from the chaff."[1] Jefferson believed, in short, that there were natural aristocrats, that their job was to manage the concerns of society, and that the best
way to get them into office was via free, fair, and open elections.

To understand Jefferson's thoughts on natural aristocracy, we should
consider his thoughts about nature and aristocracy separately before exploring the topic as a whole. Regarding nature, we need to explore Jefferson's
conception of nature as well as how he thought the human mind recognized
it. With regard to aristocracy, we face a slightly different set of questions.
First, we will consider how Jefferson defined an aristocrat. Beyond that, we
will ask how Jefferson reconciled his belief in government by natural aristo-

crats with his belief in the rights of men. The answer to that question returns us to Jefferson's theory of knowledge. There was a direct link between his political goals and how he reasoned about nature. The key to understanding Jefferson's thoughts on these subjects, we will see, is his belief that men could achieve a great deal of certainty about nature. Certainty was essential to Jefferson's hopes for the future.

Jefferson only used the term "natural aristocracy" twice: once in the letter to John Adams quoted above, and once in a letter to Joseph C. Cabell in which he enclosed a copy of the letter to Adams. He also made one ironic reference to Federalist "natural aristocrats" in a letter that he wrote to James Madison in 1793. It is possible that Jefferson simply did not consider the subject terribly important. But there is no necessary relationship between the number of times people discuss a particular idea and its importance, particularly when they have reasons for holding their tongues. Jefferson, ever the prudent politician, may have feared that speaking favorably of aristocracy, even natural aristocracy, was not likely to help his political cause. That reading grows more likely in light of other bits of evidence. The natural aristocracy letter is probably the longest letter Jefferson wrote to Adams. Moreover, the letter concludes with a strong declaration: "I have thus stated my opinion on a point on which we differ, not with a view to controversy, for we are both too old to change opinions which are the result of a long life of inquiry and reflection; but on the suggestion of a former letter of yours, that we ought not to die before we have explained ourselves to each other."[2] At the very least, assuming he was not lying to Adams, Jefferson thought he could not explain his political philosophy without addressing the question of natural aristocracy. Beyond that, there is the nature of Jefferson's comments, which seem to indicate that he had given the subject a great deal of thought, and that he considered it a matter of particular importance. Finally, it is significant that he sent a copy of the letter to Cabell in order to help him think about how to organize the University of Virginia. It is also true that Jefferson discussed the idea of natural aristocracy sometimes without actually using the term, often in his writings on education.

Jefferson liked certainty. He wrote that, of all the subjects he studied in school, mathematics was "my favorite one. We have no theories there, no uncertainties on the mind; all is demonstration and satisfaction." Certainty was central to the Jefferson Bible. Jefferson was able to march through the Gospels and abstract Jesus's teachings from those that he believed had been falsely attributed to him because the difference between the two seemed obvious. "In the New Testament," Jefferson wrote, "there is internal evidence that parts of it have proceeded from an extraordinary man; and that other parts are of the fabric of very inferior minds. It is as easy to separate those parts, as to pick out diamonds from dunghills." Upon hearing that Connecticut had repealed its religious establishment, Jefferson exclaimed that "the genuine doctrine of one only God is reviving, and I trust that there is not a *young man* now living in the United States who will not die an Unitarian." Once state-sponsored churches lost their artificial supports, Jefferson reasoned, the simple truth of Unitarianism would be clear to all. Only corruption and coercion could sustain belief in the Trinity. "It is too late in the day," he maintained, "for men of sincerity to pretend they believe in the Platonic mysticisms that three are one." Jefferson's faith in certainty also came through in the scheme of education he articulated in the *Notes on the State of Virginia:* "the best genius of the whole selected, and continued six years, and the residue dismissed. By this means twenty of the best geniusses will be raked from the rubbish annually." For such a selection to work, it must be clear who deserved to be raked from the rubbish. The idea also plays an important role in Jefferson's constitutional thought. "Let mercy be the character of the lawgiver," he wrote, "but let the judge be a mere machine."[3] Jefferson presumed that a constitution could be clear enough to be applied mechanically by a judge.

Although he craved certainty, Jefferson was not a systematic philosophic thinker. More than one scholar has characterized his position as "eclectic." In part, that was itself a philosophical position. He took pride in the fact that he had "never submitted the whole system of my opinions to the creed of any party of men whatever in religion, in philosophy, in politics, or in anything else where I was capable of thinking for myself. Such an addiction is the last degradation of a free and moral agent." To submit to any party in religion, politics, or philosophy was to surrender his freedom as a "moral agent." For example, he declared himself to be an Epicurean. Yet, contrary to classic Epicurean thought, he also believed that the universe was designed with purpose and was not a random concatenation of atoms and void.[4]

The faith that human reason could yield certainty is the key to Jefferson's understanding of nature. If he had one fundamental belief, it was probably that there was a logic in Creation that human reason could discern. That belief allowed Jefferson to reason backward from the order of the universe to its nature. Perhaps we should say that Jefferson posited what the order in the universe must be, in order for Creation to be good. Consider his letter on natural aristocracy. Jefferson reasoned that "it would have been inconsistent in creation to have formed man for the social state, and not to have provided virtue and wisdom enough to manage the concerns of society." He wrote similarly of the moral sense. "The Creator would indeed have been a bungling artist," he averred, "had he intended man for a social animal, without planting in him social dispositions." Jefferson presumed not only that Creation was ordered a particular way for a particular reason, but also that human reason could discern that order. Once men apprehended it, they could draw inferences about life on earth. This belief was connected with his belief in "the oeconomy of nature." Species endured forever because "no instance can be produced" of nature "having permitted any one race of her animals to become extinct; of her having formed any link in her great work so weak as to be broken." Mathematics had the principle of conservation of value; in nature there was the principle of conservation of species. Why would nature create a species only to let it go extinct?[5]

Jefferson's belief in the economy of nature was built upon his understanding of the scientific method. He counted Francis Bacon, Isaac Newton, and John Locke as "the three greatest men that have ever lived." What did they do? Bacon invented the scientific method, and the other two applied it to the universe and to man. Bacon's method was to employ repeated observations of the world and to draw conclusions from those observations. Those conclusions were laws of nature. Newton applied that method to discover gravity. After observing apples falling from trees to earth, and no apples falling from the earth to trees or holding still in the air, the scientific method suggested a law of nature—things tend to fall to earth. Bacon was not seeking truth in the profound sense. Correlation, he knew, is not the same thing as causation. The fact that no one had ever seen an apple fall upward did not mean that it was hypothetically impossible. Similarly, it was possible that the senses were deceived. Newton understood that truth. When people read him as saying that gravity was a property of matter, Newton complained: "Pray do not ascribe that Notion to me."[6] Whether gravity really was a law of nature, or whether it simply looked that way to human senses, was not a terribly important question to him. Functionally speaking, the laws of gravity described the world as it seemed to be.

Many of the early promoters of the scientific method had political goals.

By turning men and women away from the quest for absolute knowledge about the universe, they hoped to turn them away not only from metaphysical speculation but also from religious war. Rather than fighting over God's wishes, a never-ending and often bloody argument, men could use their intelligence to make useful improvements in the world, making it better for all. Jefferson took that hope to heart and turned it into a philosophical principle. Jefferson dropped the qualifiers from Bacon's method and regarded such scientific truth as truth itself. To reason otherwise, he implied, was to suggest that there was something wrong with Creation. Newton was friends with the Cambridge Platonists; Jefferson dismissed Plato for his mystical obscurity.[7]

What was a useful assumption for Bacon became an article of faith for Jefferson. This slippage comes through in an 1820 exchange with Adams. In that year Adams pushed Jefferson on philosophical fundamentals, applying skepticism to modern skepticism, and implicitly reminding him that the scientific method itself rested upon hypotheses impossible to verify. According to Adams, no philosophy was certain. "I insist upon it that the Saint has as good a right to groan at the Philosopher for asserting that there is nothing but matter in the Universe," Adams wrote, as "the Philosopher has to laugh at the Saint for saying that there are both Matter and Spirit." Jefferson's reply was revealing. He told Adams that his "croud of scepticisms kept me from sleep. I read it, and laid it down: read it, and laid it down, again and again: and to give rest to my mind, I was obliged to recur ultimately to my habitual anodyne, 'I feel: therefore I exist.'" Jefferson continued from there to give his materialist creed. "I feel bodies which are not myself," he wrote. "There are other existences" and "I call them *matter*. I feel them changing place. This gives me *motion*. Where there is absence of matter, I call it *void*, or *nothing*, or *immaterial space*. On the basis of sensation, of matter and motion, we may erect the fabric of all the certainties we can have or need." Later on in the same letter, he added that "a single sense may indeed be sometimes deceived, but rarely, and never all our senses together, with their faculty of reasoning." Jefferson's "habitual anodyne" was a sensational Cartesianism. Rather than finding all truth through abstract reason, à la Descartes, Jefferson found "all the certainties we can have or need" from his senses, and "their faculty of reasoning." Adams tried to remind Jefferson that the scientific method itself made certain assumptions about the nature of nature, and that a consistent skeptic must apply skepticism back against itself. Yet Jefferson ruled out of bounds Adams's questions. For him the truth science discovered about nature was the truth about nature. "According to the rules of philosophizing," he wrote, "when one sufficient cause for an effect is known, it is not within the economy of nature to employ two." In other words, Jefferson held that Occam's razor, upon which the scientific method rested, was part of the economy of nature, for God would have been a bungling artist if he had placed the secrets of nature beyond human comprehension.[8] Occam did not go that far. His razor applied to probabilities and convenience, and not to truth in the final sense.

Jefferson brought the scientific method, and its attendant certainties, to bear upon the question of aristocracy. We can almost reverse-engineer Jefferson's chain of thought from his conclusions to his assumptions. It is as if Jefferson asked: If it is to be easy to distinguish the natural from the artificial in general, and hence natural aristocrats from artificial aristocrats, what must be true? Somehow, the traits that set them apart would have to be manifest to common sense. He wrote to Adams that "I agree with you that there is a natural aristocracy among men. The grounds of this are virtue and talents." Jefferson contrasted this natural aristocracy with the "artificial aristocracy founded on wealth and birth, without either virtue or talents; for with these it would belong to the first class." Natural aristocrats were those who were truly better (more virtuous and talented) than others. Artificial aristocrats, according to Jefferson, were those who rose to the top of society for some other reason. That was why Jefferson wrote about Adams's "apostacy to *hereditary* monarchy and nobility" in the 1790s, rather than his apostasy simply to monarchy and nobility.[9] According to Jefferson, belief in aristocracy did not make one an apostate to republican principles; only belief in hereditary aristocracy did. Natural aristocrats deserved office; artificial ones did not. Yet how to distinguish the one from the other? Jefferson thought it would be obvious. "*I* think the best remedy is exactly that provided by all our constitutions," he wrote. "Leave to the citizens the free election and separation of the aristoi from the pseudo-aristoi, of the wheat from the chaff."[10]

Jefferson's thoughts and presumptions come into clearer light when we contrast them with those of Adams. "Tho' We have agreed in one point, in Words," Adams responded to Jefferson, "it is not yet certain that we are perfectly agreed in Sense. Fashion has introduced an indeterminate Use of the Word 'Talents.' Education, Wealth, Strength, Beauty, Stature, Birth, Marriage, graceful Attitudes and Motions, Gait, Air, Complexion, Physiognomy, are Talents, as well as Genius and Science and learning." For Adams, a "talent" was a quality that gave someone power or influence in society. "Any one of these Talents, that in fact commands or influences true Votes in Society, gives to the Man who possesses it, the Character of an Aristocrat, in my Sense of the Word." Adams's empiricism was broader than Jefferson's. By studying the past and by drawing upon his own experience, Adams discovered the things that seemed to help men get ahead in politics in most times and places. These things were "talents." The nature that Adams discovered was less economical than Jefferson's. To Adams, human irrationality went in predictable patterns. "Who are these 'aristoi'? Who shall judge? Who shall select these choice Spirits from the rest of the Congregation?" Adams asked.[11] Adams doubted that there would ever be agreement about the identities of the natural aristocrats. Such things were never so clear as Jefferson hoped. Ultimately, Adams wished to remind Jefferson that empiricism found its limit when one had to decide what constituted a fact. Jefferson did not take well to that criticism. To Jefferson, such questions were heretical, for they implied that politics could never have the precision of mathematics.

By implication, Adams raised a moral question. Were aristocrats better people or simply more powerful? To Adams, a political talent was something, virtually anything, that helped one get votes. If that were the case, then the word would imply nothing deeper about the moral quality of talented men, except to the extent that real virtue (which Adams believed existed) was itself a talent. Jefferson, by contrast, wished to preserve, at least in part, the ancient notion that the better sort really were better people. For him, aristocracy retained its moral dimension. Its members could include themselves among the wise and good and not merely the talented.

This effort to preserve the moral character of natural aristocracy presented a challenge to Jefferson. How could he believe in the equal rights of men and also believe that some men were morally superior? Jefferson addressed this question at the start of his letter to Adams. Adams had provoked Jefferson to write about natural aristocracy by quoting Theognis:

> My friend Curnis, When We want to purchase, Horses, Asses or Rams, We inquire for the Wellborn. And every one wishes to procure, from the good Breeds. A good Man, does not care to marry a Shrew, the Daughter of a Shrew; unless They give him, a great deal of Money with her.

Adams thought that this constituted sage wisdom. "Has Science or Morals, or Philosophy or Criticism or Christianity, advanced or improved, or enlightened Mankind upon this Subject, and shewn them, that the Idea of the 'Well born' is a prejudice, a Phantasm, a Point no point, a Grape Fly away, a dream?" he asked. To be sure, "Philosophers and Politicians, may nibble and quibble, but they never will get rid of it. Their only resource is, to controul it." Voting for people because of who their father was, or because they were famous, good-looking, or rich was, like apples falling to the ground, natural and inevitable, Adams thought. Jefferson, however, disagreed. "The passage you quote from Theognis," he replied to Adams, "I think has an Ethical, rather than a political object." Adams had mistaken a sermon for science. "The whole piece is a moral exhortation," Jefferson wrote, "and this passage particularly appears to be a reproof to man, who, while with his domestic animals he is curious to improve the race by employing always the finest male, pays no attention to the improvement of his own race, but intermarries with the vicious, the ugly, or the old, for considerations of wealth or ambition." What Adams understood as a description of human behavior, Jefferson regarded as a reprimand. Moreover, Jefferson applied the lesson narrowly, confining it to its literal context.[12] Jefferson allowed that humans often selected mates irrationally. He did not, however, think that reality suggested a larger pattern at work.

Jefferson, who claimed to believe in the rights of man, trod in perilous waters but escaped much of the danger. According to Jefferson, what "Theognis seems to recommend from the example of sheeps and asses, would doubtless improve the human, as it does the brute animal, and produce a race of veritable aristocrats. For evidence proves that the moral and physical qualities of man, whether good or evil, are transmissible in a certain degree from father to son." Were human coupling done rationally it would produce a true aristocracy of birth—a class of people born with superior mental, physical, and moral attributes that reproduced itself. Ultimately, human passions overcome reason when it comes to selecting a mate: "the equal rights of men will rise up against this privileged Solomon, and oblige us to continue acquiescence under the degeneration of the race."[13] Absent the phenomenon that Theognis decried, all men would not be created equal. If humans followed the dictates of reason when selecting their mates, the result would be a natural aristocracy of blood. Fortunately for the cause of human equality, Jefferson suggested, reason did not rule in affairs of the heart.

According to Jefferson, the natural aristocracy was not a self-reproducing class, but it was, in large part, biologically based. If natural aristocrats were the "wise and good," and if both physical and moral character was partly biological, then "the accidental aristoi produced by the fortuitous concourse of breeders" produced superior beings. By trivializing the nature of talents, Adams avoided that problem. For him there was no necessary correlation between the possession of the kinds of talents that would help one acquire office and moral worth.[14] Jefferson, by contrast, never entirely escaped from the eugenic implications of his belief in natural aristocracy. In this regard, recall that in his scheme of education, worthy students will be "raked from the rubbish." Yet he had greater hopes than Adams that the common man could be raised up. That would enable ordinary Americans both to live as free and independent citizens and, at the same time, to recognize true worth and vote it into office. While Jefferson allowed that individual men would inevitably choose wives for less than pure reasons, he thought that—given proper education, laws, and public institutions—political choices could be more clean. These hopes helped Jefferson to reconcile his belief in natural rights with his belief in natural aristocracy.

To the degree that Jefferson resolved this tension in his thought, he did so by combining his belief in the goodness of nature with a belief in historical progress. Eventually, Jefferson believed, the equal right of each man to manage his own affairs would become manifest to all reasonable men and, at the same time, men would also acquire the ability to enjoy that right. Near the end of his letter on natural aristocracy, Jefferson commented that "science is progressive." Referring particularly to political science, or perhaps the impact of other sciences on political science, he wrote that "talents and enterprise [are] on the alert. Resort may be had to the people of the country, a more governable power from their principles of subordination; and rank, and birth, and tinsel-aristocracy will finally shrink into insignificance, even" in Europe. Formerly, Jefferson implied, it made sense to separate the aristocrats into a separate house—a Lords in England, a distinct Estate in France, or a Senate in the Roman republic. Science made it possible to trust the people with more power than before. Jefferson returned to this theme in his famous last letter. "The general spread of the light of science has already laid open to every view the palpable truth, that the mass of mankind has not been born with saddles on their backs, nor a favored few booted and spurred, ready to ride them legitimately, by the grace of God," he wrote. The "palpable truth" that men were born with rights was spreading, thanks to "the light of science." Note that this truth was no longer "sacred and undeniable" (as in Jefferson's first draft of the Declaration) or even "self-evident" (as in the final version); it was now "palpable"—recognized by the senses and not the intellect. The American Revolution, Jefferson hoped, would help to spread the good news. "May it be to the world," he wrote, "the signal of arousing men to burst the chains under which monkish ignorance and superstition had persuaded them to bind themselves, and to assume the blessings and security of self-government. That form which we have substituted, restores the free right to the unbounded exercise of reason and freedom of opinion."[15]

The American Revolution constituted both a restoration of rights that had been lost due to "monkish ignorance" and a step forward to greater liberty than men had formerly enjoyed. In his letter on natural aristocracy, Jefferson suggested that human nature had a historical dimension. "Formerly bodily powers gave place among the aristoi," Jefferson wrote, but "since the invention of gunpowder has armed the weak as well as the strong with missile death, bodily strength, like beauty, good humor, politeness and other accomplishments, has become but an auxiliary ground of distinction."[16] Prior to the invention of gunpowder, physically strong men were *natural aristocrats* because they were those to whom nature had given the requisite qualities to rise. Science had changed things, and intelligence had replaced bodily strength as a defining feature of the natural aristocracy. As that change took place, it became easier for common men to enjoy their rights.

Jefferson faulted Adams for failing to recognize that change. "With respect to aristocracy," he wrote to Adams, "we should further consider that, before the establishment of the American states, nothing was known to history but the man of the old world." Adams used history as the data of his political science. Presuming that human nature did not change, he examined the historical record and drew conclusions about what was possible in human societies. Jefferson thought Adams's sample was too small. European history did not display the full range of possibilities. America was different. Unlike Europe, where people were crowded into cities, "here every one may have land to labor for himself if he chuses." Beyond that, Jefferson thought the underlying conditions of society were moving to a higher plane. Jefferson held that "the terms whig and tory belong to natural, as well as to civil history." Adams agreed, believing that any just regime had to manage the conflict between them. Jefferson thought that need not remain the case in the future. In England, he hoped that a revolution in government would bring about real change and that "the distinctions between whig and tory will disappear like chaff on a troubled ocean."[17] Natural history was progressive, Jefferson thought. The world would progress beyond the distinction between Whig and Tory. Men would progress away from politics in the classic sense.

Jefferson hoped that advances in education and politics would further the progress that science had begun. Toward the end of his letter on natural aristocracy, Jefferson turned to his plans for reforming Virginia after 1776. First, he mentioned the abolition of entails and primogeniture. By taking away concentrations of land in certain families, he "laid the axe to the root of Pseudo-aristocracy." Next on the agenda "was a Bill for the more general diffusion of learning." Had that been enacted, "worth and genius would thus have been sought out from every condition of life, and compleatly prepared by education for defeating the competition of wealth and birth for public trusts." Jefferson connected education reform with his scheme for ward republics. By breaking down Virginia into counties, and each county into smaller districts, self-government could be maximized. As much as possible, people would live as they chose or under laws that they chose directly. Education would train individual citizens to manage their own affairs, and train local leaders as well. It would also teach them to distinguish the natural aristocrats from the pretenders when they voted. Finally, Jefferson mentioned Virginia's Statute for the Establishment of Religious Freedom.[18] He then summarized:

> The law for religious freedom, which made a part of this system, having put down the aristocracy of the clergy, and restored to the citizen the freedom of the mind, and those of entails and descents nurturing an equality of condition among them, this on Education would have raised the mass of the people to the high ground of moral respectability necessary to their own safety, and to orderly government; and would have compleated the great object of qualifying them to select the veritable aristoi, for the trusts of government, to the exclusion of the Pseudalists.

Jefferson's scheme had both positive and negative elements. Certain things had only to be repealed—entails, primogeniture, and religious establishment —and truth would win. Other, positive actions had to be taken to move the citizenry up, notably his education and ward republic schemes. Partly because the education bill never came close to passage, Jefferson did not prepare a detailed plan for primary education. In his *Notes on the State of Virginia*, he suggested that basic education should include "reading, writing, and arithmetic." That would be done by dividing the state into small districts, congruent with the wards that comprised the republic. The next level, grammar school, featured "Greek, Latin, geography, and the higher branches of numerical arithmetic." All students at grammar school would remain at least a year or two. The best among them would be "raked from the rubbish" and remain in the grammar school for several more years. And above all these was the university where they would study "such of the sciences as their genius shall have led them to."[19]

The purpose of these reforms was to allow each individual to rise to the level in society for which nature had destined him. At the bottom, the least intelligent would manage their own farms, and select the best among them to manage their wards. At each geographic remove, up to the state capital, and beyond that to the U.S. capital, the more capable people would advance, with the true natural aristocrats running the system as a whole. All voters would be qualified to recognize the "veritable aristoi," and select them for the positions that suited them.[20]

Jefferson reconciled his belief in natural aristocracy with his belief in equal rights by making self-rule the fundamental right and, at the same time, suggesting that politics was not the fundamental human activity. Just as Jefferson believed that a sort of spontaneous move to religious truth would follow disestablishment, so too did he believe that a move to political order would follow the repeal of aristocratic institutions (and the implementation of his plans for education and ward republics). If, as Aristotle said, man was a political animal, then the only people who truly lived to the full potential of man were statesmen, the men who ran the political system. Perhaps the philosophers would suggest that the true philosophers were above the statesmen as beings who thought through the fundamental human problems. These men were morally superior to the average man because they lived at, and were capable of living at, a higher moral plane. But if the political system could become a machine that ran itself, if we can progress beyond Whig and Tory, if religious irrationality can be done away with merely by ending religious establishments, if educators truly can separate the best students without any significant difficulty (if talented men remained at a lower level, they would continually be causing trouble), if the law can be so clear that judges can be mere "machines," and in general that all political problems could be solved fairly and with precision, then that would no longer be the case. Human society could progress beyond the tragic choices that were the essence of classic statesmanship. If the ideal of life was Epicurean, as it was for Jefferson, politics was far less important.[21] If Jefferson resolved the tension between natural aristocracy and natural right, that is how he managed it.

In Jefferson's plan, natural aristocrats had skills superior to those of the average man, but only in the same way it is true that some run faster than others. In other words, Jefferson's solution to the problem reconciling natural rights with natural aristocracy was to trivialize politics. In the economy of nature, Jefferson thought, the problem of justice can be resolved—otherwise nature would not be economical. Once the great political problems were solved, statesmen, men above the political order, would no longer be necessary, and it would finally be possible to create a regime based upon the equality of men. Men would meet as equals in society, leaving behind the unequal ground of politics. Were that done, true statesmanship would no longer be necessary.

It is significant that Jefferson said that nature provided natural aristocrats to "manage the concerns of society" rather than to rule society. As Thomas Paine wrote in *Common Sense*, "some writers have so confounded society with government, as to leave little or no distinction between them; whereas they are not only different, but have different origins. Society is produced by our wants, and government by our wickedness; the former promotes our happiness *positively* by uniting our affections, the latter *negatively* by restraining our vices."[22] Thanks to science, Jefferson hoped, politics would become increasingly irrelevant to American life. At the same time, the political dimension of citizenship would be reduced.

According to Jefferson, science would allow mankind to move to a higher moral plane. Jefferson held that "the moral sense is as much a part of our constitution as that of feeling, seeing, or hearing." Reasoning, once again, backward from the order of creation, he held that "he who made us would have been a pitiful bungler, if he had made the rules of our moral conduct a matter of science. For one man of science, there are thousands who are not. What would have become of them? Man was destined for society. His morality, therefore, was to be formed to this object." Once Jefferson's scheme was in place, the most important political fact in America would be the moral equality of men. Absent artificial restraints in politics and religion, peace and harmony would prevail. That was God's plan: "I do believe that if the Almighty has not decreed that man shall never be free, (and it is blasphemy to believe it,) that the secret will be found to be in the making himself the depository of the powers respecting himself, so far as he is competent to them, and delegating only what is beyond his competence by an synthetical process, to higher and higher functionaries." Because men were intended to be free, Jefferson reasoned, certain things about human nature had to be true. Officeholders were "functionaries," not statesman who truly ruled, and society would become the key realm of civic life.[23]

In America, the great exception, of course, was the matter of race and slavery. It might not be a coincidence, therefore, that in the *Notes on the State of Virginia*, the only place Jefferson uses the word "statesman" is in Query 18, amid his discussion of race and slavery. Race and slavery gummed up the works of the constitutional machine. It needed management by statesmen. In his "wolf by the ears" letter, Jefferson frames the problem exactly that way: "justice is in one scale, and self-preservation is in the other."[24] Making the best of situations where self-preservation conflicts with justice is the essence of high politics, in the classic sense of the term.

Ultimately, Jefferson's hopes for the future rested upon his belief that nature, including human nature, was created with human liberty, as Jefferson understood it, in mind. Those who disagreed with Jefferson were "heretics," deniers of the "sacred and undeniable" truths about God, man, and nature. That explains Jefferson's response to Adams. Adams challenged not simply Jefferson's constitutional system, but also the presumptions about nature and history that lay beneath it. By doing that, Adams was, according to Jefferson's logic, beyond the pale. Hence Jefferson branded Adams's writings "heresies," and kept his *Defence of the Constitutions* from being published in France. Jefferson often branded opponents "heretics," or called their ideas "heresies." Why these terms? And why was it legitimate to censor Adams's writings? To Jefferson, Adams's ideas were unscientific; they ran contrary to common sense and contradicted the order of nature.[25] To put it slightly differently, Adams's sympathy for Aristotle's political thought was impossible to reconcile with the political importance Jefferson assigned to Bacon's scientific method. Were men social or political beings by nature? On the answer to that question the argument turned.

We can best understand Jefferson's point of view when we recall Ernst Cassirer's suggestion that theodicy was a political problem for men of the Enlightenment. If men were capable of living in peace, plenty, and harmony in the future, why had they seldom done so in the past? Adams's answer was the classic one: That was the way of the world. "After all," he wrote Jefferson, "as grief is a pain, it stands in the predicament of all other evil and the great question occurs what is the origin and what the final cause of evil. This perhaps is known only to omniscience. We poor mortals have nothing to do with it, but to fabricate all the good we can out of all inevitable evils, and to avoid all that are avoidable."[26] In his personal life, Jefferson found such stoicism admirable. In politics, however, Jefferson hoped that science could change the world. That was possible because there were rather fewer necessary evils than Adams supposed. Absent artificial religious supports, all would become Unitarians. Absent artificial political supports, and with the addition of a commonsensical educational system, all the great political problems would be solved, and the wise and good would be in charge.

The ultimate goal of Jefferson's science was peace, and the main assumption was that God had created a world in which universal peace was possible. Politics was the realm of argument, division, and, ultimately, war. Society was different. It was the realm of harmony and spontaneous order. "Peace is our passion, and the wrongs might drive us from it," Jefferson wrote. "We prefer trying *ever* [*sic*] other just principles, right and safety, before we would recur to war." America would lead Europe to the light. "We are destined to be a barrier against the returns of ignorance and barbarism," he wrote to Adams. "Old Europe will have to lean on our shoulders, and to hobble along by our side." Once again, clarity was key. To have just peace, there must be general agreement about justice. All parties must believe that they are getting their due, or there would not be peace. The result would be an international harmony that echoed Jefferson's domestic harmony.[27]

In his famous "Adam and Eve" letter, Jefferson wrote that "the liberty of the whole earth was depending on the issue of the contest, and was ever such a prize won with so little blood? . . . Rather than it should have failed, I would have seen half the earth desolated. Were there but an Adam and an Eve left in every country, and left free, it would be better than it now is." For our purposes, the key phrase is "in every country." Jefferson did not resolve the human race back to one pair, but rather into several nations, which presumably would be equal. For Jefferson, nations, like aristocrats, were themselves artifacts of nature. They were not political creations. From that, Jefferson foresaw the creation of a society of nations acting harmoniously rather than a balance of power maintained ultimately by the threat of war. In this society of nations the interests of nations would be clear enough to ensure peace. Reflecting on Anglo-American relations during his administration, Jefferson wrote that "no two countries upon earth have so many points of common interest and friendship; and their rulers must be great bunglers indeed, if, with such dispositions, they break them asunder." Note Jefferson's language. To fail to achieve peace was to be "bunglers"—the same term Jefferson used when discussing the order of nature. God would be a bungler if he created a natural order where peace was not possible, and men would be bunglers if they failed to be true to their natures and live in peace.[28]

Only peace, Jefferson believed, could justify modern science. "If science produces no better fruits than tyranny, murder, rapine and destruction of national morality," Jefferson informed Adams in 1812, "I would rather wish our country to be ignorant, honest and estimable as our neighboring savages are." Modern science gave man tremendous power. In their lifetimes, Adams and Jefferson had seen the ravages of smallpox and lightning reduced. The steam engine began to make transportation much more rapid. That was power for good. But suppose that man's capacity for evil was not the result of historical accident, but rather was part and parcel of his nature, as Adams suggested. "Science, literature, mechanic arts, and those fine arts . . . which you love so well and taste to exquisitely," Adams wrote to Jefferson, "have been subservient to Priests and Kings Nobles and commons monarchies and republicks. For they have all used them when they could, but as the rich had them oftener than the poor, in their power, the latter have always gone to the wall."[29] If belief in the Trinity was not due to religious establishments, and if the rise of "artificial aristocracy," as Jefferson defined the term, was not due to corrupt laws, then his hope for peace, which rested on a similar foundation, would be vain. If all was on the table, philosophically speaking, Jefferson realized, the argument about justice would never end and, for that reason, times of peace would remain precious because they were rare. There was a direct correlation between Jefferson's epistemology and his politics. If political knowledge could be had with Euclidean certainty, then, perhaps, all great political problems could be solved. Politics could be reduced from statesmanship to engineering.

What was interesting about Jefferson, of course, is that he believed so fervently in peace and harmony that, when in office, he knew how to compromise.[30] Peace was a practical goal, not a mere ideological hope. His statesmanship was more moderate than his political science. As a theorist, Jefferson had a Jacobinical streak, but as a statesman, he was moderate and practical. Two hundred years after the end of his presidency, we may rightly wonder whether Jefferson's hopes for changing the world deluded him, and it might be reasonable to ask if he was right about the future of politics and the nature of aristocracy.

Notes

1. TJ to John Adams, 28 October 1813, *AJL*, 388. Whenever Greek terms appear in these letters, I use the translation provided by Cappon.

2. TJ to Adams, 13 October 1813, *AJL*, 387–92; TJ to Joseph C. Cabell, 5 January 1815, Ford, 9:501. These two letters are the only ones that use the term "natural aristocracy" in a text-search of all Jefferson writings that are currently available. It is possible that there is another reference lurking in writings that are not, as of yet, searchable. We should also note that Adams concludes his reply to Jefferson's letter: "As I have no Amanuenses by females, and there is so much about generation in this letter that I dare not ask any one of them to copy it, and I cannot copy it myself I must beg you to return it to me." Adams to TJ, 15 November 1813, *AJL*, 402; TJ to Madison, [13 May 1793], *TJP*, 26:26. Charles Miller, *Jefferson and Nature* (Baltimore, 1988), 83, also cites the Cabell letter. Jefferson had reasons for holding his tongue. Speaking regularly about natural aristocracy might make it harder to enlighten the masses and teach them to be less deferential to elites, in addition to costing Jefferson popularity. TJ to Adams, 13 October 1813, *AJL*, 391.

3. TJ to Benjamin Rush, 17 August 1811, *TJP:RS*, 4:87. Miller notes this passage, 28, n. 18. TJ to John Adams, 24 January 1814, *AJL*, 421. TJ to Benjamin Waterhouse, 26 June 1822, *TJW*, 1459. On this idea, see Johann Neem, "Beyond the Wall: Jefferson's Danbury Address," *JER* 17 (2007): 139–54. TJ to Adams, 22 August 1813, *AJL*, 368. TJ, *Notes on the State of Virginia*, in *TJW*, 272. TJ to Edmund Pendleton, 26 August 1776, ibid., 757.

4. "Jefferson was eclectic if not at times inconsistent in his philosophy," according to Miller, *Jefferson and Nature*, 26. "Jefferson's eclectic view of the problems and subject matter of general philosophy did not commit him to any one position in philosophy of education," according to John Densford, "The Educational Philosophy of Thomas Jefferson," *Peabody Journal of Education* 38 (1961): 274. TJ to Francis Hopkinson, 13 March 1789, *TJW*, 941. Miller notes Jefferson's peculiar Epicureanism, 26. Jefferson was often reluctant to consider whether a deeper internal logic held the ideas of political, philosophic, or religious parties together. On his Epicureanism, see, for example, his comment to William Short on 31 October 1819: "I too am an Epicurean." See L&B, 15:219.

5. Henry May notes that Jefferson held that "the world was intelligently planned, benevolently intended, and understandable to man. Such a creed leaves no place for mystery, or even for mess. As a scientist Jefferson was in the habit of proving that things must be true because

their contrary would reflect on the beneficence of the Creator." See May, *The Enlightenment in America* (New York, 1976), 295. TJ to Adams, 28 October 1813, *AJL*, 388; TJ to Thomas Law, 13 June 1814, L&B, 14:142. TJ, *Notes, TJW,* 176. On the same idea, see TJ to John Stuart, 10 November 1796, *TJP,* 29:205–6. Very late in his life, Jefferson reluctantly began to accept that species could go extinct. That concession does not change the underlying point. Jefferson reasoned backwards from his presumption about what the order of creation was. It was hard to show him enough evidence to change his mind.

6. TJ to John Trumbull, 15 February 1789, *TJP,* 14:561. Newton, in Charles Gillispie, *The Edge of Objectivity: An Essay in the History of Scientific Ideas* (Princeton, N.J., 1960), 147.

7. "Speaking of Plato, I will add, that no writer, ancient or modern, has bewildered the world with more *ignes fatui,* than this renowned philosopher," TJ to William Short, 4 August 1820, *TJW,* 1436. In his essay on "Jefferson and the Republic of Letters," in *Jeffersonian Legacies,* ed. Peter S. Onuf (Charlottesville, Va., 1993), 63, Douglas Wilson notes the empiricism of Jefferson, who affirmed that "a patient pursuit of facts, and cautious combination and comparison of them is the drudgery to which man is subjected by his maker if he wishes to attain sure knowledge." In general, Jefferson objected to nonliteral readings of texts. Consider his comment on the Bible: "If histories so unlike as those of Hercules and Jesus, can, by a fertile imagination and allegorical interpretations, be brought to the same tally," he wrote, "no line of distinction remains between fact and fancy," TJ to Adams, 14 October 1816, *AJL,* 491.

8. Adams to TJ, 12 May 1820, *AJL,* 564. TJ to Adams, 15 August 1820, ibid., 567. Jefferson was dogmatic on the question of matter and spirit: "To talk of *immaterial* existences is to talk of *nothings.* To say that the human soul, angels, god, are immaterial, is to say they are *nothings,* or that there is no god, no angels, no soul. I cannot reason otherwise: but I believe I am supported in my creed of materialism by Locke, Tracy, and Stewart. . . . Jesus taught nothing of it. He told us indeed that 'God is a spirit,' but he has not defined what a spirit is, nor said that it is not *matter*" (ibid., 568). TJ to Adams, 15 August 1820, ibid., 569. This letter is in response to Adams's of 12 May 1820, ibid., 564. TJ to John Page, 16 August 1804, Ford, 10:96. Jefferson's empiricism was not so "humble" as Garry Wills contends in *Inventing America: Jefferson's Declaration of Independence* (Garden City, N.Y., 1978), 186. Similarly, Jefferson's understanding of a God who "bungleth not" is not quite what Wills describes. For a powerful critique of Wills's interpretation of Jefferson, see Ronald Hamowy's "Jefferson and the Scottish Enlightenment: A Critique of Gary Wills," *WMQ* 36 (1979): 503–23.

9. TJ to Adams, 28 October 1813, *AJL,* 388; TJ to George Washington, 8 May 1791, *TJP,* 20:291, italics added by author for emphasis. Jefferson implicitly agreed with Adams's definition of an aristocrat. Adams explained to John Taylor that "by aristocracy I understand all those men who can command, influence, or procure more than an average of votes; by an aristocrat, every man who can and will influence one man to vote besides himself." See Adams to John Taylor II, in *The Works of John Adams,* 10 vols., ed. Charles Francis Adams (Boston, 1850–56), 6:451. The common foundation of Jefferson's natural and artificial aristocrats is what Adams suggested.

10. TJ to Adams, 28 October 1813, *AJL,* 388.

11. Adams to TJ, 15 November 1813, ibid., 398. He wrote similarly to Benjamin Rush, "You see I use the word talents in a larger sense than usual, comprehending every advantage. Genius, experience, learning, fortune, birth, health, are all talents, though I know not how the word has been lately confined to the faculties of the mind." Adams to Rush, 11 November 1807, in *Spur of Fame: Dialogues of John Adams and Benjamin Rush, 1805–1813,* ed. John Schutz and Douglas Adair (Indianapolis, 2001), 107. Adams to TJ, 9 July 1813, *AJL,* 352; TJ to Adams, 28 October 1813, ibid., 387.

12. Adams to TJ, [14?] August 1813, ibid., 365. In the same letter, Adams added another translation from Theognis: "Nor does a Woman disdain to be the Wife of a bad rich Man. But she prefers a Man of Property before a good Man. For Riches are honoured." The editors of the *Spur of Fame* point out that Adams thus reversed the classical formulation, according to which the masses need to be tamed by the aristocrats; 189, n. 19. Adams to TJ, 2 September 1813, *AJL*, 371. In his reply to Jefferson, Adams split the difference: "The Proverbs of Theognis, like those of Soloman, are Observations on human nature, ordinary life, and civil Society, with moral reflections on the facts." Adams to TJ, 15 November 1813, ibid., 399.

13. TJ to Adams, 28 October 1813, ibid., 387–88.

14. In his reply to Jefferson's letter, Adams allowed that the traits of aristocracy might be inherited. Yet Adams limited the moral implications of that conclusion: "I quoted him [Theognis] as a Witness of the Fact, that there was as much difference in the races of Men as in the breeds of Sheep. . . . Surely no authority can be more expressly on point to prove the existence of Inequalities, not of rights, but of moral intellectual and physical inequalities in Families, descents and Generations. If a descent from, pious, virtuous, wealthy literary or scientific Ancestors is a letter of recommendation . . . in a man's favour, and enables him to influence only one vote in Addition to his own, he is an Aristocrat, for democrat can have but one Vote. Aaron Burr had 100,000 Votes from the single Circumstance of his descent from President Burr and President Edwards." Adams to TJ, 15 November 1813, ibid., 399.

15. TJ to Adams, 28 October 1813, *AJL*, 391; TJ to Roger Weightman, 24 June 1826, *TJW*, 1517.

16. TJ to Adams, 28 October 1813, *AJL*, 388. This historical dimension in Jefferson's thought might be related to his thoughts about natural history. On Jefferson and natural history, see James Ceaser, *Reconstructing America* (New Haven, Conn., 1997).

17. TJ to Adams, 28 October 1813, *AJL*, 391. In March, 1801, Jefferson told Joseph Priestley, the liberal English minister, that "we can no longer say there is nothing new under the sun. For this whole chapter in the history of man is new." See TJ to Joseph Priestley, 21 March 1801, *TJP*, 33:394. When the letter was published in 1813, Adams read it, and he begged to differ: "I can yet say there is nothing new under the sun, in my sense." See Adams to TJ, 14 June 1813, *AJL*, 330; TJ to Adams, 27 June 1813, ibid., 335; Adams to TJ, 9 July 1813, ibid., 353–54; TJ to Adams, 25 November 1816, ibid., 498.

18. In between these sections of the letter on natural aristocracy are a couple of paragraphs in which Jefferson argues that family and wealth matter more in New England than in Virginia. Holly Brewer notes the scope of entail in colonial Virginia in her article, "Entailing Aristocracy in Colonial Virginia: 'Ancient Feudal Restraints and Revolutionary Reform,' " *WMQ* 54 (1997): 307–46. For more on the bill for religious liberty, see my entry on "Jefferson and Religion: Private Belief and Public Policy," in the *Cambridge Companion to Jefferson*, ed. Frank Shuffelton (Cambridge, 2009), 143–54.

19. TJ to Adams, 28 October 1813, *AJL*, 388–90. Jefferson's suggestion that education would teach common men to recognize and elect the natural aristocracy contradicts Joseph Ellis's claim that Adams provoked Jefferson simply by "calling the Jeffersonian ideal of human equality a seductive delusion." See *American Sphinx* (New York, 1997), 249. TJ, *Notes*, Query 14, *TJW*, 272.

20. In 1810, he informed John Tyler that "I have indeed two great measures at heart, without which no republic can maintain its strength. 1. That of general education, to enable every man to judge for himself what will secure or endanger his freedom. 2. To divide every county into hundreds, of such size that all children of each will be within reach of a central school in it. But this division looks to many other fundamental provisions. Every hundred,

besides a school, should have a justice of the peace, a constable and a captain of the militia" (*TJW*, 1226). On Jefferson's reform scheme, in particular its educational dimension, see Richard D. Brown, "Bulwark of Revolutionary Liberty: Thomas Jefferson's and John Adams's Programs for an Informed Citizenry," and Jennings L. Wagoner Jr., " 'That Knowledge Most Useful to Us': Thomas Jefferson's Concept of Utility in the Education of Republican Citizens," in *Thomas Jefferson and the Education of a Citizen*, ed. James Gilreath (Washington, D.C., 1999), 91–102, 115–33.

21. "I wish I could subjoin a translation of Gosindi's Syntagma of the doctrines of Epicurus, which, notwithstanding the calumnies of the Stoics and caricatures of Cicero, is the most rational system remaining of the philosophy of the ancients." TJ to Charles Thomson, 9 January 1816, *TJW*, 1373. Adams, by contrast, not only was not an Epicurean but also thought there was something profoundly wrong with the philosophy. See Adams to John Rogers, 6 February 1801, *Adams Papers*, Microfilm, reel no. 118.

22. "Common Sense," in Eric Foner, ed., *Paine* (New York, 1995), 6.

23. Jean Yarbrough suggests that "Jefferson's position . . . is consistent with Enlightenment assumptions. What Jefferson objects to is not reason per se but the traditional rationalist argument that the moral and political truths necessary for men living together in society can be known *only* by reason, and in particular by intuitive reason. If this were true, then the bulk of humankind whose ability to reason is limited would be dependent on the wise few for moral knowledge." See Yarbrough, *American Virtues: Thomas Jefferson and the Character of a Free People* (Lawrence, Kans., 1998), 36. She also notes that "Jefferson devotes much more of his efforts to forming the character of the citizens than he does to thinking about the distinctive virtues republican statesmen should possess." See *American Virtues*, 103. TJ to Adams, 15 October 1816, *AJL*, 492. Yarbrough notes that Jefferson only discussed the moral sense twice, and not at great length. See *American Virtues*, 33. TJ to Peter Carr, 10 August 1787, *TJP*, 12:14–18. TJ to Joseph Cabell, 2 February 1816, *TJW*, 1380. Michael Zuckert notes that in this letter, Jefferson says that his system "constitutes truly a system of fundamental balances and checks for the government." See Zuckert's "Founder of the Natural Rights Republic," in *Thomas Jefferson and the Politics of Nature*, ed. Thomas S. Engerman (Notre Dame, Ind., 2000), 50.

24. "The man must be a prodigy who can retain his manners and morals undepraved by such circumstances. And with what execration should the statesman be loaded, who permitted one half the citizens thus to trample on the rights of the other, transforming those into despots, and these into enemies, destroys the morals of the one part, and the amor patrae of the other." TJ, *Notes*, *TJW*, 288. Note that Jefferson's concern here is the impact slavery has on the character of both master and slave. So long as slavery persisted, the ward republic scheme would not do what it was designed to do. TJ to John Holmes, April 22, 1820, *TJW*, 1434. Douglas L. Wilson notes Jefferson's belief that his times were peculiar: "The circumstances of our country at my entrance into life, were such that every honest man felt himself compelled to take a part, and to act up to the best of his abilities." See Wilson, "Jefferson and the Republic of Letters," in *Jeffersonian Legacies*, ed. Onuf, 54. Jefferson wished to create a world where such service is no longer a duty.

25. In 1791, Jefferson used the publication of Thomas Paine's *Rights of Man* as an excuse to brand Adams a heretic. Jefferson wrote that he was pleased that Paine's book would be reprinted in America, "and that something is at length to be publically said against the political heresies which have sprung up among us." TJ to Jonathan B. Smith, 26 April 1791, *TJP*, 20:290. See Joyce Appleby, "The Adams-Jefferson Rupture and the First French Translation of John Adams' *Defence*," *WMQ* 78 (1968): 1084–91. For other examples of Jefferson denouncing "heresies" see,

among many others, TJ to John Brown Cutting, 2 October 1788, *TJP,* 13:649; TJ to James Madison, 29 June 1793, ibid., 26:404; TJ to James Sullivan, 19 June 1807, L&B, 11:238; TJ to John Hollins, 5 May 1811, *TJP:RS,* 3:606; and TJ to Samuel Kercheval, 12 July 1816, *TJW,* 1396. In this context we should note that Jefferson called the Virginia statute for religious liberty "A Bill for Establishing Religious Freedom." See *TJW,* 346. Religious freedom would be the new establishment.

26. Ernst Cassirer, *The Philosophy of the Enlightenment,* trans. Fritz Koelln and James Pettegrove (Princeton, N.J., 1951), Ch. 4:1, "The Dogma of Original Sin and the Problem of Theodicy." Adams to TJ, 6 May 1816, *AJL,* 473. Jefferson accepted this tragic view as it applied to individuals. In response to Adams's comments about grief, he wrote, "I see that, with the other evils of life, it is destined to temper the cup we are to drink." See TJ to Adams, 1 August 1816, *AJL,* 483. Jefferson had a harder time accepting that politics had similar limitations.

27. TJ to John Sinclair, 30 June 1803, *TJW,* 1133. Jefferson wrote, "my hope of preserving peace for our country is not founded in the greater principle of non-resistance under every wrong, but in the belief that a just and friendly conduct on our part will procure justice and friendship from others. In the existing contest, each of the combatants will find an interest in our friendship." TJ to the Earl of Buchan, 10 July 1803, *TJW,* 1134; TJ to Adams, 1 August 1816, *AJL,* 484; TJ to Adams, 1 August 1816, ibid., 484.

28. TJ to William Short, 3 January 1793, *TJP,* 25:14. See Peter Onuf, *Jefferson's Empire: The Language of American Nationhood* (Charlottesville, Va., 2000), esp. 147–88. One way to resolve the tension in Jefferson's thought between equality and natural aristocracy is to argue that Jefferson believed in equality among nations but not individuals. Jefferson's belief in clear borders between nations may have been related to his anti-Jewish comments. Jefferson told William Short that "Moses had bound the Jews to many idle ceremonies, mummeries and observances, of no effect towards producing the social utilities which constitute the essence of virtue. . . . [He] instilled into his people the most anti-social spirit towards other nations." See TJ to Short, 4 August 1820, *TJW,* 1437–38. Jews were a distinct nation, but lived inside many other nations. They were a living contradiction to Jefferson's hope for clear national boundaries. TJ to James Monroe, 4 May 1806, L&B, 11:110. Similarly, he pointed to a revolution in England (in which "the distinctions between whig and tory will disappear"), which "effect the desired object of an honest government, one which will permit the world to live in peace, and under the bonds of friendship and neighborhood." TJ to Adams, 15 November 1816, *AJL,* 498. On Destutt-Tracy's work on ethics, Jefferson commented, "I gather from his other works that he adopts the principle of Hobbes, that justice is founded in contract solely, and does not result from the constitution of man. I believe, on the contrary, that it is instinct, and innate, that the moral sense is as much part of our constitution as that of feeling, seeing, or hearing; as a wise creator must have seen to be necessary in an animal destined to live in society." TJ to Adams, 14 October 1816, ibid., 492.

29. TJ to Adams, 21 January 1812, ibid., 291. Jefferson's choice of words ("if science") implicitly compares the world under the direction of science to the world under the direction of religion, as if science constituted the new reigning idea and not simply the quest for the truth about nature. Adams to TJ, 2 February 1817, ibid., 507.

30. Alexander Hamilton wrote that "a true estimate of Mr. J[efferson]'s character warrants the expectation of a temporizing rather than a violent system." See Hamilton to James Bayard, 16 January 1801, *AHP,* 25:323.

The Jefferson Gospel

A Religious Education of Peace, Reason, and Morality

CAMERON ADDIS

M OST OF JEFFERSON'S CONTEMPORARIES AGREED IN PRINCIPLE WITH
his core belief about education, that it should reinforce democracy by
teaching citizens and leaders about the world and their rights and responsibilities. But his notion that public education should emphasize scientific
rather than scriptural revelation was more controversial. While the First
Amendment succeeded generally in providing Americans with a pluralistic
and relatively tolerant religious landscape, they have argued ever since over
prayer, Bible instruction, and evolution vs. creationism in public schools.
Jefferson boasted near the end of his second presidential term that Americans
had "solved, by fair experiment, the great and interesting question whether
freedom of religion is compatible with order in government and obedience
to the laws." But in education these issues remained unresolved except insofar
as there was a near consensus in Jefferson's time that theologians should run
even public schools. Jefferson countered that trend in Virginia, where his
proscience agenda and religious heterodoxy clashed with the Protestant majority. Over the course of his half-century campaign to institute schools,
he developed a curriculum that turned conventional wisdom on its head,
instilling ethics based on Enlightenment universalism rather than orthodox
Christianity. Confronted with the inescapability of promoting some religious
stance (either explicitly or indirectly by omission), Jefferson endorsed a vi-
sionary faith at the University of Virginia based on general principles of

"peace, reason and morality," fending off criticism while reconciling his separationist principles with a thriving but relatively open religious culture.

Jefferson began studying law at the College of William and Mary in 1762, near the beginning of the revolt against Britain. The conflict between the colonies and mother country immersed the precocious teenager in serious matters of politics, philosophy, and religion. The Anglicans who ran the school, despite their affiliation with the established Church of England, held liberal latitudinarian religious beliefs—broad by orthodox Christian standards—and Jefferson's teachers discouraged strict Calvinism and evangelical emotion. They assigned writers who described the Christian tradition as antithetical to peace, accentuating such lowlights of fanaticism and bigotry as the Crusades, Catholic Inquisition, Thirty Years' War, and French wars of religion. Their work gave Jefferson no appreciation of how faith bolstered the spirituality and sanity of everyday believers; nor did it suggest that religions might defuse, rather than always promote, violence. He consequently developed a fairly harsh and one-sided view of organized faiths that lacked appreciation for the cohesive function of churches in society. Jefferson never argued that organized religions should not exist, however—only that society should repulse their influence or domination over the public realm. Most of the writers he read at William and Mary did not repudiate religion generally so much as they endorsed a more universal approach. Science provided a truer path to spiritual enlightenment than religion's violent past. Jefferson's *Literary Commonplace Book* prominently mentions John (Viscount) Bolingbroke (1678–1751), who argued that Christianity rested on miracles and superstition, not reason or experience. While his contemporaries studied at colleges that grew out of denominational seminaries, Jefferson read writers who saw nature as the genuine path to scientific *and* religious enlightenment. Given Jefferson's unwavering commitment to scientific theory, he no doubt would have come to embrace evolution more fully had he lived another half century (he conceded toward the end of his life that species such as the mastodon were mutable), but his religious views were similar to his contemporary William Paley's Natural Religion, or Intelligent Design in our own time.[1]

Jefferson was a deist or, more particularly, a pantheist, since he saw nature as *animated with*, rather than just *created by*, divinity.[2] It followed that his take on the American Revolution's cosmic implications strayed from the usual God and country religious nationalism one might expect from a budding

statesman. In the Declaration of Independence Jefferson kept things universal, predicating the break with Britain on "the God of Nature" rather than the
Lord or God almighty. Jefferson had both religious and political faith. His
interpretation of the Revolution was rooted in the Jewish and Puritan traditions of a chosen people acting on behalf of a progressive and benevolent
deity; the chosen people of the Declaration were the universal Enlightenment
diaspora rather than just the American Protestants of nineteenth-century
Manifest Destiny. This God buttressed his otherwise unsubstantiated claim of
natural rights such as civic freedom, landownership, and religious liberty.
Democracy and religious freedom were compatible for Jefferson because men
of the cloth, especially through their political associations with monarchies,
were another artificially imposed aristocracy designed to think for the people.

As Virginia governor Jefferson acquiesced in existing religious laws at
first, but quickly arrived at the separationist stance he maintained throughout his career—a position, he explained, not grounded in disrespect toward
religion itself, but a desire to curb the government's power over the minds of
the people and its capacity to foment war. His full-blown separation bill
(drafted in 1777) failed legislative approval in 1779 but eventually passed as the
landmark 1786 Virginia Statute of Religious Freedom, which forbade even a
nondenominational inter-Protestant establishment and outlawed religious
discrimination against anybody, including "Jew, Muhametan & Hindu." Simultaneously, he introduced his first education bill, which called for public
schooling to "diffuse knowledge" among an informed citizenry, but it failed
partly because it proposed a non-Christian curriculum.[3]

Jefferson connected secular education to independent-minded republican politics in the *Notes on the State of Virginia*, writing that youth were too
undeveloped for anything but indoctrination in the religious realm. "Instead
of putting the Bible into the hands of the children at an age when their
judgments are not sufficiently matured for religious inquiries, their memories may here be stored with the most useful facts from Grecian, Roman,
European and American history." (Some might argue that elementary students are similarly unprepared for anything but indoctrination in history.)
Students delayed studying science (religion's proxy) until the university level,
when they were ready for its mental rigor, while early language training would
serve as "instruments for [its] attainment." While reading, writing, and arithmetic would be taught in each school, special attention would be given to
history books that would alert students to various forms of tyranny, both

monarchical and spiritual, and encourage them to resist it in both forms. Like the *philosophes* he read at William and Mary, Jefferson not only wanted biblical instruction omitted but also hoped to demonstrate organized religion's absurdity and disruptiveness by selectively tracking its checkered past. In Jefferson's mind, religions retained their power by suppressing thought and causing "millions of innocent men, women, and children" to be "burnt, tortured, fined, [and] imprisoned," making "one half the world fools, and the other half hypocrites."[4] For the time being he conveniently avoided confronting how these heterodoxical views might interfere with his endorsement of local, participatory democracy: he simply preferred plans that would "keep elementary education out of the hands of fanaticizing preachers, who in county elections would be universally chosen."

Jefferson also served on the board of his *alma mater*, William and Mary, where he eliminated the divinity department and fired the education professor because he feared Anglican influence on local elementary teachers. Yet he also called for a post in ecclesiastical history because, while cautioning against indoctrination, he valued knowledge *about* religions.[5]

In public, Jefferson embraced the social benefits of Jesus's teaching and stayed loosely connected to the church establishments, attending Anglican or Episcopalian churches in Washington and Virginia and a Unitarian church in Philadelphia and making financial contributions.[6] He maintained correspondences with Presbyterians as well. Privately he edited the Bible by omitting supernatural passages from the New Testament. He wrote to Ezra Stiles, a Congregationalist and natural theologian scientist from Rhode Island, "I am of a sect by myself, as far as I know."[7] The Federalists attacked Jefferson's views in the 1796 and 1800 elections, so as president he avoided drawing undue attention to his personalized sect. He encouraged, but did not demand, national prayers, and he authorized the War Department to fund Presbyterian missionaries among the Cherokee. He allowed churches to use the Supreme Court and War and Treasury offices for services, contributed liberally to area churches, and attended services himself at the Episcopalian Christ Church, which met in a tobacco barn near Capitol Hill. (Buildings were scarce during the first years of Washington, D.C.) Throughout his presidency, he retained popularity among Baptists and Methodists because of his assertion of religious freedom in his "wall of separation" phrase and their minority status within certain regions such as New England.[8] On the education front his main efforts were steered, for the time being, toward establishing a strong science curriculum and Republican stronghold at the new military academy at West Point.

In retirement, Jefferson was freer to express himself and to recharge his efforts at establishing education in his home state. The earlier emphases established at William and Mary and espoused in *Notes on the State of Virginia* —generally undermining sectarian authority while endorsing religious studies and science—marked Jefferson's subsequent plans for public education and found expression in the curriculum, faculty, architecture, and religion of the University of Virginia. His 1814 plan for the Albemarle Academy (a proposed private school in Charlottesville) included a department of "Theology and Ecclesiastical History" that could train ministers, probably because of its private status and dependence on private donations. His last comprehensive public plan in 1817 disallowed any state-sponsored "religious instruction, reading or exercise." Teachers would be drawn from the laboring classes, including the sickly, crippled, or aged, but not the ministry.[9] Finally, the pioneering Rockfish Gap Report of 1818 outlined the curriculum of the University of Virginia, depriving religious denominations of the status as the organizing principle behind higher education that they had enjoyed for at least a millennium. At Jefferson's university, the God of Jehovah would be dethroned and supplanted by the universal god of the *philosophes*. The document stated that "in conformity with the principles of Virginia's Constitution, which places all sects of religion on an equal footing . . . we have proposed no professor of divinity." The professor of ethics would handle "proofs of the being of God, the creator, preserver, and supreme ruler of the universe, the author of all the relations of morality, and of the laws and obligations these infer."[10] Jefferson might have also mentioned the provinces of science and history, for the school's novel attempt to inculcate morals through untraditional means spread across the curriculum.

It is difficult now to appreciate the radicalism of this new arrangement. By the 1820s, the trend was in the opposite direction: all American colleges, public or private, required chapel attendance, and most schools had originated around seminaries or divinity departments. Christianity took its role in running colleges for granted even in France, where anticlericalism and devotion to reason had fueled its revolution. Without strong colleges, it was impossible for Christians to retain their legitimacy in the elite circles they strove to be part of and affect, so they embraced education; their students, in turn, often embraced religion. Between 1802 and 1815, major evangelical awakenings occurred at campuses such as Yale, Williams, Middlebury, Princeton, and Dartmouth. The *North American Review* noticed the revolutionary character of the Rockfish Gap Report in 1820 and commented upon it favorably, if pessimistically. Edward Everett wrote that the journal's readers would be gratified to view portions of the report since this was the "first instance, *in the world*, of a university without any such [orthodox religious] provision."[11] Others had implemented nondenominational curricula before but, like the founding generation's experiment in representative democracy, Jefferson had few successful precedents to build on in erecting an Enlightenment college.

In the 1750s, Benjamin Franklin had the idea nearest to what Jefferson later advocated. The Franklin Academy, which later grew into the College of Philadelphia, started out nonsectarian, but rivalries between Presbyterians and Anglicans beset its lay board. In 1776 it was rechartered by Presbyterians, who broadened its curriculum and renamed it the University of Pennsylvania. King's College in New York (later Columbia) espoused nondenominational intentions early on but ended up run by a consortium of Anglicans and Presbyterians. Princeton's seminary, opened in 1812, became the stronghold for Presbyterianism during the remainder of the century, and had satellites throughout the South, including Virginia's Hampden-Sydney. Colleges that tried to establish a nonsectarian grounding in the upper South became hotbeds of controversy. The University of North Carolina began as a nondenominational institution in 1795, but early in the nineteenth century, Presbyterians took over its board and faculty. The school's president and a professor were accused of infidelity and run out of Chapel Hill by hostile Protestants who, in conjunction with the 1800 legislature, cut off funding to the school for five years until it was taken over by a Princeton graduate. As late as 1900 the University of North Carolina was attacked by John Kilgo, president of Methodist Trinity College (later Duke), as an organ of Jeffersonian infidelity.[12] Denominations also clashed with religious libertarians in the western part of Jefferson's home state, in what is now Lexington, Kentucky. Presbyterians there started a seminary that became Transylvania University, a relative beacon of philosophy on the frontier. Through his friend John Breckenridge, Jefferson saw to it that Unitarian Harry Toulmin was elected its president in 1794, but Presbyterians ousted him within two years.[13] Jefferson admired

Transylvania's successful interlude but, by 1815, regarded Franklin's University of Pennsylvania as the best college in the United States and closest to his vision (and subsequently our own) of a true university. His goal was to improve on it, emulate its medical school, and set up an institution centered on science and the humanities in his hometown of Charlottesville.[14]

Those plans threatened to unravel nearly twenty years of hard work on the part of administrators to stamp out all but the most watered-down Enlightenment philosophy on America's campuses. These reformers now focused their attention on the infidel they considered the heir apparent to Thomas Paine, who had died in 1809. Jefferson's religion was similar, after all, to the deism Paine corrupted young minds with in *The Age of Reason* (1794). Jefferson was also trying to hire radicals such as Thomas Cooper on the faculty (jailed during the Alien & Sedition riots in 1799, Cooper was an agnostic but known to the public as a deist because of his association with Joseph Priestley). After colleges managed to snuff out Paine's popularity during the revivals of the early nineteenth century, Jefferson and his associates emerged as the foremost public symbols of the old discredited radicalism. Yale president Timothy Dwight was the most outspoken, fearing that the religion of Paine and Jefferson would unravel the delicate balance between liberty and order in the young republic, separating "the meat from the drink." Dwight and like-minded administrators were grouped in among the same men of the cloth whom Jefferson claimed were "pant[ing] to reestablish the Holy Inquisition" by challenging his plans for the University of Virginia.[15]

His enemies spoke in similar hyperbole, but Jefferson was only an infidel, as they charged, by the strictest definition of the term: he did not believe in scriptural revelation or the supernatural elements of Judaism, Christianity, or Islam. He rejected Jesus's divinity as a product of mythic "lore," but he admired his social philosophy, as evidenced by his unusual cutting-and-pasting of the Bible (removing the supernatural components of the New Testament). Denying any sort of direct communication from the heavens, his critique of Jewish people's faith—the bedrock of the desert religions—was that "the fumes of [their] disordered imaginations were recorded in their religious code, as special communications of the deity." Formal Christianity, constituted by an unbroken string of "dupes and imposters" (led by Paul and culminating in his contemporary Calvinists) had corrupted Jesus's doctrines.[16] In retirement, he continued to deny Christ's divinity, or even that Christ himself had any pretension of divinity.[17] Nevertheless, Jefferson avoided atheism at his university by implementing a philosophy typical of early nineteenth-century colleges, including those of the Presbyterians: the Scottish Common Sense school.[18] This program was the main conduit connecting Enlightenment philosophy to Jeffersonian America. It reacted against skepticism about the limits of human knowledge by embracing the moderate vision of a rational and perceptible order. Common Sense conveniently doubled as common ground with his critics and dovetailed reasonably well with Jefferson's reliance on inborn morality and morals derived from studying nature and history rather than gleaned from outside supernatural forces.

Jefferson optimistically argued that the moral foundation lay *within* and relied on instinct rather than coercion. Consequently, he did not see the controversy over the University of Virginia's curriculum as a debate between religious morality and secular amorality or apathy. Christianity, for him, actually cheapened the process of personal development because ethics enmeshed in superstitions lost their true meaning. Historians, scientists, and classical writers had broader perspectives and were better suited to awaken and develop ethics, or what Jefferson (as opposed to later deists and historians) meant by the phrase "natural religion." Drawing on atheist philosopher Baron d'Holbach, he wrote to John Adams that the world would be better off without organized religion; the moral precepts "necessary for a social being" were "innate in man" and "part of his physical constitution."[19] This moral philosophy connected to politics insofar as religions destroyed the sense of independence and responsibility requisite in a republican society.

He reminded his nephew Peter Carr of the importance of morals, but advised him to "question with boldness even the existence of a god; because, if there be one, he must more approve the homage of reason, than that of blindfolded fear."[20] If Jefferson oversimplified the situation when he wrote that the "dogmas on which the particular religions differ ... are unconnected to morality," he did so in the hope that the University of Virginia would provide a universal constellation of values that "all sects could agree on," avoiding discrepancies in dogma and superfluous detail.[21] His universal cause, whether he realized it or not, was rooted in the monotheistic tradition of the Scriptural faiths and their early attempts to unify by condensing and co-opting provincial religions (the same back-to-basics essentialism later inspired the Protestant Reformation). Jefferson merely expanded this notion to include all major faiths, recognizing that their contradictory details presented "artificial systems that had to be swept clean." Ideally, dogmatism would be swept clean while still exposing students to the best and most important ideas of prominent theologians through his university's course on moral philosophy, or ethics. Jefferson enlisted James Madison, a former divinity student, to compile a large and comprehensive list of works, both pagan and Christian, dating from the first centuries after Jesus. Here, Madison tempered Jefferson's own dogmatism in the same way he tried to with the university's law curriculum, where he advocated avoiding "the two extremes, by referring to selected Standards." When Jefferson wrote Madison that "it is in our Seminary that the Vestal flame is to be kept alive," he did so on behalf of a political curriculum that promoted not just republicanism, but also states' rights tracts such as the Virginia & Kentucky Resolutions and John Taylor's *Constitution Construed*.[22] While no Tories made their way into the university's law school, Madison compiled a broad cross-section of western theology. His topics ranged from original sin, deism, natural theology, Moravians, and Quakers to the Catholic Council of Trent; his authors included Aquinas, Leibniz, Luther, Calvin, Newton, and Penn.[23]

Madison concurred that broadening the students' exposure to religion was important; he also agreed that an ethics course was the proper venue. As a state institution, the University of Virginia could not have a divinity department, which Madison considered a direct violation of their 1786 Statute for Religious Freedom. Madison preferred overcoming short-term charges of irreligion to allowing any sect to monopolize religion, an alternative that would have ensured "an arena of theological gladiators."[24] Complementing their ethics course, their university would also emphasize rationalism as expressed by the French Physiocrats, who shared Jefferson's dream of an agrarian utopia and hoped to use mathematics and reason to structure society and solve its problems. For Jefferson, the most compelling part of Physiocratic theory was sensationalist philosophy, which argued that the human brain was comprehensible entirely (and exclusively) through the study of its chemistry. "Sensationalist" P. J. G. Cabanis, Monsieur Flourens, whom Jefferson met in Auteuil at the salon of Madame Helvétius, especially intrigued him.[25] Cabanis introduced Jefferson to positivism, the theory that natural phenomena and their properties form the bases of all true knowledge.

Cabanis argued in *Rapports du physique et du moral de l'homme* (1802) that thoughts and emotions are entirely chemical. He sent the book to Jefferson during his presidency, who ten years later still referred to the book as the "most profound of all human compositions."[26] Twenty years later Jefferson spelled out his (strangely modified) position in a letter to Adams:

> On the basis of sensation, of matter and motion, we may erect the fabric of all the certainties we can have or need. I can conceive thought to be an action of a particular organisation of matter . . . to say that the human soul, angels, god, are immaterial, is to say they are nothings, or that there is no god, no angels, no soul. . . . At what age of the Christian church this heresy of immaterialism, this masked atheism, crept in, I do not know. But a heresy it certainly is. Jesus taught nothing of it. He told us indeed that 'God is a spirit,' but he has not defined what a spirit is, nor said that it is not matter.[27]

Rather than using materialism to deny the existence of God and souls, Jefferson used it to support his pantheism.[28] He did not hold that God created the world and then retired from the scene, as did many deists in the seventeenth and eighteenth centuries. Instead, he believed that God continued to create and sustain the world moment by moment. Jefferson even hoped to further this materialism by including the University of Virginia's departments of ideology (English, rhetoric, and fine arts) and government under the heading of zoology. Zoology, in turn, subdivided into the physical and the moral. Jefferson was certain that "the faculty of thought belongs to animal history, is an important part of it, and should there find its place."[29]

He never subsumed the humanities or social sciences under zoology, but Jefferson hired sensationalist professor John Patton Emmet. Emmet, the son of Irish political rebel Thomas Addis Emmet, was one of the most promising scientists in the United States. In 1822 he received a medical degree from New York University with a dissertation titled "An Essay on the Chemistry of Animated Matter." He was unable to find work for three years because he argued that the proximate cause of all organic formation is chemical affinity. By not accounting for an ultimate cause, or "vital [theistic] principle," Emmet outraged the profession, who accused him of heresy. The *American Medical Recorder* condemned Emmet as a materialist and infidel. It was the last time anyone challenged the vital principle in print until 1844 but, tellingly, he found employment at Jefferson's university in 1825 as a professor of chemistry and medicine.[30]

The University of Virginia's architecture matched its Enlightenment curriculum. Jefferson spent his retirement absorbed in designing and overseeing construction of the campus. Referring to the Rotunda, the university's focal point, *New Yorker* architecture critic Paul Goldberger wrote that "if Jefferson had never done anything else, if he had never been President, if he hadn't written the Declaration of Independence, if he had never designed Monticello, if he had only designed this building, he would be a critical figure in American history."[31] At the head of the campus's rectangular lawn, or "academical village," the Rotunda displaced the traditional college chapel with a library and a proposed planetarium, the Enlightenment temple's sanctuary. Controversy surrounded not just the building's high cost, but also the predominance of the expansive, domed library at the chapel's expense. The larger-scale Roman Pantheon on which he modeled it was a pagan temple dedicated to the planetary gods, and unlike the upward-reaching spires of gothic cathedrals, the Rotunda's spherical dome suggested earth and nature. A small and humble room in the basement (directly under the library) set aside for worship, drawing, and music was all that sufficed for a chapel. The library, banished to the third floor at William and Mary, was front and center at Jefferson's university, leaving no doubt that reason prevailed over revelation. In his design, according to a modern commentator, "the human is at the center, and the library is the mind of the university—the repository of wisdom, knowledge of the past, and ideas for the future."[32]

Jefferson integrated organized religions into the plan as well. He defused opposition to the campus by inviting all area denominations to build seminaries, on an equal basis, around the outskirts of the university's campus. Students could attend any of the surrounding chapels, while seminarians, in turn, were welcome to attend classes at the university. Virginia jurist St. George Tucker had suggested the idea years earlier, as had Samuel Knox, a Maryland clergyman whom Jefferson had tried unsuccessfully to hire as a faculty member (Knox was runner-up to Samuel Stanhope Smith in the American Philosophical Society's 1796 contest to design the best educational system; he was also a staunch supporter of Jefferson's notion of religious liberty).[33] Jefferson called for bridging the "chasm now existing" between science and religion by giving theological students "ready and convenient access and attendance on the scientific lectures of the university; and to maintain by that means those destined for the religious professions on as high a standing of science, and of personal weight and respectability as may be obtained by others from the benefits of the University." Privately, Jefferson wrote to former revolutionary Thomas Cooper—whose aforementioned aborted hiring had caused a firestorm—that access to a sound education for ministers-in-training would "soften their asperities, liberalize and neutralize their prejudices, and make the general religion a religion of peace, reason and morality."[34] As Jefferson cynically predicted, jealousies among the sects, and their collective refusal to validate his experiment in ecumenicalism, precluded them from accepting his offer early on. No religious organizations affiliated themselves with the university until the YMCA in 1858, because each desired a monopoly. Nonetheless, the plan secured state funding for the university. Jefferson's sponsor in the state legislature, Joseph Cabell, informed him that his "suggestion regarding religious sects has had a great influence. It is the Franklin [rod] that has drawn the lightning from the cloud of opposition."[35]

As administrators such as Madison discovered when the school opened in 1825, more clouds lay on the horizon. For a variety of reasons, stemming from a disagreement between the students and European professors over how disrespectfully to treat the campus slaves, and generally including belligerent and insubordinate attitudes among the sons of Virginia's planters, the university suffered a disciplinary meltdown in its first years. Jefferson's final year turned out to be the school's first. Jefferson suffered the indignity of realizing that his naïve experiment in student self-policing had failed, and that his own great-great-grandnephew—Wilson Miles Cary—presented himself as a rioting ringleader and stood first to be dismissed.[36] Jefferson had carefully dispersed the professors' dwellings amidst the student dorms on the lawn, but found that most youth were not interested in philosophizing about the Enlightenment in their professors' parlors after hours the way that he had in Williamsburg. Instead, they were interested in tossing bottles of urine through their professors' windows. Vandalism and professor-floggings were typical at contemporary religious colleges as well, making it difficult to link the University of Virginia's disciplinary problems to its ethics course or lack of a proper chapel.[37]

Not so disease, which, especially in an era of rudimentary medicine, could be traced to supernatural causes. The University of Virginia suffered from the inherent disadvantage of any party subject to fundamentalist criticism, which is that any and all misfortune could easily be attributed to divine retribution. (The *philosophes* made subtler distinctions concerning the nature of causality, rendering them unable to return such charges in kind.) The spread-out design Jefferson had implemented, partly to avoid epidemics, failed in the late 1820s when a typhoid epidemic killed several students and slaves. (A year later, after a cholera outbreak, a cadaver, stolen from the medical school, wasted away to the skeleton, was found in a pond, the ice and water from which were drawn to the dormitories.)[38] This provided an excellent opportunity for area Episcopalians and Presbyterians, who were angling for greater influence on campus. The Episcopalians at William and Mary had revised their message, making it more evangelical than their Anglican brethren in England or Revolutionary American precursors, and were now led by Reverend William Meade.[39] As the Assistant Bishop-elect of the Diocese of Virginia, Meade seized on the stricken students' eulogy as an opportunity to lash out at the school, with particular aim taken at its founder. Just as Presbyterians capitalized on a Richmond theater fire in 1811 to accentuate the evils of the acting profession, Meade suggested that Jefferson's infidelity had killed the students. At one point he admitted that making such a direct link would be "idiotic" since true Christians die tragically, too, but he then went on arguing exactly that. Meade noted that God "takes part in all the trivial affairs of men, and actually appoints all the accidental and seemingly irregular occurrences of life." He asked the students and faculty assembled in the Rotunda if it amounted to "superstition or weakness to wonder if these visitations have not been sent to show the rulers thereof, their entire dependence on God? The design of God, therefore, in these dispensations, and the use to be made of them by us, are as plain as they are important. When God visits us with the rod of affliction, it is that we may search our hearts, and try our ways, and turn to him."

Meade considered Jefferson and the "dignified and philosophic" French revolutionaries the "most diligent, indefatigable and daring enemies of all religion which the world ever witnessed." He compared them unfavorably to Enlightenment Christians such as Locke, Bacon, and Newton. He linked Jefferson to the French Revolution and its "war against everything holy and venerable." Meade equated Jefferson's deism with atheism because (for natural theologians), God is "at best . . . the soul of the world, not the creator of it." In France "the poison took effect; the contagion spread far and wide and among all classes general infections prevailed." Meade hoped that the University of Virginia could avoid that fate and turn to Christianity, not allowing the "goddess of reason" to "set up in the form of a lewd prostitute in the great hall of atheistic legislation." He later soft-pedaled the message of this eulogy in his memoirs, but Meade's speech had a great effect at the time.[40] Despite protests on the part of both students and faculty to the tenor of the bishop's sermon, his criticisms (along with the fear of more typhoid) hurt recruiting efforts enough to make the board consider hiring a full-time chaplain.

The board decided to rotate a chaplaincy among the four main Protestant denominations: Methodist, Baptist, Episcopalian, and Presbyterian.[41] Methodists and Baptists such as James B. Taylor (who served in 1839) coveted the post, although many evangelicals claimed that the campus was an improper training ground. Beginning in 1835, voluntary contributions from the students and faculty supported chaplains who performed Sunday services, weekly lectures, and a "monthly concert for prayer." That same year a Sunday school and Bible society began. Ministerial candidates won small scholarships beginning in 1837 and ministers could stay on campus. When Presbyterian William Maxwell addressed the university's Bible group in 1836, he said that if the school was going to be the "nursery of republican patriots" that Jefferson and Madison had envisioned, then the Bible should be required, for it is the "best statesmen's manual I know." The Bible would also help prevent the spirits of corruption and abolition from infecting the campus, "and twenty other spirits I will not name—all mingling their drugs together, with infernal incantations, in the caldron of confusion, on purpose to brew up the blackest storm that has ever threatened to destroy the vessel of state in which we are all embarked." The board initially rejected the idea of constructing a chapel because other denominations voiced their intention to bar Unitarians, and that violated their view of Jefferson's legacy and his university's core principle of religious freedom and toleration.[42]

Jefferson's model of a religious liberty survived at least in this compromised form. His successors in effect diluted his purer ecumenicalism down to the statewide model Patrick Henry had proposed (and George Washington supported) in the 1780s: religious worship was voluntary and pluralistic, but only within mainstream Protestantism. The faculty prohibited Sabbath-breaking in 1828 and Protestant theologians played an increasingly big role on campus as the nineteenth century wore on.[43] In addition to Jefferson's original sparse worship room, which was proving too small, one of the gyms under the Rotunda terraces was converted into a nondenominational chapel in 1837. Strict impartiality was observed among the Protestant sects, and many students were enthusiastic about the ministers. One recorded that "Mr. Hammet preached for us yesterday and the Sunday preceding—gives general satisfaction, shown by the overflowing crowds which throng from the Univ.

& country & town to hear him. Our room is far too small to contain them and many are obliged to stand."[44] Chaplain Taylor, in turn, attended free lectures in classics, philosophy, and chemistry. In 1832 he helped to establish the Virginia Baptist Seminary, which became Richmond College and later the University of Richmond.

Dissatisfied even with this qualified ecumenicalism, clergymen kept Jefferson's university in their crosshairs. Some lambasted the decline in religion at the institution after 1835, even though a revival was arguably mounting. Journals criticized the hiring of Catholic and Jewish professors: Hungarian Charles Kraitser in 1840 and Englishman J. J. Sylvester in 1841. Revolutionary France still cast its shadow a half century after the Reign of Terror. North Carolina Episcopalian Francis Lister Hawks, who considered himself a mortal enemy of Jefferson's, viewed the school as an "alliance between the civil authority and infidelity," a subject on which "revolutionary France has once read to the world an impressive lesson." Echoing Bishop Meade, Hawks accused Jefferson of "poisoning the stream at the fountain." In 1837, Professor George Tucker published his own more favorable Jefferson biography to counter Hawks. As editor of the *New York Review and Quarterly Church Journal*, Hawks issued a rebuttal, citing Tucker's failure to depict Jefferson as a hater of Christianity. The students, as a whole, sided with Hawks, refusing to erect a statue of Jefferson at his university for twenty-five years after his death.[45]

The school and its founder remained easy targets, but clergy who actually visited the campus got a different impression. The Reverend Septimus Tuston claimed to experience "nothing but kindness and courtesy" during his stay there.[46] S. H. Tyng (1800–1885), an Episcopal minister and newspaper editor from Philadelphia, confirmed the school's religious enthusiasm in an 1840 account. Tyng was a tough audience: Henry Ward Beecher once characterized him as "the one man I am afraid of," and his hatred for Jefferson prevented him from touring Monticello's interior. In his first letter home from Charlottesville, before he had visited the campus, Tyng wrote:

> I have never heard his name spoken with so little respect, and so much aversion, as in this very neighborhood [Charlottesville] in which he lived and died. I had never conceived his character so bad as I have found it here. His plans are all defeated. The religion of Jesus triumphs over all opposition. The whole spirit of the community has

awakened against the spirit and tendency of Mr. Jefferson's example. All his greatness has perished and is forgotten because he was an infidel.

Tyng changed his mind about the University of Virginia, if not Jefferson, after preaching there. Although he thought the university was set up in "direct and designed hostility to Christianity," he found that most of the faculty and students were practicing Christians, including Jefferson's biographer, Tucker. In the Rotunda Tyng preached to what he called the "most attentive and interested auditory of [his] entire priesthood. Not a single college in New England would've furnished me with such an attentive and respectful audience."[47] Travel writer Harriet Martineau commented on the controversy that the humanist university caused in the North, but pointed out after visiting that the students heard a wider variety of sermons than at denominational schools. Agreeing with one of Jefferson and Madison's longtime contentions about society as a whole, she concurred that the voluntary nature of church services actually increased their attendance.[48]

Countrywide, likewise, the duo's radical commitment to liberty aided rather than curbed religions. While Jefferson's private fusillades against organized faith could be irrational and vindictive, the free religious market that he helped to create thrived over the succeeding two centuries, if not in the forms he imagined (he was mistaken that ending church establishments would usher in a Unitarian age).[49] Then, as now, such libertarian commitments were often confused with crusades against religion itself, conflicting with the wishes of the electorate. Presbyterian John Holt Rice did not want to "cool the zeal of a single individual [Jefferson]," but he reminded newspaper readers in the 1820s that "THE UNIVERSITY OF VIRGINIA BELONGS TO THE PEOPLE OF VIRGINIA. It is their money which has founded, and will endow their institution; it is their children who are to be educated there; it is they and their posterity, who are to partake of the good or suffer the evil, which it will produce." Rice argued that the people who run a public college have no right to make independent hiring and curricular decisions. The university was "the property of the people, and they will see to it that infidelity, whether open or disguised under a Christian name, shall not taint its reputation and poison its influence."[50] Whereas for Jefferson religious freedom was fundamental to civic freedom, Rice's version included the freedom of the Protestant majority to pursue its interests by influencing the democratic system—that was the "free exercise thereof" portion of the First Amendment that Jefferson helped Madison pen. Jefferson's crusade against denominational control brought him into direct conflict, in other words, with his endorsement of participatory democracy.

The multitude of American religions, far more pronounced in our time (Virginia had few Jews and no Muslims or Hindus when its landmark religious statute passed in 1786), make any agreement on religious curriculum in public schools difficult, only underscoring the need to embrace Jefferson's broader vision. His crusade for a religious education that transcended the merely doctrinaire remains a worthy cause with which, according to some polls, a growing number of American theologians and their followers agree.[51]

Notes

1. Jefferson would have been appalled by Creationists' use of Intelligent Design as a cover for infiltrating Christianity into science curriculums—he was, after all, trying to disprove extinction with fossils, not Scripture.

2. Historian Joyce Appleby describes Jefferson well as a "believing freethinker." Appleby, *Thomas Jefferson* (New York, 2003), 88.

3. On the goal and scope of the religious freedom law, see TJ, *Autobiography*, 6 January 1821, *TJW*, 40; TJ to George Wythe, 13 August 1786, L&B, 5:396.

4. TJ, *Notes on the State of Virginia*, ed. William Peden (New York, 1982), 146–47, 159–60; TJ to Anne Cary Bankhead, 24 February 1823, L&B, 18:255.

5. TJ to Joseph Cabell, 28 November 1820, in *Early History of the University of Virginia, as Contained in the Letters of Thomas Jefferson and Joseph C. Cabell*, ed. Nathaniel Francis Cabell (Richmond, Va., 1856), 187; *TJP*, 2:535–42.

6. TJ to Benjamin Waterhouse, 19 July 1822, and 8 January 1825, Ford, 10:220–21, 336.

7. TJ to Ezra Stiles, 25 June 1819, L&B, 15:203.

8. On New Year's Day 1802 President Jefferson received a 1,235-pound "mammoth cheese" (4' x 15") from the Baptist congregation of Cheshire, Massachusetts, led by Elder John Leland.

9. TJ to Peter Carr, 7 September 1814, L&B, 19:211–21; TJ to Cabell, 6 January 1818, Jefferson Papers, Swem Library, College of William and Mary; TJ to Cabell, 24 October 1817, in *Early History of the University of Virginia*, ed. N. F. Cabell, 84; Darren Staloff argues that excluding ministers was Jefferson's primary motive in the state's assuming control over education. Staloff, "The Politics of Pedagogy: Thomas Jefferson and the Education of a Citizen," in *The Cambridge Companion to Thomas Jefferson*, ed. Frank Shuffelton (Cambridge, 2009), 134.

10. The Rockfish Gap Report was known officially as the "Report of the Commissioners Appointed to Fix the Site of the University of Virginia." For the full fifty-one-page report, see the TJ Papers (Series 3, Film 8, #1567), Special Collections, University of Virginia Library, University of Virginia. For a condensed version, see Peterson, ed., *The Portable Thomas Jefferson* (New York, 1975), 332–46.

11. Edward Everett, "University of Virginia," *North American Review* 36 (January 1820): 130.

12. President David Kerr and Professor William R. Davie lost their jobs before Joseph Caldwell assumed the presidency. See J. H. Hobart to Joseph Caldwell, 30 November 1796, University Archives, Wilson Library, University of North Carolina at Chapel Hill; Joseph Caldwell to Thomas Y. Howe, 8 November 1796, ibid.; Joseph Caldwell to Treasurer Haywood, 23 March 1822, ibid.

13. Niels Henry Sonne, *Liberal Kentucky, 1780–1828* (New York, 1939); Thomas Cooper to Dr. F. Ridgley, 12 February 1816, Thomas Cooper Papers, Special Collections, Douglas Gray Jr./Francis Carrick Thomas Library, Transylvania University; *Kentucky Gazette*, 19 January 1816.

14. On the University of Pennsylvania (Jefferson called it the University of Philadelphia), see TJ to Caspar Wistar, 25 August 1814, TJ Papers, Lib. Cong.

15. John Holt Rice, "On the Unitarian Controversy," *Virginia Literary and Evangelical Magazine* 5 (January 1822): 31, 276–77; TJ to William Short, 4 August 1820, TJ Papers, Lib. Cong.

16. TJ to William Short, 4 August 1820, TJ Papers, Lib. Cong.; TJ to William Short, 13 April 1820, TJ Papers, Lib. Cong.

17. For a conversation Jefferson had toward the end of his life with atheist Samuel Whitcomb on the fine line between denouncing Christian revelation while maintaining faith in God, see William Peden, "A Book Peddler Invades Monticello," *WMQ* 3, no. 6 (1949): 633–34; quoted in Kevin Hayes, *Road to Monticello: The Life and Mind of Thomas Jefferson* (Oxford, 2008), 593.

18. Henry F. May, *The Enlightenment in America* (New York, 1976). May referred to *Common Sense* as part of the "moderate Enlightenment."

19. TJ to James Fishback, 27 September 1809, TJ Papers, Lib. Cong.; TJ to Thomas Law, 13 June 1814, L&B, 14:139, 143; TJ to John Adams, 5 May 1817, *AJL*, 512; see TJ, "On the Writings of the Baron d'Holbach on the Morality of Nature and That of the Christian Religion," *Free Enquirer* 2 (1830): 102–3; Hayes, *Road to Monticello*, 582–83.

20. TJ to Peter Carr, 10 August 1787, *TJP*, 12:15–16; TJ to Fishback, 27 September 1809, TJ Papers, Lib. Cong.

21. To Adams he described these as the "deism taught us by Jesus of Nazareth in which all agree constitute a true religion." TJ to Adams, 5 May 1817, *AJL*, 512.

22. Madison cautioned that "with respect to the Virginia document of 1799, there may be more room for hesitation . . . [it] might excite prejudices against the University as under Party Banners, and induce the more bigoted to withhold from it their sons." Madison to TJ, Feb. 8, 1825, in *The Republic of Letters: The Correspondence between Jefferson and Madison, 1776–1826*, 3 vols., ed. James Morton Smith (New York, 1995), 3:1925–26. In the eighteenth century, *seminary* was often used in the educational rather than strictly religious sense of the word. *Vestal* contrasts the purity of republicanism with what he called the "infection" of Federalism or "consolidationism." TJ to Madison, Feb. 17, 1826, ibid., 1965.

23. TJ to William Short, 31 October 1819, L&B, 15:221; TJ to Madison, 8 August 1824, and Madison to TJ, 10 September 1824, in *Republic of Letters*, ed. Smith, 3:1896–901.

24. Madison to Edward Everett, 19 March 1823, in *The Writings of James Madison*, 9 vols., ed. Gaillard Hunt (New York, 1900–1910), 9:124–30.

25. E. Brooks Holifield, *The Gentleman Theologians: American Theology in Southern Culture, 1795–1860* (Durham, N.C., 1978), 58–59; Gilbert Chinard, *Jefferson et les idéologues d'après sa correspondance inédite avec Destutt de Tracy, Cabanis, J.-B. Say, et Auguste Comte* (Baltimore, 1925), 25, 231.

26. TJ to Thomas Cooper, 10 July 1812, TJ Papers, Lib. Cong.

27. TJ to Adams, 15 August 1820, *AJL*, 567–68.

28. Adrienne Koch described Jefferson as fluctuating between materialism and "vitalistic pantheism." Koch, *The Philosophy of Thomas Jefferson* (New York, 1943), 98; Edwin S. Gaustad, *Sworn on the Altar of God: A Religious Biography of Thomas Jefferson* (Grand Rapids, Mich., 1996), 35.

29. TJ to Augustus Woodward, 24 March 1824, in *The Writings of Thomas Jefferson*, 8 vols., ed. H. A. Washington (Washington, D.C., 1854), 7:339–40. At other times, Jefferson combined science and history or law and botany under history. See Daniel P. Jordan, "President's Letter," *Monticello* 11 (Spring 2000): 2.

30. George Tucker, *Memoir of the Life and Character of John P. Emmet, M.D., Professor of Chemistry and Materia Medica in the University of Virginia* (Philadelphia, 1845); Jefferson distrusted physicians generally, but he respected the more empirically minded and, toward the end of his life, grew close to another University of Virginia medical professor, Dr. Robley Dunglison. See Dunglison, *Autobiographical Ana* [manuscript diary], Special Collections, University of Virginia Library.

31. *Jefferson's Other Revolution*, History Channel, 17 June 2006; Goldberger, "Jefferson's Legacy: Dialogues with the Past," *New York Times*, 23 May 1993, 2:33.

32. Mark Wenger, "Thomas Jefferson, the College of William and Mary, and the University of Virginia," *Virginia Magazine of History and Biography* 103 (July 1995): 374; Patricia C. Sherwood and Joseph Michael Lasala, "Education and Architecture: The Evolution of the University of Virginia's Academic Village," in *Thomas Jefferson's Academical Village: The Creation of an Architectural Masterpiece*, ed. Richard Guy Wilson (Charlottesville, Va., 1993), 71.

33. "Report and Documents Respecting the University of Virginia," *Journal of the Virginia House of Delegates, 1822–23*, 3–4; "Jefferson to President and Director of Literary Fund," 7 October 1822, TJ Papers, Special Collections, University of Virginia Library; Minutes of the Board of Visitors for the University of Virginia, 7 October 1822, L&B, 19:414–16; St. George Tucker, "Sketch of a Plan for the Endowment and Establishment of a State-University in Virginia," 4 January 1805, Tucker-Coleman Papers, Swem Library, College of William and Mary.

34. "Report and Documents respecting the University of Virginia," *Norfolk & Portsmouth Herald*, 31 January 1823; TJ to Thomas Cooper, 2 November 1822, L&B, 15:405–6.

35. Cabell to TJ, 3 February 1823, in *Early History of the University of Virginia*, ed. N. F. Cabell, 273.

36. Cary was Jefferson's nephew on the paternal side, the son of Thomas Mann Randolph's sister.

37. On Jefferson's plans for using the professors to help police the students and to host them in small groups in their quarters for dinner, see Jefferson to the Trustees of the Lottery for East Tennessee College, 6 May 1810, *TJP:RS*, 2:365–66; Stephen J. Novack, *The Rights of Youth: American Colleges and Student Revolt, 1798–1815* (Cambridge, Mass., 1977).

38. Dunglison to Madison, 19–25 March 1829, University of Virginia Chronological File, University Archives, Special Collections, University of Virginia Library; Minutes of the University of Virginia Faculty, 22 January, 6 and 25 February 1829, ibid., 418–41.

39. William Meade to John Hartwell Cocke, 29 March 1827, Cocke Family Papers, Special Collections, University of Virginia Library.

40. Meade, *Sermon, Delivered in the Rotunda of the University of Virginia on Sunday May 24, 1829 On the Occasion of the Deaths of Nine Young Men, Who Fell Victims to the Diseases Which Visited That Place During the Summer of 1828, and the Following Winter* (Charlottesville, Va.,

1829), Rare Pamphlets #315, Special Collections, University of Virginia Library; Meade, *Old Churches, Ministers and Families,* 2nd ed. (Philadelphia, 1910), 53–54.

41. "Student Petition" in Proctor's Records, 1830 and Rector and Visitors' Minutes, 17 July 1833, 299, University Archives, Special Collections, University of Virginia Library.

42. Joseph Martin, *A New and Comprehensive Gazetteer of Virginia and the District of Columbia* (Charlottesville, Va., 1836), 123; William Maxwell, *An Address Delivered before the Bible Society of the University of Virginia, May 13th, 1836* (Charlottesville, Va., 1836), 9, 11; John B. Minor, "University of Virginia," Part 3, *The Old Dominion: A Monthly Magazine of Literature, Science and Art* 4–5 (15 May 1870): 260; Meade, *Old Churches, Ministers and Families,* 56; George Tucker to Cabell, 18 March 1835, Cabell Deposit, and William Cabell Rives to John Hartwell Cocke, 2 August 1839, Cocke Family Papers, Special Collections, University of Virginia Library.

43. Minutes of the University of Virginia Faculty, 8 July 1828, 335, University Archives, Special Collections, University of Virginia Library.

44. Gessner Harrison to Dr. Peachy Harrison, 1 April 1833, Tucker-Harrison-Smith Family Papers, Special Collections, University of Virginia Library.

45. Francis Lister Hawks, ed., *A Narrative of Events Connected with the Rise and Progress of the Protestant Episcopal Church in Virginia* (New York, 1836), 179; Hawks, "The Character of Jefferson," *New York Review and Quarterly Church Journal* 1 (March 1837): 5, 7, 14–15; some students disagreed with Hawks, arguing in the student newspaper that a statue should be built. *The Chameleon* 1 (9 and 16 May 1831), n.p.; Peterson, *The Jefferson Image in the American Mind* (New York, 1962), 127–28.

46. Septimus Tuston, "University of Virginia," *New York Observer,* [1837?], University of Virginia Chronological File, University Archives, Special Collections, University of Virginia Library.

47. Tyng was influential in the Sunday school movement, and St. Paul's Church in Philadelphia was known as "Tyng's Theater" from 1829 to 1834; S. H. Tyng, "Correspondence from Charlottesville," *Episcopal Recorder* (Philadelphia), 27 May 1840, 46, Archives of the Episcopal Church, Austin, Texas; Tyng, "For the Episcopal Recorder," *Episcopal Recorder* (Philadelphia), 20 June 1840, 50, ibid.

48. Harriet Martineau, *Retrospect of Western Travel,* 2 vols. (New York, 1838), 203–7.

49. TJ to Benjamin Waterhouse, 26 June 1822, *TJW,* 1459; Johann Neem, "Beyond the Wall: Jefferson's Danbury Address," *JER* 17 (2007): 139–54; Richard A. Samuelson, "What Adams Saw Over Jefferson's Wall," *Commentary* 104, no. 2 (August 1997): 52–54.

50. Rice, "Literature and Science," *Virginia Evangelical and Literary Magazine* 2 (January 1819): 46–47.

51. See Part II of the Pew Forum's 2008 American Religious Landscape Study at http:// pewforum.org/.

West from West Point

Thomas Jefferson's Military Academy
and the "Empire of Liberty"

CHRISTINE COALWELL McDONALD AND ROBERT M. S. McDONALD

T HOMAS JEFFERSON SELECTED MERIWETHER LEWIS TO LEAD THE CORPS of Discovery because he was the least unqualified person for the job. In January 1803, when Jefferson asked Congress to fund an expedition up the Missouri to the Pacific, the army captain was twenty-eight. In his brief military career he had served west of the Appalachians, where he had gained some familiarity with Native American cultures. Then, for nearly two years, he had worked as Jefferson's secretary, demonstrating diligence, fidelity, and raw intelligence. Other than Lewis "no man within the range of my acquaintance," Jefferson remembered decades later, "united so many of the qualifications necessary" for the expedition's "successful direction." Yet no man—not even Lewis—knew all that would be needed to undertake successfully an enterprise so fraught with danger. Jefferson, however, thought that Lewis could learn.[1]

From April through June, Lewis visited Pennsylvania to purchase supplies for the expedition and seek the tutelage of some of the new nation's leading "natural philosophers"—men whose broad engagement with the cutting edge of science had earned them prominence as members of the American Philosophical Society, over which Jefferson had presided since 1797. From Andrew Ellicott, he learned astronomy, mathematics, and surveying. From Charles Willson Peale, he learned natural history. Under the watchful eye of Robert Patterson, he continued his development as a mathematician and surveyor. He also studied under Benjamin Rush, the noted medical doctor and anthropologist of Indians. Then he visited Benjamin Smith Barton, the University of Pennsylvania's resident botanist and taxidermist.[2] After little more than a month Lewis had completed his makeshift education as an explorer; then, on his way back to Washington, he invited William Clark to join the enterprise as co-commander. By August he was on his way to St. Louis, where he and Clark would prepare to ascend the Missouri and venture into the unknown.

Twenty-seven years later, Captain Benjamin Bonneville also ventured west. Like Lewis, he was a young army officer. His mission, also, was to explore the country to the "Rocky Mountains and beyond." Yet he needed to undertake no pilgrimage to Philadelphia in search of some special and supplementary education to prepare him for his task since, unlike Lewis, he was a graduate of the United States Military Academy at West Point, founded by Jefferson in 1802. Ellicott, whom Lewis had sought out in 1803, had served as mathematics professor there from 1813 until his death in 1820. Bonneville, who had studied under Ellicott, also completed course work at the academy in astronomy and natural philosophy with Jared Mansfield, Jefferson's friend and correspondent. Alden Partridge, West Point's superintendent, schooled Bonneville in the principles of engineering. Much that Lewis had made such an extraordinary effort to learn Bonneville had mastered as a result of his education as a cadet. Bonneville was, to be certain, a new breed of army officer, one better prepared than Lewis to chart and conquer what Jefferson described as America's "Empire of liberty."[3]

It was probably no coincidence. Jefferson, who wrote in 1821 that he had always considered his military academy "of major importance to our country," never explained why.[4] For nearly two centuries, neither did historians. Only in recent years have two theories emerged. The first is that Jefferson founded West Point to Republicanize the Federalist-leaning Army; the second is that he established West Point in order to advance the cause of education.[5] Here, we offer a third interpretation, one that views republicanism and education as complementary in Jefferson's mind—as the end and the means of Jefferson's ambitions for the West. Certainly Jefferson's efforts in behalf of West Point—his selection of the faculty who then shaped the curriculum and involved him in the promotion of a scientific group called the U.S. Military Philosophical Society—suggests his support for an academy that would advance his efforts to expand, explore, secure, and develop the frontier for liberty-loving Americans. If so, then West Point did not let him down. Under his patronage and through the leadership of the men he placed in charge, the academy developed and disseminated knowledge that equipped army officers to consolidate and extend the successes of Lewis and Clark. Its graduates occupied positions of national prominence in diverse fields such as road surveying, railroad engineering, exploration, prospecting, and harbor improvement. Over 85 percent of the United States Army's Corps of Topographical Engineers received their education at Jefferson's school on the Hudson River. Taken together, the alumni did more than any other single group to chart the trans-Mississippi West and open up the American frontier.[6]

Prior to his presidency, Jefferson weighed several different proposals for a national military academy, none of which the government implemented. One appears to have sparked his imagination while another provoked his resistance and a third his scorn. Overlooking his reaction to the first of these proposals and misreading his opposition to the others, a long line of historians have mischaracterized Jefferson as a longstanding opponent of a school for future army officers. Even the most recent and most careful of these scholars describes it as "ironic, to say the least, that President Jefferson drafted and signed the legislation" that established West Point.[7] The irony disappears, however, in the face of Jefferson's consistent desire that any national academy embrace a curriculum designed to advance very particular ambitions for America's future.

Maybe the real irony is that one of the earliest proposals for a military academy, authored by General Frederick William von Steuben and considered by Congress in the spring of 1783, seems to have fascinated Jefferson but was scuttled by a committee chaired by Alexander Hamilton, the Continental Army veteran and future treasury secretary often characterized as the military academy's greatest champion. Steuben's proposal—the most ambitious of several suggested—provided for an academy of 120 cadets, two-thirds of whom would see service as infantry officers while the remaining portion would be divided in equal numbers between cavalrymen and artillerists or engineers. Their instruction would come from professors of mathematics, history and geography, law, science, and "eloquence and *belles lettres,*" as well as teachers of architecture, horsemanship, drawing, dancing, music, fencing, and French.[8] Broad and classical in its nature, the plan failed to win favor with Hamilton's committee, which included James Madison, Samuel Holten,

James Wilson, and Oliver Ellsworth.[9] "The benefits of such institutions rarely compensate for the expense," the committee determined, since "military knowledge is best acquired in service" and only "those branches of service which are of a more scientific nature, the professors proposed to be attached to the Corps of Engineers, will produce substantially all the utility to be expected from academies." Thanks to Hamilton's committee, the movement for a national military academy stagnated.[10]

Jefferson, meanwhile, appears to have taken an interest in Steuben's plan. When he was elected as a delegate to Congress shortly after the report of Hamilton's committee, Steuben's idea for an academy caught his attention. Somehow, perhaps through Madison, he obtained the particulars of Steuben's proposal.[11] In his notes Jefferson detailed the proposed academic organization for the academy, listing the faculty positions projected by Steuben— and even the salaries that Steuben had recommended. While his notes focus primarily on Steuben's ideas, at a few junctures Jefferson jotted down his own thoughts. Considering the efficacy of adding military instruction to civilian institutions, he asked, "will it not be better to improve colleges into them?" In his notes he provided no answer. He did, however, record his response to "whether the Confed[e]r[ation] gives powers from military peace establ[ish]m[en]t." Here he referenced approvingly the fifth clause of Article Nine, which makes clear that "Congress may agree on the numbers of land forces &c." This document, misdated by the keepers of his papers in the Library of Congress and ignored by historians, does not reveal Jefferson's opinion of Steuben's plan. It does, however, suggest that Jefferson, even at this early date, was open to and interested in the establishment of a military academy.[12]

If in 1783 Jefferson stood more ready than Hamilton to embrace a proposal to establish an academy, then ten years later their roles reversed. The reason might well be that, in 1793, the proposal was backed by Hamilton, whom Jefferson had come to regard as the leader of a pro-British, counter-revolutionary movement that threatened to sabotage the nation's republican experiment. "The ensuing year will be the longest of my life," Jefferson predicted in 1792.[13] Already he had expressed to President George Washington his desire to step down as secretary of state, but later he decided to stay "in order to keep things in their proper channel and prevent them from going too far." Soon perpetually opposed to Hamilton and his Federalist allies, Jefferson would assume the role that Washington had requested: he stood as a "check" against Hamilton, who, as he told Washington, was a closet monarchist and considered the Constitution "a shilly shally thing of mere milk and water, which could not last, and was only good as a step to something better." As Jefferson observed, "Hamilton & myself were daily pitted in the cabinet like two cocks" readying themselves for battle.[14]

In this hostile atmosphere, calls on the national level for a school for future officers resurfaced. In November 1793, at a cabinet meeting convened to consider the contents of Washington's fifth annual message, Jefferson recorded that "it was proposed to recommend the establishment of a military academy. I objected that none of the specified powers given by the const[itutio]n to Congress would authorize this."[15] As a result, when Edmund Randolph prepared a draft of Washington's speech that included the clause recommending a military academy, the president, as Jefferson observed, "said he would not chuse to recommend any thing against the constitution, but if it was *doubtful,* he was so impressed with the necessity of this measure, that he would refer it to Congress, and let them decide whether the const[itutio]n authorized it or not."[16]

How serious were Jefferson's objections to a military academy? According to the most thorough scholar of his constitutionalism, his opposition had less to do with the Constitution than Jefferson's "instinctive, but not well-considered, knee-jerk reaction" against what he considered to be yet another proposal by Federalists to stamp their imprint on the new nation's government. Jefferson tended to interpret narrowly the portions of the Constitution granting powers to the federal government. Meanwhile, he viewed broadly the Constitution's clauses guaranteeing rights and limiting federal action. Yet Jefferson generally had no problem entrusting the national government to exercise sweeping powers in areas, such as international trade and national defense, over which it held exclusive authority. It was both "necessary and proper" for Congress to establish a military academy to exercise its power "to raise and support armies." He opposed at the time the founding of one because it seemed to possess too much potential to be entrusted to Hamilton.[17]

Jefferson's hostility to a Hamiltonian academy made good sense in the context of the 1790s. It was Hamilton, after all, who urged Washington to dispatch 15,000 troops—a force larger than the one that defeated the British at Yorktown—into western Pennsylvania to quell the Whiskey Rebellion. Hamilton, too, would during the Adams administration take charge of the "New Army," fill its ranks with Federalists, and in 1799 threaten to march it south to "put Virginia to the test." Like other American revolutionaries, Jefferson viewed the military not only as a defender of liberty but also as one of its greatest potential threats. The less influence Hamilton had on it, the better.

While Hamilton looked east toward England for a model for America, Jefferson saw America's future in the West. Hamilton envisioned a European-style empire that featured a powerful and centralized government, bustling cities, large-scale manufacturing, a robust navy backing oceanic commerce, and a standing army always ready to combat foes on far-flung battlefields. Jefferson, on the other hand, cared less about overpowering other nations and more about securing America's character. He dreamed of small-town "ward republics" where men governed themselves, small-scale "manufactories" where free laborers enjoyed viable options for alternative employment, and independent farmers whose harvests so much filled the mouths of Europeans that they would never be able to choke out words hostile to the United States. His aim was liberty, and he never relinquished the belief that, the more power government possessed, the less there remained for individuals to exercise over their own decisions. As if Hamilton's ambitions for an Old World future were not obvious enough, he once let slip his eastward orientation when, in a memorandum to Washington, positioned the United States with Canada on "our left" and Latin America on "our right." Jefferson, meanwhile, believed that the differences between American and European political forms constituted "a comparison of heaven and hell," with that of England somewhere in the middle. He looked not across the Atlantic but beyond the Mississippi for "important aids to our treasury, an ample provision for our posterity, and a wide-spread field for the blessings of freedom and equal laws."[18]

Different visions of America's future prompted competing notions of how best to educate America's future officers. Consider Jefferson's hostility to Secretary of War James McHenry's January 5, 1800, report on "certain measures and arrangements . . . indispensable to the improvement of our military system." These included a plan for a military academy authored by the former treasury secretary two months earlier. The establishment of a military academy, Hamilton believed, was "of prime importance." Recognizing "the near approach of a Session of Congress," Hamilton had sent to McHenry a draft of his proposal in order to acquire his support in obtaining the "legislative Sanction" necessary for its implementation.[19]

Hamilton initially proposed an academy consisting of five components: a "Fundamental School," a "School of Engineers & Artillerists," a "School of Cavalry," a "School of Infantry," and a "School of Navy." When the scheme reached the House of Representatives, however, it was reduced to four by combining the schools of cavalry and infantry. The military academy was intended for "Cadets of the Army, and young persons who are destined for military and Naval service." Each cadet would attend the Fundamental School for a period of two years where he would be taught, as Hamilton envisioned, elements of arithmetic, algebra, geometry, the laws of motion, mechanics, geography, topography, surveying, the design of structures and earthworks, and tactics.[20] McHenry reported to Congress that "the Fundamental School is designed to form Engineers, including Geographical Engineers, Miners, and officers for the Artillery, Cavalry, Infantry, and Navy; consequently, in this school is to be taught all the sciences necessary to a perfect knowledge of the different branches of the military art." Graduates of the Fundamental School would then advance to study at the "School of Engineering and Artillerists," "School of Infantry and Cavalry," or the "School of the Navy." The scheme, as McHenry noted, had been based "upon those of institutions of a similar nature, from which the nations who have founded them derive the most decided advantages." Its inspiration, in other words, was European.[21]

Jefferson, whose academy at West Point would comprehend the subjects embraced by Hamilton's Fundamental School as well as the engineering program, nevertheless rejected the Old World elements of the institution proposed by McHenry on January 5. Jefferson had no patience for the "branches of science, formerly esteemed" and still "valued in Europe, but useless to us for ages to come." These, he told Joseph Priestley, "may be now omitted." That meant scuttling "almost the whole of the institution proposed to Congress by the Secretary of war's report of the 5th." What America needed, he thought, was a "University on a plan so broad & liberal & *modern,* as to be worth patronising [*sic*] with the public support." For such an institution, the "first step" would be "to obtain a good plan." There must be "a judicious selection of the sciences, & a practicable grouping of some of them together, & ramifying of others, so as to adopt the professorships to our uses, & our means." The school he imagined, to be located in the "upper & healthier country" near Monticello, two decades later would take shape as the University of Virginia. Two years later, however, these principles would guide the organization of the United States Military Academy at West Point.[22]

At nearly the same time that Meriwether Lewis studied under some of the most knowledgeable members of the American Philosophical Society, Jefferson called on Jonathan Williams, with whom he had served as an officer of the same society, to take command as the first superintendent of West Point.[23] It was in Paris that Jefferson had first met Williams, a grandnephew of Benjamin Franklin, and Jefferson noted that he "resembled his relative Dr. Franklin in many points of Character and Mind." Despite Williams's moderate Federalist leanings, his reputation as a man of science now made him a natural choice for Jefferson, who assured Williams after receiving his *Treatise of Artillery*, that he was "very happy to see the corps . . . profit by his example and pursue the line of information he has so well pointed out."[24]

Other faculty members were chosen within months. The group included, most notably, Jared Mansfield to teach mathematics.[25] For the infant academy's educational success, only the appointment of Williams as superintendent eclipsed the importance of the recruitment of Mansfield, who had been educated at Yale and had recently authored *Essays Mathematical and Physical*. The work covered subjects West Point cadets would need to master, including algebra, geometry, calculus, and nautical astronomy, all of which facilitated the determination of time, longitude, and latitude.[26]

As the commencement of classes approached, preparations continued to be made at West Point and in Washington. After consulting with Jefferson, Secretary of War Henry Dearborn sent to Williams a list of books for the institution's library. Williams acknowledged his receipt of Dearborn's list, which contained "the President[']s remarks in the Margin," and went to work procuring the titles for the library. In time, he predicted, West Point would possess "every Book of merit that is extant" on the subjects its curriculum embraced.[27]

In August of 1802 Williams sent Decius Wadsworth, a major appointed to the academy, on a trip from West Point to Washington, instructing him to impress upon Dearborn the "absolute necessity of a drawing master" and to drop "a hint or two about a French teacher."[28] Within months Jefferson would approve authorization "to appoint one teacher of the French Language and one teacher of Drawing to be attached to the Corps of Engineers."[29] That Jefferson signed off on an instructor of drawing to be attached to the academy was no accident. As one scholar notes, during the nineteenth century "military officers were expected to sketch battlefields and design fortifications. Officers of the Army's Corps of Topographical Engineers, which organized exploring expeditions, were expected to return with the information needed to map the expanding American West." For these reasons, "the

Military Academy at West Point incorporated art into its curriculum within a year after its creation." Jefferson had favored the idea at least as early as 1783, when his "Memo on Military Academies" included an instructor of drawing among the proposed faculty. His support twenty years later for the addition of art to the academy's curriculum proved particularly valuable. Although the Corps of Discovery did not count among its members any formally trained artists, future military expeditions west would make a point of including them. And in 1832 William Clark would make a point of assisting artist George Catlin, a West Point graduate, in his efforts to document the "looks and modes" of the American Indian and—in an attempt to paint subjects described in the journals of the Lewis and Clark expedition—retrace parts of their route.[30]

Instruction in French also prepared cadets for missions in the West, for it provided a means not only to understand advanced studies of engineering, many of which were published in France, but also to communicate with the francophone inhabitants of the Louisiana Territory. In the first years at the academy, the first consideration carried less weight than the second. Neither Mansfield nor George Barron, the early mathematics instructors, spoke French; their primary textbooks, moreover, were printed in English. Other texts, some of which had been published originally in French, were later assigned; nearly all, however, were available to cadets in translation. Why, then, was the language considered necessary at West Point, especially at a time when prejudices aroused by the French Revolution had caused instruction in French at other U.S. colleges to wither? While it is true that knowledge of French benefited professional engineers who wished to consult their field's leading works, the acquisition of Louisiana and its sizeable French-speaking population provided another motivation. The journals of Lewis and Clark testify to the value of French in the western territories. In September of 1805, for example, when they assembled a group of chiefs and warriors from the Salish tribe, they noted that "what we Said had to pass through Several languages before it got in to theirs." Their English was translated into French, then to Hadatsa, then to Shoshone, and finally to Salish. When the Salish responded, the chain of communication reversed. This group of Indians had never met a white man, but their neighbors' neighbors knew well the French fur traders long established in the vicinity of the Mississippi.[31]

Not all such encounters yielded peaceable outcomes, a fact that could not have surprised Jefferson. He supplied Lewis and Clark with nearly 100 "peace medals" that featured his profile on one side and, on the other, hands shaking between the words "peace" and "friendship." Lewis and Clark distributed these medals to tribal leaders who seemed to acknowledge American sovereignty and Jefferson's status as their new "great father." On one occasion, however, after a group of Piegan Blackfeet warriors attempted to steal American horses and fired upon the Americans, Lewis left a peace medal on the chest of a slain Piegan so that whoever recovered his body "might be informed who we are." Americans would secure their new empire by persuasion if possible but through force if necessary. Jefferson sent to the West soldiers commanded by officers with language skills, but not legions of unarmed linguists.[32]

He also sent a relatively large number of young men from the farthest reaches of American settlement. The students of the early academy had a western character. By April of 1805, as Lewis and Clark prepared to enter the Rocky Mountains, the school's ranks had been augmented by only twelve new cadets, and fully half of them hailed from the Louisiana Territory. Lewis had recommended all six. Auguste Pierre Chouteau, Charles Gratiot, Pascal Vincent Bouis, Louis Loramier, Augustus Loramier, and Louis Vallé—all sons of prominent St. Louis families—had met the explorer during the winter of 1803–4.[33] Theodore Crackel maintains that Lewis recommended these men in order to "bind these families to the new nation—and to the administration." This may have been the case, but Lewis and Amos Stoddard, the commandant of Upper Louisiana, could not have failed also to recognize that these men, like their fathers before them, could play an active role in opening up the western territory of North America. What better young men could be chosen to secure the republic's claim on the West than individuals from the edge of the frontier?[34]

The academy was to be prominent in the North as well as the South, in the East as well as the West. "Our guiding star," Superintendent Williams explained, "is not a little mathematical School, but a great national establishment. . . . We must always have it in view that our Officers are to be men of Science, and as such will by their acquirements be entitled to the notice of learned societies." As a result, in November 1802 he convened the faculty and cadets "for the purpose of considering the propriety of forming a Society for promoting Military Science," which soon became known as the U.S. Military Philosophical Society. At the Society's next meeting, on July 4, 1803, Jefferson and Dearborn were elected as members.[35]

Williams formalized the Society's mission and bolstered its membership. It aimed, he wrote, "to collect and preserve the Military science" deduced by veterans as well as citizens "who may have gathered scientific fruits in the course of their travels." It existed "under the auspices of the President of the United States" for the purpose "of establishing and perpetuating a repository so evidently beneficial to our country." Within a short period of time senators and congressmen joined the rolls; judges, men of science, and officers of all the military branches were represented. Members soon included John Adams, DeWitt Clinton, James Madison, Henry Dearborn, Gouverneur Morris, Albert Gallatin, John Jay, James Monroe, Eli Whitney, Robert Fulton, and Joel Barlow.[36] William Clark, who had returned from his journey to the Pacific, acknowledged his acceptance of membership in 1807. So did General Caleb Swan, with whom Clark had spent time in Ohio while preparing for the expedition. He wrote that he felt "flattered with a belief, that I may possibly make some communication . . . that may be beneficial to our Country, and aid future military commanders." Swan, the author of *Some Accounts of the Northwest Lakes of America,* then offered a gift. He said he would soon send to the Society a description of his activities during the past eight years, including his adventures with Major General Anthony Wayne, with whom he had "lately explored the Country of the Native Savages to the Pacific Ocean." Captain Zebulon Pike, who had heard about the Society from Jefferson, sent to Williams artifacts that he had collected on his last expedition to the Red River. This was only the first of gifts to the group from Pike. He dedicated his 1810 book, *An Account of Expeditions to the Sources of the Mississippi and through the Western Parts of Louisiana,* to the president and members of the U.S. Military Philosophical Society.

Williams was ardently committed to the proposition that he and his faculty were educating men to render great services to the nation. "The Science of an Engineer," he told a cadet, "is applicable to almost every profession in Life." The study of engineering prepared a man to work as "a draughtsman, a Surveyor, a Navigator, an Architect, and a Calculator on any subject." Cadets who succeeded in the rigorous coursework enjoyed the prospect of a valuable position in the corps of artillerists or engineers, but they also faced examinations.

The "Internal Regulations for the Military Academy," written by Williams in 1810, set the examination requirements for such a commission. Fifteen points covered all aspects of cadet life, from acceptable uniform to rules of parade, terms of disobedience, and, most important, academic standards. The scholarly requirements included mastery of "Arithmetic, Logarithms, the Elements of Algebra, Geometry, Trigonometry, Mensuration of heights and distances, Planometry, Stereometry, Surveying, Artificer's work, and Conic Sections." Academy graduates needed to know French in order "to pronounce the language tolerably, and to translate from English to French, and French into English, with accuracy." They had to be able to handle a musket, correctly aim artillery, and comport themselves on a battlefield.

The War of 1812 brought the end of Williams's career as superintendent. Like many others, he left the academy to battle the British. West Point, however, had a bright future. Due to the adoption of the "Act Making Further Provision for the Corps of Engineers," signed by James Madison on April 29, 1812, it grew in strength and importance. The cadets of the military academy would be appointed directly to the Corps of Engineers. The authorized number of students increased to 250; the faculty roster surged as well. Three new professors were added who, if not engineering officers, could be retained from other branches of service. They included a professor of natural and experimental philosophy, a professor of mathematics, and a professor of engineering.[37]

Especially important was the professor of natural and experimental philosophy. Williams had proposed the establishment of such a position as early as 1805. He asked again in 1808, when Jefferson communicated the request to Congress. Although legislators would drag their heels until 1812, both the academy's founder and its first superintendent recognized the crucial nature of this post, for it related particularly to the field of western exploration. Referring to the ongoing expeditions of Lewis and Clark, William Dunbar, and Zebulon Pike, Jefferson described their leaders as "persons qualified expressly to give us the geography of the rivers with perfect accuracy, and of good common kno[w]le[d]ge and observation in the animal, vegetable & mineral departments." These attributes, he thought, were essential in an explorer. As James Ronda writes, "Jefferson never claimed that Lewis belonged to the fraternity of 'Scientific men.'" He did, however, think that "the young army officer was a keen naturalist. And natural history, with its techniques of observation, collection, description, and classification, was what

Jefferson had in mind. Natural history emphasized useful knowledge, the sort of learning that could be applied to the benefit of human kind." The addition of a faculty member in this field meant that such a "keen naturalist" would be found at West Point. In 1812 Mansfield, who had been serving as general surveyor of Ohio and the Northwest Territory, accepted the position and returned to the academy. With Ellicott, the former mentor of Lewis who had been appointed professor of mathematics, Mansfield commenced, as John C. Greene writes, "the process of giving the West Point cadets the kind of scientific training that would enable them to carry on the tradition of scientific exploration inaugurated by Lewis and Clark."[38]

There is abundant evidence of the important role played by the Corps of Engineers in extending into the western territories Jefferson's "empire of liberty." The achievements of West Point graduates in exploration, mapping, and the building of canals, bridges, roads, and railways had no parallel. Francis Wayland, president of Brown University, noted in 1850 that "although there are more than 120 colleges in the United States, the West Point Academy has done more to build up the system of internal improvements in the United States than all the [other] colleges combined." George Ticknor, a reform-minded Harvard professor, in the 1820s recognized Jefferson's school on the Hudson as America's premier center for engineering—an institution with standards high enough to "cast a reproach on any of the colleges in the country."[39]

The testimonials of Wayland and Ticknor suggest much about the vision of a long line of men—including Hamilton, Washington, Du Pont, Williams, and Jefferson most of all—who recognized the important contributions engineers could make to the nation. They understood, as Mansfield observed, that "the Engineer Corps will not, as they ought not, suppose that they are unqualified for any *scientific task*" for "an Engineer should be qualified for any work of art." He maintained that a proficient engineer—with a sound education—should consider himself nothing less than "Omni-Accomplished."[40] Former President John Adams agreed. In 1821, he congratulated the Corps of Cadets "on the great Advantages you possess for attaining eminence in Letters and Science as well as Arms" for, as he said, "the habits you have acquired well qualify you for any course of Life you may choose to pursue."[41]

Adams's prediction proved correct; the early graduates of Jefferson's military academy distinguished themselves in numerous fields. Yet it was in the West that their educations prepared them to contribute most to the new nation's development. In 1830 the United States Military Academy Board of Visitors declared that West Point's purpose was to supply not only "efficient officers" but also to furnish "a corps of engineers capable of giving wholesome direction to the spirit of enterprise which pervades our country. It ought to furnish science for exploring the hidden treasures of our mountains, and ameliorating the agriculture of our valley." These were, as Forman writes, the "basic goals of the Military Academy."[42]

A year later Benjamin Bonneville, Class of 1815, decided to explore the new Northwest. The War Department supported his decision, gave him two years' leave, and Major General Alexander Macomb, a former instructor at the academy, sent detailed instructions about how best to get "every information which you may conceive would be useful to the Government." In 1835 Bonneville returned and submitted his report. Oregon's Willamette Valley he described as "one of the most beautiful, fertile and extensive vallies in the world." It was ideal "wheat corn and tobacco country," he thought. "If our Government ever intends taking possession" of this Eden, "the sooner it shall be done the better." Bonneville's report was among the best the government had ever received on the region. It enchanted its readers and eventually helped to entice thousands of settlers across the continent.[43]

James Duncan Graham, Class of 1817, served as first assistant to Major Stephen Long on his 1818 expedition to the Rockies aboard the *Western Engineer*, the steamboat on which their scientific corps embarked on the expedition. Graham, a topographical engineer, in 1839 surveyed and explored the boundary between the U.S. and Texas. He charted the British western provinces soon thereafter and in 1850–51 made a second mapping trip to the Mexican border.[44]

Other West Pointers would follow in the Northwest, including Hartman Bache, '18; Washington Hood, '27; Henry Wallen, '40; Joseph Dixon, '58; and John Parke, '49. Gouverneur Warren, Class of 1850, explored the Upper Missouri, Dakotas, Nebraska, and eventually created the first comprehensive map of the West.[45] In California, William Warner, '36; George Horatio Derby, '46; Robert Williamson, '48; and J. L. Kerby Smith, '57, participated in scientific expeditions. James Simpson, '32, covered more of the West than any other West Pointer. His track over California would produce the present-day route of California's State Highway 50. In the Southwest, the Class of 1831's William H. Emory created a map so accurate that it stands as "one of the landmarks in western American cartography," according to one scholar.[46]

Infantryman-explorer Randolph Marcy, Class of 1832, in 1852 discovered the source of the Red River.[47] William Franklin, Class of 1843, enlarged John Frémont's landmark map by adding the territory between the Platte and Arkansas Rivers.[48] Soldier and explorer Joseph Ives, Class of 1852, led an 1857 expedition up the Colorado River that resulted in valuable contributions to scientific understanding of the region.[49] Joseph Johnston, '28; John Macomb, '32; William Smith, '45; and Nathaniel Michler, '48, also explored the Southwest. On the Mississippi, Henry L. Abbot, Class of 1852, with A. A. Humphreys, Class of 1831, made a lasting contribution through their 1861 "Report upon the Physics and Hydraulics of the Mississippi," which investigated flood protection.[50] These men were only a few of many military academy graduates who opened up the West by following in the footsteps of Meriwether Lewis and William Clark.

The West Point graduates whose scientific educations enabled them to explore, map, and secure Jefferson's empire helped to establish what would be only an elusive republic. If, as Drew McCoy has written, for Jeffersonians the point of territorial expansion was for America to halt the familiar pattern of historical progression, to acquire arable land in order to forestall the corpulent vice of unbridled commerce and prolong the nation's moment as a sturdy and independent yeoman's paradise—"to expand across space rather than develop through time"—then the officers produced by Jefferson's military academy achieved only short-term success.[51] Obedient to their orders, they performed as instructed. Yet their fidelity, proficiency, and bravery on America's advancing frontier did not, in the end, match their skill as inventors, engineers, and entrepreneurs.

Although many helped to open the West to farmers, many others back east laid the groundwork for revolutions in transportation and manufacturing that transformed the nation from an agrarian republic to a commercial empire. In other words, they accelerated the new nation's progression from a land-based society of sturdy, middling yeomen to a capital-intensive, mechanized nation of millionaires and wage laborers. Stability, tradition, and deference to the well-born gave way in an increasingly dynamic and democratic environment. While some men continued to build fortunes through the acquisition of land, a growing number enriched either themselves or their nation—or both—through the more fluid transfer of cash and goods and produce as well as ideas and innovations.[52]

Among this new breed, West Point alumni occupied important positions.

Richard Delafield, Class of 1818, a member of the Army Corps of Engineers, helped to mastermind the completion of the National Road, which connected the bustling docks of Baltimore with the proliferating farms of Ohio. Numerous graduates of the academy contributed to the design and construction of the C. & O. and Erie canals. William Gibbs McNeill, Class of 1817, was a topographical engineer who, like George Washington Whistler, Class of 1819, laid the groundwork for the system of railroads to which many other West Pointers during the nineteenth century would lend their expertise, nearly 60 as chief engineers and at least 22 as railroad company presidents. Less remembered are the successful efforts of a member of the Class of 1829 to help devise a plan to abate silt buildup at the crucial Mississippi River port of St. Louis. His name was Robert E. Lee.[53]

While some West Point graduates maintained commercial waterways, others mapped them. Alexander Dallas Bache, Class of 1825, became an expert on America's bustling Atlantic ports. A grandson of Franklin and a relative of Williams, this chief of the Coast and Geodetic Survey, originally devised by Jefferson, took over from Ferdinand R. Hassler, a former West Point mathematics instructor. Bache also established standardized U.S. weights and measures, presided over the American Philosophical Society, and helped to establish the Smithsonian Institution. Then there were the several alumni of Jefferson's school who distinguished themselves as inventors, such as Andrew Talcott, an 1818 graduate who devised the zenith telescope, and Ormsby McKnight Mitchel, an 1829 graduate who helped to pioneer the development of refracting telescopes. Their scientific achievements, while facilitated by the same sort of astronomical training that Lewis had received from Ellicott, had less to do with exploring the far West than with charting the far reaches of the heavens.[54]

Yet the accomplishments of another West Point alumnus connected more closely with the vision of the institution's founder. This 1830 graduate of Jefferson's academy spent much of his early army career stationed at Missouri's Jefferson Barracks. As a lieutenant he fought Indians in the Black Hawk War until, after resigning his commission, he worked as an architect and civil engineer in St. Louis, part of which he represented in the Missouri House of Representatives. During the Mexican War he answered his country's call, returned to military service, and fought as far west as Sacramento. He made his way back to Missouri, where he had been born, and worked as the national government's chief surveyor. In the Civil War he cast his loyalties with the South and, in many respects, maintained his fidelity to Jefferson's vision of a decentralized and enlightened republic. Afterwards, he served as commandant and professor of mathematics at the Kentucky Military Institute. Thus this individual, who devoted his life to the maintenance, mapping, and expansion of the West—and who applied himself to the study of the scientific principles crucial in all these tasks—helped to establish America's dominion over the far reaches of its continental empire. The first-born son of one famous explorer, his father had christened him in honor of another. His name was Meriwether Lewis Clark.[55]

Notes

1. TJ to ——, 29 November 1821, *The Writings of Thomas Jefferson,* ed. H. A. Washington, 9 vols. (New York, 1854), 7:224.

2. Paul Russell Cutright, "Meriwether Lewis Prepares for a Trip West," *Bulletin of the Missouri Historical Society* 23 (1966): 3–20. Maj. Gen. Alexander Macomb to Capt. B. L. E. Bonneville, 29 July 1831, Bonneville File R.G. 46, National Archives, as quoted in William H. Goetzmann, *Exploration and Empire: The Explorer and the Scientist in the Winning of the American West* (New York, 1966), 149.

3. TJ to George Rogers Clark, 25 December 1780, *TJP,* 4:237–38. For the War Department instructions to Benjamin Louis Eulalie Bonneville, see Goetzmann, *Exploration and Empire,* 149. See also George W. Cullum, *Biographical Register of the Officers and Graduates of the U.S. Military Academy at West Point, N.Y.* (New York, 1891–), 1:144–50. For a list of instructors at the United States Military Academy at West Point during the period of Bonneville's training, see Sidney Forman, *West Point: A History of the United States Military Academy* (New York, 1950), 36–37. See also Peter Michael Molloy, "Technical Education and the Young Republic: West Point as America's École Polytechnique, 1802–1833," (Ph.D. diss., Brown University, 1975), 350.

4. TJ to Jared Mansfield, 13 February 1821, TJ Papers, Lib. Cong.

5. See Theodore J. Crackel, "The Founding of West Point: Jefferson and the Politics of Security," *Armed Forces and Society* 7 (Summer 1981): 529–43, and Jennings L. Wagoner Jr. and Christine Coalwell McDonald, "Mr. Jefferson's Academy: An Educational Interpretation," in *Thomas Jefferson's Military Academy: Founding West Point,* ed. Robert M. S. McDonald (Charlottesville, Va., 2004), 118–53. For earlier treatments, see Stephen E. Ambrose, *Duty, Honor, Country: A History of West Point* (Baltimore, 1966), 18; Thomas J. Fleming, *West Point: The Men and Times of the United States Military Academy* (New York, 1969), 16; Dumas Malone, *Jefferson and His Time,* 6 vols. (Boston, 1948–81), 5:510–11.

6. Forman, *West Point,* 81; William H. Goetzmann, *Army Exploration in the American West, 1803–1863* (Austin, Tex., 1991), 13. Goetzmann's excellent study focuses on the role of the Topographical Engineers, not the contributions of the United States Military Academy. For the declared mission of the United States Military Academy for "exploring the hidden treasures of our mountains," see *American State Papers, Military Affairs,* 4:603, as quoted in Forman, *West Point,* 81.

7. Matthew Moten, *The Delafield Commission and the American Military Profession* (College Station, Tex., 2000), 26.

8. Friedrich Kapp, *The Life of Frederick William von Steuben: Major General in the Revolutionary Army* (New York, 1859), 515–19.

9. Alexander Hamilton to George Washington, 9 April 1783, *AHP*, 3:322–23. Hamilton informed Washington that the committee was to be composed of "Messrs. [James] Maddison, [Samuel] Osgood, [James] Wilson, [Oliver] Elseworth and myself" (ibid., 322, n. 1). It is uncertain that Osgood served his entire term on the committee; see 23 October 1783, *Journals of the Continental Congress, 1774–1789*, ed. Worthington C. Ford et al., 39 vols. (Washington, D.C., 1904–37), 25:722.

10. *Journals of the Continental Congress*, April 1786, 30:215. On 27 April 1786, Col. Christian Senf delivered to Congress a letter from Adrian De Nys of Utrecht, which "offer[ed] the raising of a regiment of regular troops in Europe for the service of the United States," which Senf's letter explains are to be used in "establishing a military academy in the United States." Jefferson was in contact with Senf. Senf delivered to Secretary of the Congress Charles Thomson "a care box" from Jefferson; see TJ to André Limozin, 8 October 1785, and TJ to Charles Thomson, 8 October 1785, *TJP*, 8:598–99. There is no evidence to suggest that the letter from Adrian De Nys of Utrecht was among the items Jefferson directed Senf to deliver to Thomson or Congress.

11. Lincoln to Steuben, 27 April 1783, in John McAuley Palmer, *Washington, Lincoln, Wilson: Three War Statesmen* (Garden City, N.Y., 1930), 67. Lincoln informs Steuben that "the Committee have under consideration your observations."

12. TJ, Memorandum on Military Academies, 1783 [misdated 23 November 1793], TJ Papers, Lib. Cong. Jefferson in this document reflects on Steuben's entire plan for Military Academies and Manufacturers. When he references "5th Art. of Confedn. 'Congress may agree on numbers of land forces &c.,'" Jefferson cites article nine, section five of the Articles of Confederation, which maintains that "the united states in congress assembled shall never . . . agree upon the number of vessels of war, to be built or purchased, or the number of land or sea forces to be raised, nor appoint a commander in chief of the army or navy, unless nine states assent to the same."

13. TJ to Martha Jefferson Randolph, 22 March 1792, *TJP*, 23:326.

14. TJ, "Notes of a Conversation with George Washington," 1 October 1792, ibid., 24:433–36; TJ to Walter Jones, 5 March 1810, *TJP:RS*, 2:272.

15. TJ, "Notes of Cabinet Meeting on the President's Address to Congress," 23 November 1793, *TJP*, 27:428. See also "Materials for the President's Address to Congress," [ca. 22 November 1793], ibid., 421–24.

16. TJ, "Notes of Cabinet Meeting on the President's Address and Messages to Congress," 28 November 1793, ibid., 27:453–55.

17. David N. Mayer, "'Necessary and Proper': West Point and Jefferson's Constitutionalism," in *Thomas Jefferson's Military Academy*, ed. McDonald, 54–76.

18. Hamilton to George Washington, 15 September 1790 (enclosure), *AHP*, 7:52–53; TJ to Joseph Jones, 14 August 1787, *TJP*, 12:34; TJ, "Third Annual Message," 17 October 1803, *TJW*, 512. See also Gerald Stourzh, *Alexander Hamilton and the Idea of Republican Government* (Stanford, Calif., 1970), 191–201; Joyce Appleby, "Thomas Jefferson and the Psychology of Democracy," in *The Revolution of 1800: Democracy, Race, and the New Republic*, ed. James Horn, Jan Ellen Lewis, and Peter S. Onuf (Charlottesville, Va., 2002), 160.

19. Hamilton to James McHenry, 23 November 1799, *AHP*, 24:69–75; *U.S. House Journal,* 14 January 1800, Appendix, 1397–404.

20. Hamilton to McHenry, 23 November 1799, *AHP*, 24:69–75.

21. *U.S. House Journal,* 14 January 1800, Appendix, 1397–404. Jefferson, given his swift implementation of the Military Peace Establishment Act of 1802 (as we shall see), appears to have recognized the importance of the Fundamental School and the School of Engineering and Artillerists.

22. TJ to Joseph Priestley, 18 January 1800, *TJP*, 31:319–23.

23. TJ to Benjamin Smith Barton, 27 February 1803, ibid., 16–17; TJ to Caspar Wistar, 28 February 1803, ibid., 17–18; TJ to Benjamin Rush, 28 February 1803, ibid., 18–19; TJ to Robert Patterson, 2 March 1803, ibid., 21. See also Andrew Ellicott to TJ, 6 March 1803, ibid., 23–25. For an examination of Lewis's education before the expedition, see Cutright, "Meriwether Lewis Prepares for a Trip West," 3–20.

24. TJ to Jonathan Williams, 14 March 1801, USMA Archives.

25. See Henry Dearborn to Jared Mansfield, 7 June 1802, "War Department Letters Relating to the U.S. Military Academy 1801–1838"; Dearborn to Williams, 11 June 1802, ibid.; Dearborn to Williams, 8 July 1802, ibid.; Dearborn to Joseph B. Varnum, 8 July 1802, ibid.; Dearborn to Williams, 28 July 1802, ibid.

26. See John C. Greene, *American Science in the Age of Jefferson* (Ames, Iowa, 1984), 143; *Dictionary of American Biography Base Set* (American Council of Learned Societies, 1928–1936), Jared Mansfield entry; *Catalogue of the Library of Thomas Jefferson,* comp. E. Millicent Sowerby, 5 vols. (Washington, D.C., 1955), 4:33–34.

27. Williams to Dearborn, 9 August 1802, Papers of Jonathan Williams, Lilly Library, Indiana University (microfilm available at the U.S. Military Academy Library, West Point, N.Y.); Williams to Decius Wadsworth, 13 May 1802, ibid.

28. Williams to Wadsworth, 13 May 1802, ibid.

29. See *Statutes at Large,* 2:206–7, quoted in Edgar Denton III, "The Formative Years of the United States Military Academy, 1775–1833" (Ph.D. diss., Syracuse University, 1964), 35.

30. Joan Carpenter Troccoli, ed., *West Point Points West* (Denver, 2002), i; Troccoli, "West Point and the Early Art of the American West," in *West Point Points West,* ed. Troccoli, 19, 20, 23. See also TJ, "Memo on Military Academies," 23 November 17[8]3 (misdated 1793), TJ Papers, Lib. Cong.

31. For information regarding the various texts used at the United States Military Academy, see Molloy, "Technical Education and the Young Republic," 256–57. See also Forman, *West Point,* 21–22, 52, 138. The exchange with the Salish is described in *The Lewis and Clark Journals: An American Epic of Discovery,* ed. Gary E. Moulton (Lincoln, Neb., 2003), 202, 202, n. 28; see also Duncan and Burns, *Lewis and Clark,* 137.

32. [Meriwether Lewis,] Journal entry for 27 July 1806, *The Journals of the Lewis and Clark Expedition,* ed. Gary E. Moulton, 13 vols. (Lincoln, Neb., 1983–2001), 8:135. For a narrative of the encounter with the Piegan Blackfeet, see James P. Ronda, *Lewis and Clark among the Indians* (Lincoln, Neb., 1984), 238–43.

33. Williams to Dearborn, 19 April 1805, as quoted in Cullum, "Early History of the United States Military Academy," in Cullum, *Biographical Register of the Officers and Graduates of the U.S. Military Academy,* 3:504. For the state of the academy upon Williams's return in April 1805, see ibid., 504–5. Information regarding the appointments of Auguste Pierre Chouteau, Charles Gratiot, Pascal Vincent Bouis, Louis Loramier, Augustus Loramier, and Louis Vallé may be found in Donald Chaput, "The Early Missouri Graduates of West Point: Officers or Merchants?"

Missouri Historical Review 72 (1978): 262–70, and George T. Ness Jr., "Missouri at West Point: Her Graduates through the Civil War Years," *Missouri Historical Review* 38 (1944): 163–69.

34. Crackel's examination of the appointments may be found in *Mr. Jefferson's Army*, 109–10. For information regarding records of Lewis's recommendations, see *Letters of the Lewis and Clark Expedition*, 170–71n. What did the St. Louis cadets accomplish? Young Auguste Pierre Chouteau after graduation in June of 1806 served in the southwest frontier as the aide-de-camp to Brigadier General Wilkinson and then accompanied an expedition to Fort Mandan; he returned to St. Louis in 1807, after which he left the Army to pursue a career as an Indian trader. Charles Gratiot left St. Louis with the Osage delegation to visit President Jefferson in May of 1804, after which he attended West Point and graduated in 1806. Gratiot, of all the St. Louis appointees, enjoyed the most distinguished career. After receiving his appointment as a second lieutenant, he served as assistant engineer in the construction of the defenses of Charleston Harbor before returning to West Point where, in 1810, he became the acting superintendent of the academy during Williams's absence. Gratiot would eventually reach the rank of colonel and chief engineer of the U.S. Army. In honor of his contributions, Ft. Gratiot on the St. Clair River and Gratiot County in Michigan were among other places named for him. Pascal Vincent Bouis graduated in 1806, and although Bouis would have a short career in the military, his reputation at West Point was one of scientific honor. In 1805 he translated the mathematician Pothenot's trigonometric theorem, adding some additional information for surveyors; in 1806 this work was enthusiastically received by the Military Philosophical Society. The Loramier brothers, sons of the commandant of the district of Cape Girardeau, never made any notable military achievements, and Augustus did not even graduate from the Academy. It is, however, interesting to note that Louis Loramier Jr. was the first Native American to graduate from West Point. Stoddard apparently objected to the appointment, noting that young Loramier "exhibited too much of the Indian in his color"; nevertheless, Loramier—whose father was French and mother was Shawnee—graduated in 1806. Loramier would return to Cape Girardeau after serving three years as a second lieutenant on the western frontier. The last cadet appointed during this period from St. Louis was Louis Vallé, who entered West Point in 1805 and graduated in 1808. Vallé declined his commission upon graduation to, as Chaput writes, "join the more lucrative, powerful frontier forces controlled by his family." See William Clark to Henry Dearborn, 18 May 1807, *Letters of the Lewis and Clark Expedition*, 411. Clark notes that Chouteau was of "late an Officer" in his letter to Dearborn, 1 June 1807, ibid., 414. For information regarding Charles Gratiot's accompanying the Osage delegation to Washington, see Charles Gratiot to William Morrison, 12 May 1804, ibid., 189n. For information regarding Gratiot's army career, see Cullum, *Biographical Register of the Officers and Graduates of the U.S. Military Academy*, 1:70–71. See also Chaput, "The Early Missouri Graduates of West Point," 264. For information regarding Cadet Bouis's scientific contributions, see Molloy, "Technical Education in the Young Republic," 295. Information regarding Louis Loramier and his brother Augustus may be found in Chaput's "The Early Missouri Graduates of West Point," 265, 270. For information regarding Stoddard's prejudice against the young cadet, see Crackel, *Mr. Jefferson's Army*, 110. For additional information on these cadets, see Cullum, *Biographical Register of the Officers and Graduates of the U.S. Military Academy*, #13, Pascal Vincent Bouis, p. 69; #14, Auguste Chouteau, p. 69; #16, Charles Gratiot, p. 70–71; #25, Louis Loramier, p. 76; and #35, Louis Vallé, p. 87.

35. Papers of the United States Military Philosophical Society, New-York Historical Society.

36. "Letter of information to candidates for admission into the society," 31 May 1805, Minutes of the U.S. Military Philosophical Society, New-York Historical Society. George Izard accepted his membership and showed his respect for the society by writing that "The Men of

distinguished Science who are already in the Bosom of the Society insure success to its labors and consequent advantage to our country"; see the correspondence section, 17 January 1806, ibid. Jefferson accepted his role as "perpetual patron" in his letter to Williams, 25 December 1802, ibid. For the invitation, see Williams to TJ, 12 December 1802, ibid. For a register of members, also see ibid., collection at the New-York Historical Society.

37. Denton, "The Formative Years of the United States Military Academy," 79–80; Emory Upton, *The Military Policy of the United States* (2nd impr.; Washington, D.C., 1907), 94, as quoted in ibid., 79. See also Forman, *West Point,* 36–37.

38. Williams to Albert Gallatin, 19 September 1805, Papers of Jonathan Williams; TJ to C. F. de Volney, 11 February 1806, *TJW,* 1159–60; James P. Ronda, *Jefferson's West: A Journey with Lewis and Clark* ([Charlottesville, Va.,] 2000), 37–38; Greene, *American Science in the Age of Jefferson,* 143–44.

39. Goetzmann, *Army Exploration in the American West;* Francis Wayland, as quoted by R. Ernest Dupuy, *Sylvanus Thayer: Father of Technology in the United States* (West Point, N.Y., 1958), 14; George Ticknor, as quoted in ibid., 15. Wayland's "Report to the Corporation of Brown University" can be found in *American Higher Education: A Documentary History,* ed. Richard Hofstadter and Wilson Smith (Chicago, 1961).

40. Mansfield to Williams, 22 August 1805, Papers of Jonathan Williams.

41. John Adams, Address to the Cadets of the USMA & Citizens of Boston, August 1821, Special Collections, USMA Library.

42. *American State Papers, Military Affairs,* 4:737, as quoted in Forman, *West Point,* 81.

43. Maj. Gen. Alexander Macomb to Capt. B. L. E. Bonneville, 29 July 1831. Bonneville File R.G. 46, National Archives, as quoted in William H. Goetzmann, *Exploration and Empire,* 149. Bonneville's report as contained in File R.G. 46, as quoted from ibid.

44. "James Duncan Graham," *Dictionary of American Biography Base Set* (American Council of Learned Societies, 1928–1936). For more information about the Long Expedition of 1819, see Goetzmann, *Exploration and Empire,* 58–64.

45. Goetzmann, *Army Exploration in the American West,* 59.

46. Ibid., 142.

47. Ibid., 377.

48. Ibid., 115.

49. "Joseph Christmas Ives," *Dictionary of American Biography Base Set.*

50. "Henry Larcom Abbot," *Dictionary of American Biography Base Set.* Maj. Gen. W. M. Black, "The Problem of the Mississippi", *North American Review* (December 1927), as quoted in *Dictionary of American Biography.*

51. Drew R. McCoy, *The Elusive Republic: Political Economy in Jeffersonian America* (Chapel Hill, N.C., 1980), 62.

52. TJ to Francis Adrian Van De Kamp, 11 January 1825, *The Works of Thomas Jefferson,* ed. Paul Leicester Ford, 12 vols. (New York, 1904–5), 10:337. For suggestive accounts of the Market Revolution's democratic consequences, see Gordon S. Wood, *The Radicalism of the American Revolution* (New York, 1992), 229–369, and Joyce Appleby, *Inheriting the Revolution: The First Generation of Americans* (Cambridge, Mass., 2001).

53. R. Ernest Dupuy, *Men of West Point: The First 150 Years of the United States Military Academy* (New York, 1951), 32–38.

54. Ibid., 44–47.

55. Cullum, *Biographical Register of the Officers and Graduates of the U.S. Military Academy,* 1:459.

Thomas Jefferson, Colporteur
of the Enlightenment

FRANK SHUFFELTON

W HEN THOMAS JEFFERSON'S BOYHOOD HOME, SHADWELL, BURNED on February 1, 1770, he most mourned the loss of his library. In a letter to his college friend, John Page, he calculated "the cost of the books burned to have been £200. sterling. Would to god it had been the money; then had it never cost me a sigh!"[1] There were books that he had inherited from his father, classical literature that he had first read during his school days, law books and notebooks that he had collected to support his legal practice, and works from writers like Lord Bolingbroke and Lord Kames that permanently shaped his sense of himself and his place in the world. Losing the law books was a setback to his legal career, but to lose the larger library was in a very real sense to lose a piece of himself. He wasted no time in beginning to rebuild his library, sending off two orders for books to Fearon Benson and Thomas Waller of London later in the spring. He appealed to "them most earnestly to lose not a day in sending them."[2]

When he took a census of his collection on August 4, 1773, he counted 1,256 volumes located in the northwest and northeast corners of the library room of Monticello, including 18 "lying about" and another 42 "lent out."[3] All his life Jefferson literally surrounded himself with books. His slave Isaac remembered that "Old Master had abundance of books; sometimes would have twenty of 'em down on the floor at once—read fust one, then tother. Isaac has often wondered how Old Master came to have such a mighty head;

read so many of them books; and when they go to ax him anything, he go right straight to the book and tell you all about it."[4] When he sold his library to the nation in 1815 to become the basis of the Library of Congress, he had acquired an additional 5,500 volumes.

As the presence in the 1773 census of 42 volumes "lent out" suggests, Jefferson's books did not constitute a solitary retreat. On the contrary, books became a medium through which Jefferson communicated with an extended body of friends and associates in the transatlantic world. He loaned books to others, invited them to use his library, bought books for them, recommended lists of books that they might read for various purposes, and encouraged the creation of libraries that would make books available to larger publics. It was in this sense that Jefferson stood out as a "colporteur," a term that needs some special interpretation to apply to his activities. Colporteurs were traveling booksellers in the years from the seventeenth to the nineteenth century who sold at public fairs and markets a wide range of popular materials: Bibles, chapbooks, cookbooks, medical books, primers, almanacs, manuals, romances, fairy tales, and tales of adventure. Colporteurs were on the bottom rung of the business of book distribution, and the materials they carried were often of a dubious character, yet they spoke to the imaginative desires and needs of ordinary people. In a revolutionary age, however, these desires often underwrote or prophesied enormous political and social change.[5] Jefferson was not usually dealing in popular or trashy materials when he provided books or reading lists to others, but he was responding to the imaginative and intellectual needs of people who desired to change themselves and the world they lived in. Jefferson was a colporteur of the Enlightenment itself, of that central movement of the eighteenth century that sought, in the words of Immanuel Kant, "man's release from his self-incurred tutelage. . . . *Sapere aude!* 'Have courage to use your own reason!' " said Kant, "That is the motto of enlightenment."[6] For Jefferson, the practice of freedom and his faith in the progress of the human mind—the ultimate fruits of reason according to Enlightenment belief—was grounded in his wide reading and in the books he wanted to make available to others.

Jefferson early on acquired a reputation as a bibliographic authority. Edmund Randolph, his contemporary, noted that "it constituted a part of Mr. Jefferson's pride to run before the times in which he lived. . . . He had been ambitious to collect a library, not merely amassing a number of books, but distinguishing them in subordination to every art and science." Even more impressive, Randolph maintained, was the fact that "this library was at this time more happily calculated, than any other private one, to direct to objects of utility and taste, to present to genius the scaffolding, upon which its future eminence might be built, and to approve the restless appetite which is too apt to seize the mere gatherer of books." Jefferson's success as a lawyer was based on his extensive reading in the law, whereas his colleague and sometime rival Patrick Henry relied on his natural powers of oratory. As Randolph observed, "Mr. Jefferson drew copiously from the depths of the law, Mr. Henry from the recesses of the human heart."[7] Aspiring lawyers frequently called on Jefferson for advice; he responded with recommendations for a heavy course of reading and study.[8] One of the earliest and most interesting recognitions of Jefferson's knowledge of books, however, came in a request from Robert Skipwith, the brother-in-law of his future wife. Skipwith asked Jefferson to recommend volumes for a gentleman's library "suited to the capacity of a common reader who understands but little of the classicks and who has not leisure for any intricate or tedious study."[9] Jefferson replied with a list of books that would have cost eight times as much as Skipwith intended but which, he pointed out, could be acquired over a period of several years.

Given Skipwith's admission of little knowledge of the classics, Jefferson only recommended English language texts, either by origin or in translation. He was himself a devoted reader of the classics in the original languages. In 1800 he wrote to Joseph Priestley that "to read the Latin & Greek authors in their original is a sublime luxury; and I deem luxury in science to be at least as justifiable as in architecture, painting, gardening or the other arts. I enjoy Homer in his own language infinitely beyond Pope's translation of him. . . . I thank on my knees him who directed my early education for having put into my possession this rich source of delight."[10] After he sold his library to the nation in 1815, he immediately began assembling a new library in which the classics played a major part. Many of his recommendations, however, followed Skipwith's preferences for lighter reading; he included more contemporary fiction than he ever recommended to anyone else. Yet he also included a selection of more serious titles that would challenge many readers and that could prove useful in the years ahead, books that Skipwith "might in time find convenient to procure."[11] Jefferson himself was not a great reader of fiction, but he justified Skipwith's taste while elevating it at the same time by offering a defense of the utility of fiction "to fix . . . the principles and

practices of virtue." "When any original act of charity or gratitude, for instance, is presented either to our sight or imagination," wrote Jefferson, "we
are deeply impressed with it's beauty and feel a strong desire in ourselves of
doing charitable and grateful acts also. On the contrary when we see or read
of any atrocious deed, we are disgusted with it's deformity, and conceive an
abhorrence of vice. Now every emotion of this kind is an exercise of our
virtuous dispositions, and dispositions of the mind, like limbs of the body
acquire strength by exercise."[12] This letter lays out two of Jefferson's primary
criteria for a library, its potential usefulness and its ability to support the
growth of the human mind, reflected by his comment that the library could
be acquired over a period of years during which Skipwith might add responsibilities and areas of interest. At the same time it implicitly agrees with
him on a third criterion, its inherent pleasurableness. If the recommendations for him reflected Jefferson's pleasures to some degree, they ultimately
accommodated Skipwith's, but libraries for Jefferson were always associated
with pleasure.

Utility was always an essential measure for Jefferson's recommendations
for his friends' reading, but he did not overlook the importance of enjoyment, of the power of books to engage the better feelings of readers. He could
prescribe a rigorous course of reading for a young student of the law that
began with recommendations to familiarize himself with the natural sciences, ethics, and religion early in the morning, move on to four hours of
reading in the law, and to follow with an hour of reading politics and the rest
of the afternoon reading history. Presumably there would be a break for
dinner and exercise, but "from Dark to Bed-time" the student was advised
to read "belles lettres, criticism, Rhetoric, Oratory," especially Shakespeare,
"who must be singled out by one who wishes to learn the full powers of the
English language."[13] This recommendation, originally drafted when Jefferson
was only recently released from his own studies of the law, undoubtedly
reflected his own strenuous reading habits. For a different sort of recipient, a
later letter about a course of reading for a young woman is equally revealing,
both for its seriousness and its accommodation of the role of pleasure and
feeling in reading appropriate for a woman. Responding in 1818 to a request from Nathaniel Burwell about "a plan for female education," Jefferson
warned against the "inordinate passion prevalent for novels" in which "reason and fact, plain and unadorned, are rejected." Nevertheless, he admitted
that some novels are "interesting and useful vehicles of sound morality." He

recommended *Don Quixote, Gil Blas,* Marmontel's *Contes Moreaux,* and novels by Anna Laetitia Barbauld, Maria Edgeworth ("they are all good," he noted), Madame de Genlis, and William Godwin's *Caleb Williams.* The reading list begins with a number of works in classical and modern history, with the classical titles recommended in translation. It also included several works in French, such as the sermons of Massillon and Bourdaloue, Fénelon's *Télémaque,* and the plays of Molière, Racine, and Corneille. Shakespeare, Dryden's tragedies, Milton's *Paradise Lost,* Pope's works, and James Thomson's *The Seasons* also enter the list. Except perhaps for the fiction recommendations, this selection is hardly au courant in 1818—he included neither Wordsworth nor Coleridge nor any other contemporary poets—but it does provide a plan of reading that suits what a well-educated woman would find morally instructive and imaginatively engaging. Utility and pleasure remained the criteria, but here accommodated to a woman's taste and background, with a special emphasis on the cultivation of sentiment.[14]

Jefferson divided his recommendations for Skipwith into nine categories. "Fine Arts" amounted to the largest; when combined, the categories of ancient and modern history ranked second. Among the fine arts selections, he recommended the novels of Smollett, Fielding, Richardson, and Sterne—his own favorite novelist—as well as *Don Quixote,* Rousseau's *La nouvelle Héloise,* and *Emile* in translation, together with a number of other popular contemporary works of fiction. He included an extensive list of dramatists—he may well have frequently encountered Skipwith at the playhouse that he attended when in Williamsburg while the court and the legislature were in session. Pope, Milton, Chaucer, Spenser, and Dryden joined a crowd of eighteenth-century poets, and the category of fine arts also found room for books on gardening and painting. The categories of "Politicks" and "Law" together included only eleven titles, but they provided a foundational course of citizenship for a progressive Virginia gentleman in 1771. Montesquieu's *Spirit of the Laws* accompanied his treatise on the rise and fall of Roman government. They joined with Locke and the writings of Algernon Sidney to ground readers in thinking about republican forms of government. Lord Kames's *Principles of Equity* and William Blackstone's *Commentaries on the Laws of England* would have been useful for the inevitable encounters a Virginia planter would have with the law, whether as jurist, juryman, or as a citizen before the court.

The list also reflects Jefferson's own reading at the time. His legal commonplace book suggests that he had been reading Montesquieu not long before, and his recommendations under the category of "Religion" speak to his own tendency toward skepticism at this time. The Bible was included under the category of "Antient History," while the religious recommendations included Epictetus, Cicero's *Tusculan Disputations*, Hume's *Essays*, Lord Bolingbroke's philosophical works, and Kames on natural religion, none of which would have supported traditional notions of piety or religion. Two volumes by William Sherlock represent the sole appearance of orthodox Christian writing, unless you count Laurence Sterne's seven volumes of sermons (and the author of *Tristram Shandy* was hardly a traditional Christian).[15] Jefferson's advice for Skipwith paralleled recommendations that he later made for his nephew Peter Carr. "Fix reason firmly in her seat," he wrote, "and call to her tribunal every fact, every opinion. Question with boldness even the existence of a god; because, if there be one, he must more approve the homage of reason, than that of blindfolded fear. . . . Read the bible then, as you would read Livy or Tacitus."[16] A library not only reflected the mind of its makers, it also had the power to shape the minds of its users. Yet Jefferson did not intend it to be a means of propagandizing for his own views in any blatant manner. The books that he recommended to Skipwith on religion could not simply be reduced to the level of tracts urging disbelief; they would make a reader think and reexamine his or her own principles. The Skipwith library was a collection to grow on, "an exercise of our virtuous dispositions" that went well beyond responding to moral fictions.

With its larger network of book dealers, Jefferson continued to purchase books even more enthusiastically when he arrived in Philadelphia in 1775. Douglas L. Wilson has noted that he recorded in 1776 more purchases in his Memorandum Book than he had in any previous year.[17] By 1783 the library contained 2,640 volumes, nearly double the size it had been a decade earlier. He acquired books from the estates of Virginians such as Peyton Randolph, Richard Bland, and William Byrd, who had accumulated important libraries of their own. He purchased books from friends such as John Randolph, who left the country at the outbreak of the Revolution, or even from enemies such as Governor Dunmore. His library became in effect an archive of the history of book collecting in Virginia. It connected him to its past even as he was working to create a different future. In the years following the Revolution, however, Jefferson arrived at a clearer sense of how the exercise of reason in pursuit of knowledge could be an instrument of social formation, and in the same period he discovered how a library could reflect the human mind and become an instrument of progress.

He had always been interested in enlarging the bounds of sociability by inviting correspondents from Skipwith to Joseph Priestley to Maria Cosway, the English artist he met in Paris, to take up residence in the neighborhood of Monticello, but it was through the medium of epistolary exchanges that he developed a network of intellectually inclined friends who became, in effect, citizens of that great Enlightenment institution, the republic of letters. In the early 1780s he received a questionnaire from the secretary of the French legation in Philadelphia asking for information on Virginia, and he began compiling information for his book *Notes on the State of Virginia* by gathering information from various correspondents. His book project established transatlantic relationships with readers in France, where it was first published, and it enhanced intellectual and imaginative bonds among the American correspondents who contributed to his knowledge. A crucial problem for the American nation in its first years was to establish feelings of shared citizenship across disparate spaces among the thirteen states and even within the territory of a large state like Virginia. Trade had long assisted this development, and the Revolutionary war effort provided a shared sense of trial and achievement among its veterans, but Jefferson, who was neither a merchant nor a military man, worked to create national bonds within a network of information and learning. A further problem for the new nation was to create a respectable position for itself in the world, and Jefferson's network of intellectual exchange formed transatlantic connections as well.

In the early 1780s Jefferson gained access to the most remarkable literary accomplishment of the Enlightenment, the French *Encyclopédie, ou Dictionnaire raisonné des sciences, des arts et des métiers,* edited by Denis Diderot and Jean Lerond D'Alembert. In gathering material for *Notes* he hoped to obtain a copy of the *Encyclopédie* but was at first deterred by the wartime difficulties involved in Atlantic shipping. In December 1780, however, he learned that merchants in Alexandria had a 28-volume set for sale for the sum of fifteen hogsheads of tobacco or £90,000 in inflated American currency. He jumped at this opportunity, and he hoped to make these books available for public use rather than merely for a part of his own collection.[18] The *Encyclopédie,* which had a considerable impact on his thinking, was prefaced with a "Preliminary Discourse" by D'Alembert, who sought to explain the organization of the contents as part of a "tree of knowledge" that would reveal the connections between the various sciences, arts, and trades. The "Preliminary Discourse" began with an account of how the human mind over time acquired knowledge about itself in a series of steps and categories, the terms of which D'Alembert drew from the writings of Sir Francis Bacon. Since "memory, reason (strictly speaking), and imagination are the three different manners in which our soul operates on the objects of its thoughts," the *Encyclopédie* would accordingly be organized with three simultaneously operating systems of reference. The articles would be listed alphabetically according to the name of the science to which the article belongs, but they would also be referenced to their position among the branches of the "tree of knowledge," which was represented by an accompanying chart expanding the categories of memory, reason, and imagination. Meanwhile, a system of cross-references, *les renvois,* would connect them to other articles discussing related bodies of knowledge.[19] With its numerous links and references, the *Encyclopédie* aspired to become the information highway of the eighteenth century, but it was structured according to a model of the human mind itself.

Jefferson began to organize his own library by subject according to the *Encyclopédie*'s categories of memory, reason, and imagination. His 1783 catalogue applied these categories respectively to books on history, philosophy, and the fine arts, ultimately divided into forty-six specific subcategories.[20] He later claimed that he "took the basis of its distribution from Lord Bacon's table of science," but he seems in fact to have followed the model of the *Encyclopédie.* D'Alembert had made a point of differing from Bacon by placing reason before imagination in the list of faculties of the human mind, just as Jefferson later did. Because Jefferson's library, like the *Encyclopédie,* was shaped to a model of the mind, it would be open to whatever the mind might later conceive. When he explained his system of classification to George Watterston, the librarian of Congress, he emphasized its relative ease of use but also its adaptability to further expansion. As he noted, his catalogue reflected his own reading habits: "Thus the law having been my profession, and politics the occupation to which the circumstances of the times in which I have lived called my particular attention, my provision of books in these lines, and in those most nearly connected with them was more copious, and required in particular instances subdivisions into sections and paragraphs, while other subjects of which general views only were contemplated are thrown into masses. A physician or theologist would have modified differently."[21] Future acquisitions could be added to the library simply by refining and expanding the subdivisions.

If the library was a record of the progress of the human mind, for Jefferson it was a machine oriented toward the future, the world that progress might bring to us, much as the *Encyclopédie* was for D'Alembert. For the latter the tree of knowledge was also a map of the world but a map with many gaps. "The universe is but a vast ocean," D'Alembert wrote, "on the surface of which we perceive a few islands of various sizes, whose connection with the continent is hidden from us." The human problem was to make the connections that would produce the kind of future knowledge that Bacon thought "should contribute to making us happier or better."[22] Jefferson thought one of the advantages of his classification system was that "when we wish to consider a particular [subject], of seeing at a glance the books which have been written on it, and selecting those from which we effect most readily the information we seek."[23] Just as he might have hoped that Robert Skipwith would connect the dots when he read the recommended books on religion, so Jefferson recognized the library as a means of connecting disparate bits of knowledge that could make people happier or better.

Making connections, so important in the *Encyclopédie*, became a major theme in Jefferson's library and in his life. His correspondence networks gave him pleasure and enlarged his vision of the world, and this correspondence frequently involved books. Before he left for France in 1784 to serve as an envoy with John Adams and Benjamin Franklin, he supplied books to James Madison and James Monroe. Madison, obviously thinking about American constitutional problems, had expressed particular interest in "whatever may throw light on the general Constitution and droit public of the several confederacies which have existed."[24] Monroe purchased a small but wide-ranging collection that included volumes, mostly in French, which Jefferson had previously lent to various members of Congress. Among them were works of the Swiss physician Samuel Tissot, the Marquis de Chastellux's treatise on public happiness, a book on chess, Emeric Vattel's *Questions de Droit Naturel*, the works of the abbé Mably, and Pieter van Muschenbroek's *Cours de Physique Experimentale et Mathematique*.[25] Jefferson must have been confident that when he arrived in Paris he would readily be able to replace these volumes, and indeed he immediately began acquiring books. Among the entries in his Memorandum Book for July 31, 1784, the day he landed in Le

Havre, is an expenditure of four francs ten sous for books, and one of his first purchases in Paris a week later was fifty-eight francs worth of books from Jean Claude Molini, who dealt mainly in Italian books.[26]

In the last months before he left America, Jefferson acquired books and information to take with him across the Atlantic. In Philadelphia he thanked his friend Charles Thomson for helping him acquire several volumes of the journals of Congress and mentioned that if he had *Notes on the State of Virginia* printed in Paris, he would both send Thomson a copy and "take the liberty of adding some of your notes."[27] A Dutch visitor, Gijsbert Karel van Hogendorp, talked with him in New York and gave him a list of questions concerning American commerce that Jefferson adapted and used to query informants in the New England states. Since his mission in Europe was to negotiate treaties of amity and commerce, this would be useful to him and the replies would assist him in answering van Hogendorp's questions. In New Haven he called on Reverend Ezra Stiles, the president of Yale, for a discussion of fossils and of the bones of the mammoth, and he also received from the author John Trumbull a copy of his satiric poem *McFingal*. Trumbull wished "for the honour of being approved by a Gentleman, who joins to his public virtues, so great a share of literary merit," but, he owned, "I depend more on the partiality of patriotism to the productions of our native country."[28] For Jefferson, Enlightenment colportage—the exchange of information and ideas—was ultimately an act of patriotism that would be no simple matter of one-way traffic across the Atlantic, flowing from east to west, but a mutually enriching process that furthered the enlightenment of both Europeans and Americans. If Jefferson was interested in importing the latest European thinking to America, he was equally interested in exporting American knowledge to Europe.

Paris, however, provided a book market unlike any Jefferson had encountered in provincial America. The variety of offerings was enormous, and the entries in his memorandum books suggest that he bought books more frequently here than at any other time or place in his life. Jean Claude Molini's Italian bookshop, a valuable stop for an apprentice diplomat who was brushing up on his languages, was only his first visit to a Paris book-dealer. In the subsequent months and years he spent many hours haunting bookshops and the barrows of dealers along the Seine and identifying favorites such as Jacques-François Froullé. When he wrote to Samuel Harrison Smith in 1814, proposing to sell his library to Congress as replacement for the one the

British had burned earlier in the year, he described those days of book hunting. "While residing in Paris," he recounted, "I devoted every afternoon I was disengaged for a summer or two, in examining all the principal bookstores, turning over every book with my own hand, and putting by everything which related to America, and indeed whatever was rare and valuable in every science." In addition, he noted, "I had standing orders during the whole time I was in Europe, on its principal book-marts, particularly Amsterdam, Frankfurt, Madrid and London, for such works relating to America as could not be found in Paris."[29] One result of these book-buying forays was a stream of paper going back across the Atlantic to a network of friends and acquaintances interested in politics, science, and commerce. Several correspondents received copies of Jean-Baptiste Dubucq's pamphlet on trade with the West Indies, for example; Charles Thomson, the secretary of the American Philosophical Society, received "a pamphlet on the subject of animal magnetism," and Ralph Izard of South Carolina obtained the *Bibliothèque Physico-Économique*.[30] This only samples books and pamphlets sent during Jefferson's first months in Paris; in subsequent years the flow continued. By the time he returned home from France, he had added more than 1,850 titles to his library in addition to those he had sent to his friends.[31]

In 1783, the year before Jefferson left for France, he and Madison together drew up a list, containing over 300 titles and based on the most recent catalogue of his own library, of "books proper for the use of Congress." An economy-minded set of legislators rejected the proposal to purchase what would have been the first Library of Congress, however.[32] The first title on this list was a new project then underway in Paris, the *Encyclopédie Méthodique*—published in serial form by a remarkable book entrepreneur, Charles-Joseph Panckoucke.[33] With its first volume appearing in 1782, the *Encyclopédie Méthodique* was designed as a new and enlarged edition of the *Encyclopédie* of Diderot and D'Alembert. While the entries within Diderot's encyclopedia were arranged in alphabetical order, the *Méthodique* was organized in sets of alphabetized topical volumes referred to as dictionaries. Originally intended to encompass fifty-three volumes, by the time publication ceased in 1832 it ran to one hundred sixty-six and a half, and it purported to offer the most up-to-date information and thinking on a vast array of topics. In 1783 Jefferson had suggested that Panckoucke set up an agent in Philadelphia to take subscriptions for the *Encyclopédie*. This came to nothing, but once in Paris Jefferson lost little time in acquiring Panckoucke's encyclopedia. Three weeks after his

arrival in Paris he repaid his friend the Marquis de Chastellux for a subscription to the *Encyclopédie Méthodique,* which he had arranged even before he
left America.[34] Jefferson maintained his subscription until he sold his great
library in 1815, and while he was in France he also arranged to supply volumes of Panckoucke's *Encyclopédie* to friends in the United States. He regularly passed on new installments to Benjamin Franklin, James Madison the
statesman and James Madison the president of William and Mary College,
James Monroe, Francis Hopkinson, Edmund Randolph, and Dr. James Cur-
rie, among others. He would soon become more closely involved with the
Encyclopédie Méthodique than merely serving as a book agent, however.

A few months after his arrival in France, he tried to persuade his friends
Madison and Monroe to join him the following summer. "Say that the whole
[cost of the trip] would be 200 guineas," he told Madison. "You will for that
have purchased the knowledge of another world."[35] Jefferson was no star-
struck tourist in Europe, however. Already in November of 1784 he delivered
the first of his many warnings against sending young Americans to Europe.
"From what I have seen here I know not one good purpose on earth which can
be effected by a young gentleman's coming here," he informed Charles Thomson. "He may learn indeed to speak the language, but put this in the scale
against the other things he will learn and evils he is sure to acquire and it will
be found too light. I have always disapproved of a European education for our
youth from theory: I now do it from inspection."[36] The Europe that Jefferson
found attractive was suitable only for fully formed republicans, and it was
particularly found in its book culture. Writing to Charles Bellini, he decried
the lack of "domestic happiness. . . . In lieu of this are substituted pursuits
which nourish and invigorate all our bad passions, and which offer only
moments of extasy amidst days and months of restlessness and torment." He
considered Europe "very much inferior . . . to the tranquil permanent felicity
with which domestic society in America blesses most of it's inhabitants,
leaving them to follow steadily those pursuits which health and reason approve, and rendering truly delicious the intervals of these pursuits." Setting
aside for the moment Jefferson's vision of American domestic happiness as a
patriotic fantasy, the conclusion he drew from this was that "in science, the
mass of people is two centuries behind ours, their literati half a dozen years
before us. Books, really good, acquire just reputations in that time, and so
become known to us and communicate to us all their advances in knowledge.

Is not this delay compensated by our being placed out of the reach of that swarm of nonsense which issues daily from a thousand presses."[37]

If Jefferson arrived in France eager to immerse himself in a world of really good books and to spread the news of them to his friends back home, he also was determined to combat the "swarm of nonsense" about America that issued from European presses. He battled misleading and deceptive anti-American accounts in British newspapers, and in his *Notes on the State of Virginia* he launched a frontal assault on the potentially most damaging slur on American possibilities. His *Notes* originated as answers to a questionnaire circulated in 1780 by the secretary to the French legation seeking information on the American states. As he developed his extensive answers to the queries, Jefferson undertook to refute the assertions of George Louis LeClerc, the Comte de Buffon, the leading French natural historian, that the supposedly wet and cold climate of the New World produced only small and degenerate life forms, including the human beings who lived there. In Query 6, the longest in the book, Jefferson amassed detail about the relative sizes of European and American animals, about the climate, and about the cultural accomplishments of both Indians and European Americans in order to prove Buffon wrong. He even obtained from General John Sullivan of New Hampshire the prepared skeleton, hide, and antlers of a moose to give Buffon as evidence of large animals in America. Refuting Buffon was important because his theory of degeneration, if true, did not promise much for future American citizens, who would be condemned to physical and mental inferiority. In addition, many other Europeans shared Buffon's theories of American degeneration. Since Buffon stood as the most prominent and authoritative exponent of these theories, however, it was logical to direct a counterargument toward him.

The Abbé Raynal had promulgated this theory in his popular and widely reprinted *Histoire des Deux Indes,* a book that Jefferson characterized as "the effusions of an imagination in deliris."[38] In 1785 Jefferson published a limited edition of his *Notes on the State of Virginia* that criticized Raynal as well as Buffon and other French naturalists. In January of 1786 the Duc de La Rochefoucauld sent a letter introducing Jean Nicolas Démeunier, who was preparing the dictionary on *L'économie politique et diplomatique* for the *Encyclopédie,* and noted that Démeunier had already written and published articles on North and South Carolina in the first of the four volumes that would cover this topic. Would Jefferson speak with him and share information about America for articles in preparation for the rest of the volume?[39] Jefferson was unhappy to discover that Raynal was a major source for much of Démeunier's information, and in several meetings and a lengthy set of written responses he tried to set him straight. He drafted an extensive set of replies to Démeunier's first queries by January 24, answered a second set by early February, and made extensive observations on the draft of Démeunier's article on the United States. He also made sure that Démeunier had access to a copy of *Notes* for his article on Virginia. As a result, the article on the United States swelled in length. France received forty pages in the printed version and England fifty, but the United States, younger and more sparsely populated, occupied eighty-nine pages.[40] The article on Virginia was longer than any other state's entry and drew heavily on *Notes on the State of Virginia*. Jefferson's intervention was not wholly successful, however, for as he later observed when forwarding the volume to a correspondent, "with respect to the article (Etats unis) of the Encylopedie now inclosed I am far from making myself responsible for the whole of the article. The two first sections are taken chiefly from the Abbé Raynal, and they are therefore wrong exactly in the same proportion."[41]

Jefferson wanted to get the facts right. He wrote extensively to correct the estimates of the population of the American states, for example, and on the extent and variety of the American postrevolutionary debt. As a diplomat, he also wished to put the best face possible on American affairs. Referring to the debt, he remarked that "those who talk of the bankruptcy of the U.S. are of two descriptions. 1. Strangers who do not understand the nature and history of our paper money. 2. Holders of that paper-money who do not wish that the world should understand it." His attempts to suggest that the United States was fiscally sound were a bit like his own efforts late in life to optimistically understate the seriousness of his own financial situation when he was, for all practical purposes, bankrupt. Similarly, his assurance that "the Confederation is a wonderfully perfect instrument, considering the circumstances under which it was formed," does not quite conform to the growing realization in America in the mid-1780s that the Articles of Confederation had serious defects. He and John Adams were desperately trying to arrange loans from European bankers in order to keep the new nation afloat; it was crucial to maintain that the United States was politically stable and able to pay its debts. Jefferson's facts were more reliable than the Abbé Raynal's, but they were not entirely free from what is now called "spin."[42]

In other areas Jefferson's observations were colored by his own ideological biases. Writing in the world of the *philosophes*, he himself took on the role of *philosophe*, aware that facts were always embedded in the context of specific political realities only made visible to rational analysis. Explaining why Rhode Island, the smallest state, was so often able to block "useful proposition[s]," he asserted that "the cultivators of the earth are the most virtuous citizens and possess most of the amor patriae. Merchants are the least virtuous, and possess the least of the amor patriae." Because of its geography, "there is not a single man in Rhode island who is not a merchant of some sort."[43] Well, not exactly accurate as to detail, but if the United States was to be thought of as a republican experiment, then it might seem appropriate to apply as explanatory tools republican concepts like the importance of the virtuous citizen and the public good.

Jefferson was also careful to explain the system of indentured servitude by which immigrants were able to pay for their passage across the Atlantic by entering into labor contracts. He echoed the argument of Guillaume de Crèvecoeur by describing the system of indenture as a progressive means of individual self-improvement that, rather than being a flaw in the American scheme, was a testimony to its promise. "So desirous are the poor of Europe to get to America, where they may better their conditions that, being unable to pay their passage, they will agree to serve two or three years, on their arrival there, rather than not go," he wrote. "During the time of that service they are better fed, better clothed, and have lighter labour than while in Europe." Yet some claimed "that these people are deceived by those who carry them over." The truth was that, in America, "this deception" was never "heard of. The individuals are generally satisfied in America with their adventure, and very few of them wish not to have made it."[44] Remarks like these accorded with the general tenor of Jefferson's observations for Démeunier. They insisted on the progressive quality of American life, on the general improvement of conditions for ordinary people. His observations, concerned with getting right the details of present-day America, also conveyed a strong sense of what America might become, of its true character as a land that would make good on its promising beginnings. It was the duty of the *philosophe* to delineate just where that promise revealed itself.

Admitting to the existence of slavery in America, Jefferson optimistically asserted the existence of growing sentiment in favor of abolition in the South, particularly in Virginia, where "I flatter myself it will take place there at some period of time not very far distant."[45] Jefferson was aware that abolition would be more difficult than this. His fears of antagonizing his fellow Virginians over his strictures on slavery in *Notes* hindered him from circulating the book widely at home, but the enlightened circles of Paris allowed him to extend his imagination about the possible future of America. If Jefferson was a *philosophe,* at least for a moment in his life, then consider that the French *philosophes* were not mere theorists but frequently men of affairs active in business, politics, and the professions. Jefferson had always his eye on the future, but as a shrewd politician he was aware of the necessity of persuading his fellow citizens of the possibilities and rewards of a democratic future. Keeping the passions of men on his side was essential, and a promising way to do this was to engage the republic of letters on behalf of America.

In describing the affair of the Cincinnati, the organization of Revolutionary War officers that threatened to be the foundation for a hereditary elite, he concluded by asking Démeunier "to avail us of his forcible manner to evince that there is evil to be apprehended even from the ashes of this institution, and to exhort the society in America to make their reformation complete; bearing in mind that we must keep the passions of men on our side even when we are persuading them to do what they ought to do."[46] Julian Boyd has noted that, although Jefferson described himself as "one who was an enemy to the institution from the first moment of it's conception," he went on to pen "what is probably the best apology for the origins of the Society of the Cincinnati ever written."[47] Jefferson created a sentimental narrative that posited the origins of the Society in a burst of affection and benevolence that broke out among the officers as they were about to disperse at the end of the war. They formed their organization in order to enjoy "the pleasure of seeing each other again, by the sweetest of all consolations, the talking over the scenes of difficulty and of endearment they had gone through." They would additionally be able to support their brothers who had fallen into economic hardship. Washington, moved by this expression of "benevolence and friendship," thought it would be an "instrument the more for strengthening the federal band, and for promoting federal ideas." When the Society came under attack as a danger to a republican, egalitarian society, Washington urged his fellow officers to suppress the Cincinnati; their opposition "was observed to cloud his face with an anxiety that the most distressful scenes of the war had scarcely ever produced." However, when the acceptances of membership arrived from the French officers who had been invited to join, it seemed impossible to undo what had been done, other than to recommend various reforms to accord with the republican spirit of the country. In America, Jefferson concluded, "no other distinction between man and man had ever been known, but that of persons in office exercising powers by authority of the laws, and private individuals. . . . But of distinctions by birth or badge they had no more idea than they had of the mode of existence in the moon or planets. They had heard only that there were such, and knew that they must be wrong." Jefferson's apology for the Cincinnati successfully connected a story of overflowing heartfelt sentiment with one of national unity and republican principle even as it subtly suggested that the undemocratic distinction it promised was a European and not an American problem. The Society retained its life because of the eager embrace of the French officers, and the threat it posed to republicanism was most to be felt "in Europe only, where the dignity of man is lost in arbitrary distinctions."[48] Jefferson's recasting of the story of the Cincinnati as a tale of "benevolence and friendship" attempted to engage the passions of men in both America and France with a narrative of sentiment and republican, rational principle. In America the members of the Cincinnati would be among the leaders of the new governments, and their support for republican principle would be crucial. In France the gentle critique of "arbitrary distinctions" could be useful and appreciated in enlightened circles.

In the case of Démeunier's dictionary, he had some success as well in reaching out to an enlightened audience, despite his failure to completely eradicate the traces of the Abbé Raynal. Most of his suggestions made their way into the published version, including some mildly radical bits such as the text of the Virginia Statute for Religious Freedom and Jefferson's praise of an American federalism that had been accused of lacking "energy"—the ability to forcefully exert power when necessary. Jefferson admitted this was true but a mere "inconvenience. On the other hand," he stated, "that energy which absolute governments derive from an armed force, which is the effect of the bayonet constantly held at the breast of every citizen, and which resembles very much the stillness of the grave, must be admitted also to have it's inconveniences. We weigh the two together, and like best to submit to the former. Compare the number of wrongs committed with impunity by citizens among us, with those committed by the sovereigns in other countries, and the last will be found most numerous, most oppressive on the mind, and most degrading of the dignity of man."[49] These were potentially dangerous words in France of the *ancien régime,* but Jefferson must have been persuasive when delivering them to the man who was one of the *censeurs royal* and the secretary to the king's brother. When Démeunier thanked Jefferson for meeting with him and commenting so extensively on his manuscript, he praised his lively and diligent attention to his text and congratulated America on having such a citizen. "I count as moments of pleasure and good fortune those in which you have allowed me to listen to you," he concluded, and in the published article on Virginia he cited Jefferson as one of its citizens "les plus respectables . . . par ses lumières"—the most respectable for his enlightenment.[50] If Jefferson found pleasure in his books, he found as much or more in talking with his friends and acquaintances about the core values of the Enlightenment, about the dignity of man, and the value of learning for the virtuous citizens of a republic.

Jefferson's involvement with the *Encyclopédie Méthodique* as consumer, unofficial book agent, and consultant for the volume on political economy and diplomacy did not lead to the abolition of slavery in Virginia or to the perfected republic that he dreamed of in which the dignity of man was always honored, and it certainly did not initiate the French Revolution. But his work was a commitment to the future, to what the philosopher and critic Jürgen Habermas has often described as the unfinished project of the Enlightenment, the pursuit of reason and justice that is yet to be fully realized. In the *Encyclopédies,* both Diderot's and Panckoucke's, had been planted the seeds of things to come. The *Encyclopédie Méthodique,* like its predecessor, was a project that aimed to affect society from the top down by encouraging an elite to use its reason about all of life's activities in the hope that reason would spread itself beyond this elite. Jefferson claimed that in America "no other distinction between man and man had ever been known, but that of persons in office exercising powers by authority of the laws, and private individuals. Among these last the poorest labourer stood on equal ground with the wealthiest Millionary."[51] If he was confident of the ordinary man's ability to govern himself, he also believed that the benefits of formal learning might be spread down from intellectuals and leaders in the sciences and professions. His schemes for public education in Virginia sketched out a hierarchy of schools from the most basic level to the university, but the university was the only one he saw into existence. Robert Darnton has described "browsing through the *Méthodique* [as] like strolling through a university: first one passes the small but elegant mathematics building; Art and Music stands to the left, History and Literature to the right; the natural sciences dominate a vast quadrangle near the gymnasium and swimming pool; and beyond them loom the law and medical schools."[52] There were many influences and motives for Jefferson's last great Enlightenment project, the University of Virginia, but it is not beyond reason to see one of its roots in his activities in France in the 1780s. At the center of his design for the university's buildings was the Rotunda that would house the library, complete with books that he had himself selected. He surely knew that a university's students and even its faculty come and go, but its library is its heart.

Notes

An earlier version of this essay was published by Fulcrum Publishing and appeared as "Taking the Enlightenment Abroad: Thomas Jefferson in France" in *The Libraries, Leadership, and Legacy of John Adams and Thomas Jefferson,* ed. Robert C. Baron and Conrad Edick Wright (Golden, Colo., 2010), 113–32.

1. TJ to John Page, 21 February 1770, *TJP,* 1:34–35. Kevin Hayes, *The Road to Monticello* (New York, 2008), argues convincingly, however, that not all of Jefferson's books were destroyed in the fire.

2. TJ to Thomas Adams, 20 February 1771, *TJP,* 1:61.

3. *Jefferson's Memorandum Books,* ed. James A. Bear Jr. and Lucia Stanton, 2 vols. (Princeton, N.J., 1997), 1:332.

4. "Memoirs of a Monticello Slave," in *Jefferson at Monticello,* ed. James A. Bear Jr. (Charlottesville, Va., 1967), 12.

5. My notion of the colporteur owes largely to Ernst Bloch, author of *The Principle of Hope,* which speaks to a theory of "anticipatory illumination." See Jack Zipes, "Introduction," in Ernst Bloch, *The Utopian Function of Art and Literature* (Cambridge, Mass., 1988), xi–xliii.

6. Kant, "What Is Enlightenment?" in *Foundation of the Metaphysics of Morals and What Is Enlightenment,* trans. Lewis White Beck (Indianapolis, 1959), 85. The meaning and significance of the Enlightenment has been troubled, to say the least, in the last half century; for a review of different interpretations, see Richard Butterwick, "Peripheries of the Enlightenment: An Introduction," in *Peripheries of the Enlightenment,* ed. Butterwick, Simon Davies, and Gabriel Sanchez Espinosa (Oxford, 2008), 1–16.

7. Edmund Randolph, "Edmund Randolph's Essay on the Revolutionary History of Virginia (1774–1782)," *Virginia Magazine of History and Biography* 43 (1935): 122–23.

8. Cf. TJ to John Minor, 30 August 1814, Ford, 9:480–84. Note also letter of 5 February 1769 to Thomas Turpin, *TJP,* 1:25.

9. Robert Skipwith to TJ, 17 July 1771, ibid., 74–75.

10. TJ to Joseph Priestley, 27 January 1800, ibid., 31:340.

11. On Jefferson's attempt to meet Skipwith's expectations but also to include his own preferences, see Douglas L. Wilson, "Thomas Jefferson's Library and the Skipwith List," *Harvard Library Bulletin*, New Series 3 (Winter 1992–93): 56–72.

12. TJ to Skipwith, 3 August 1771, *TJP*, 1:76–81.

13. TJ to Minor, 30 August 1814, Ford, 9:480–84. The original plan of study was written out much earlier, probably around 1770, and included in this letter on additional pages.

14. TJ to Nathaniel Burwell, 1 April 1818, TJ Papers, Lib. Cong. The letter has been widely reprinted, but not so the attached reading list. I am grateful to Christine Coalwell McDonald for pointing this out to me.

15. TJ to Skipwith, 3 August 1771, *TJP*, 1:76–81.

16. TJ to Peter Carr, 10 August 1787, ibid., 12:15.

17. Douglas L. Wilson, *Jefferson's Books* (Charlottesville, Va., 1996), 23.

18. TJ to D'Anmours, 30 November 1780, *TJP*, 4:168; Amable and Alexander Lory to TJ, 16 December 1780, ibid., 211; TJ to John Fitzgerald, 27 February 1781, ibid., 5:15. TJ's *Notes on the State of Virginia* is available in several editions, including *Notes on the State of Virginia*, ed. William Peden (1787; Chapel Hill, N.C., 1954).

19. D'Alembert, *Preliminary Discourse to the Encyclopedia of Diderot*, trans. Richard N. Schwab (Chicago, 1995), 50, 57.

20. Wilson, *Jefferson's Books*, 36–41.

21. TJ to George Watterston, 7 May 1815, *TJW*, 1367.

22. D'Alembert, *Preliminary Discourse to the Encyclopedia of Diderot*, 49, 75. On the metaphor of the map in the *Encyclopédie*, see David Bates, "Cartographic Aberrations: Epistemology and Order in the Encyclopedic Map," in *Using the Encyclopédie: Ways of Knowing, Ways of Reading*, ed. Daniel Brewer and Julie Candler Hayes (Oxford, 2002), 1–20.

23. TJ to Watterston, 7 May 1815, *TJW*, 1367.

24. James Madison to TJ, 16 March 1784, *TJP*, 7:37.

25. List of Books Sold to James Monroe, 10 May 1784, ibid., 240.

26. Bear and Stanton, eds., *Jefferson's Memorandum Books*, 556, 558.

27. TJ to Charles Thomson, 21 May 1784, *TJP*, 7:282.

28. John Trumbull to TJ, 21 June 1784, ibid., 317.

29. TJ to Samuel Harrison Smith, 21 September 1814, *TJW*, 1353.

30. TJ to James Monroe, 6 February 1785, *TJP*, 7:640; TJ to Richard Henry Lee, ibid., 644; TJ to Charles Thomson, 11 November 1784, ibid., 518. Izard to TJ, with Reports on the Trade of South Carolina, 10 June 1785, ibid., 195.

31. Douglas L. Wilson, "Thomas Jefferson's Library and the French Connection," *Eighteenth-Century Studies* 26 (1993): 682.

32. Report on a Committee to Prepare a List of Books for Congress, [24 January 1783,] *TJP*, 6:216. See also Fulmer Mood, "The Continental Congress and the Plan for a Library of Congress in 1782–83: An Episode in American Cultural History," *Pennsylvania Magazine of History and Biography* 72 (1948): 3–24.

33. For Panckoucke's career, see Suzanne Tucoo-Chala, *Charles-Joseph Panckoucke et la Librairie Française, 1736–1798* (Pau, France, 1977). For Panckoucke and the *Encyclopédie Méthodique*, see Robert Darnton, *The Business of Enlightenment: A Publishing History of the Encyclopédie, 1775–1800* (Cambridge, Mass., 1979), esp. 395–459.

34. TJ to David S. Franks, [March or April 1783,] *TJP*, 6:258; Bear and Stanton, eds., *Jefferson's Memorandum Books*, 560.

35. TJ to James Madison, 8 December 1784, *TJP,* 7:559.

36. TJ to Charles Thomson, 11 November 1784, ibid., 519.

37. TJ to Charles Bellini, 30 September 1785, ibid., 569.

38. "Notes on the Letter of Christoph Daniel Ebeling," *TJP,* 28:509.

39. La Rochefoucauld to TJ, 4 January 1786, ibid., 9:150.

40. "The Article on the United States in the *Encyclopédie Méthodique*" in ibid., 10:9. This editorial note by Julian P. Boyd on the exchanges between Jefferson and Démeunier is the best account of this episode.

41. TJ to G. K. van Hogendorp, 25 August 1786, ibid., 299.

42. TJ, Answers to Démeunier's First Queries, 24 January 1786, ibid., 17, 14.

43. Ibid., 16.

44. TJ, Jefferson's Observations on Démeunier's Manuscript, [22 June 1786,] ibid., 31–32.

45. TJ, Answers to Démeunier's First Queries, ibid., 18.

46. TJ, Jefferson's Observations on Démeunier's Manuscript, ibid., 54.

47. "The Article on the United States in the *Encyclopédie Méthodique,*" ibid., 6.

48. TJ, Jefferson's Observations on Démeunier's Manuscript, ibid., 48–52.

49. TJ, Answers to Démeunier's First Queries, ibid., 19–20; for the French translation of this passage, see "The Article on the United States in the *Encyclopédie Méthodique,*" ibid., 8.

50. Démeunier to TJ, [26 June 1786,] ibid., 65. Literally, "Lorsque Je Songe à la vivacité de Son Zele, Je Felicite L'Amerique d'avoir un pareil Citoyen, et Je Compte pour des momens de plaisir et de bonheur, Ceux où il m'est permis de L'ecouter."

51. TJ, Jefferson's Observations on Démeunier's Manuscript, ibid., 52.

52. Darnton, *The Business of Enlightenment,* 451. On the "top-heavy diffusion process" of the Enlightenment, see p. 526.

"Presenting to Them Models for Their Imitation"

Thomas Jefferson's Reform of American Architecture

CRAIG A. REYNOLDS

F ROM HIS EARLIEST DAYS IN WILLIAMSBURG TO HIS RETIREMENT AT Monticello, Jefferson never rested in his attempts to reform American architecture. In his influential *Notes on the State of Virginia*, Jefferson lamented the architecture that surrounded him, stating that "the genius of architecture seems to have shed its maledictions over this land." Jefferson was not only concerned with the manner by which buildings were erected, but also he was troubled by Americans' apparent lack of taste and appreciation of aesthetics.[1] He could imagine only one means by which to cultivate his countrymen's sensibilities. "How is a taste in this beautiful art to be formed in our countrymen," he asked James Madison, "unless we avail ourselves of every occasion when public buildings are to be erected, of presenting . . . models for . . . study and imitation?"[2]

It is within these words that we find the root of Jefferson's architectural reform and the manner by which he chose to enlighten his fellow countrymen. He relied directly on the powerful custom of erecting new buildings in imitation of existing ones. He recognized that, in the absence of formal institutions in which Americans could be trained in the architectural arts, setting forth models for imitation was the most practical manner in which to educate the amateur builders and civic leaders of the new American nation. Although Jefferson gained renown for creations such as Monticello, the Virginia capitol, and the University of Virginia, his best success in architecture may well have been the establishment of his building program into a didactic system of architectural prototypes, each of which served to enlighten the citizens of the young republic as appropriate architectural expressions of the democratic ideology Jefferson himself had championed in documents such as the Declaration of Independence and the Virginia Statute for Religious Freedom. For Jefferson, architecture was another element of Enlightenment discourse. The American built environment that Jefferson had envisioned would come to serve as a philosophical narrative championing the inherent rights of all, liberty chief among them.

At the heart of Jefferson's architectural movement was his ability to conjoin vernacular custom with the architecture of antiquity. By looking to classical models, specifically those described by the Italian Renaissance architect Andrea Palladio, Jefferson reinterpreted many of the standard public buildings of Virginia into temple forms. More specifically, his reeducation of American builders was achieved through the design and construction of his Virginia State Capitol, the U.S. Capitol, the University of Virginia, and the numerous temple-form county courthouses of Virginia. All of these served as didactic models both for builders and the general citizenry.

Aside from Jefferson's ability to link the vernacular with the classical, his architectural reform rested on two other principles that radically altered the American built environment. The first is the use of permanent materials, such as brick or stone, for the construction of buildings. The second is the use of the classical orders as ornament. Normally composed of a base, column, capital, and entablature, these followed one of five standard design schemes (i.e., Doric, Tuscan, Ionic, Corinthian, or composite).

Yet Jefferson's reliance on setting models amounted to merely a starting point. Of greatest importance is why and how he set out to reform American architecture. Uncovering Jefferson's reasons for reforming architectural practice in America is immensely difficult, in part because he never explicitly revealed them. In fact, his motivations have never been fully explored or explained by scholars of Jeffersonian architecture. Several possibilities stand out, however. Among these was Jefferson's desire to elevate the architectural arts by professionalizing the practice. For Jefferson, setting models was only part of the reform process. In order to perpetuate these reforms for future generations, he recognized America's need to progress from a system that employed the talents of colonial gentleman amateurs to one that used educated professionals. This is especially true with regard to an unprecedented federal building campaign that resulted in the architectural standardization of various government buildings, including courthouses, post offices, and customhouses during the first half of the nineteenth century.

Jefferson's desire to professionalize architectural practice is coupled with his goal to establish a universal standard of design and style emblematic of American, and more specifically Jeffersonian, democratic principles. Thus, architecture was meant to serve as a broad visual narrative. More specifically, Jefferson used architecture as a vehicle that promoted his philosophical agenda, creating for the populace a tangible representation of the abstract Enlightenment principles that formed the basis of American liberty.

It is well known that Jefferson wished to distance America from Europe, its religious and monarchical governance, and its "monkish ignorance and superstition." The light of freedom would shine the brightest in America and serve as a beacon for the rest of the world, with Jefferson's temple-form buildings dedicated to liberty rather than deity. For Jefferson, a monumental neoclassical building program, adhering to Palladio's fixed proportional system of architectural elements, would constitute a clear and rational representation of humanity's right of self-governance.[3]

Jefferson rejected accepted architectural practices in Virginia by suggesting alternative models of worthy architecture through his designs for the Virginia State Capitol, U.S. Capitol, University of Virginia, and his home state's courthouses. These courthouses, in particular, deserve attention, for they constitute not only the most understudied and underappreciated of his designs but also the most potent architectural models. Seen and used most frequently by common citizens, these courthouses—like Jefferson's other public buildings—served as monuments to openness and transparency, justice and just proportions, and the egalitarian belief that easily accessible and inexpensive materials could contribute to the construction of buildings both solid and, like the nation Jefferson also helped to construct, built for the ages.

Among the many difficulties in studying Jefferson and his architecture is that he did not leave us a single authoritative source. Students of Jefferson must piece together his architectural vision from a wide and seemingly unending body of letters, notes, drawings, and, of course, his buildings. Jefferson's *Notes on the State of Virginia* gives the reader one of the only focused glimpses of the built environment of eighteenth-century Virginia. In this book, Jefferson very deliberately identified what he viewed as the errors of design and construction in Virginia's public and private buildings.[4]

Unfortunately, a series of myths have been told and retold to the effect that, as a reformer, Jefferson wished to return to the pure origins of architecture, to revive the architecture of republican Rome for the new American republic, to apply the innovations of the French architectural avant-garde of the late eighteenth century in his own nation, to create a new American style—or to do all of these things in one mighty swoop. These supposed goals are fantasies perpetuated by a failure to read fully Jefferson's writing and study his many pages of architectural plans. If the achievement of these assumed ideals were his goal, then surely he would have left some indication. As in his *Notes,* Jefferson was normally direct about his critique of American architecture, yet he leaves us no link between his architectural reforms and those supposed goals. Instead, Jefferson reminded his countrymen that the Maison Carrée, from which his Virginia State Capitol is derived, dates to the Roman imperial period—"the time of the Caesars"—and not from the Roman republic. Furthermore, Jefferson even declared as his favorite the Doric order of the Imperial Baths of Diocletian. Whether a building dated to the Roman empire or Roman republic mattered less to Jefferson than technical issues such as proper architectural proportions and form, the use of appropriate materials, and how an edifice might serve as a model for future builders.[5]

In Jefferson's *Notes,* his discussion of Virginia architecture seems disorderly, leaving readers once again to piece together the many facets of his architectural thought process. In general, however, the topic of Virginia architecture falls under "Query XV: Colleges, Buildings, and Roads." Within this query, Jefferson divided architecture into three sections: private buildings, public buildings, and private buildings once more. The common thread between the three is Jefferson's two key principles: to promote masonry construction over perishable wood and to promote the use of the orders as ornament.

As the *Notes* suggest, Jefferson's loyalty to the orders reflected a larger devotion to architectural principle. He probably believed that the "moderns," the architects who renewed the architecture of antiquity from the Renaissance onward, had not equaled the "ancients'" architectural achievements. The only exception, for Jefferson, was Palladio, whose handling of the orders struck him as the best in history. Based on his affection for Palladian architecture, it seems that Jefferson had worked out a hierarchy of building types. At the top were the greatest public buildings, the statehouses, which Jefferson wanted to make models of the purest ancient forms, the "cubic" and "spherical" temple forms. On the next level down stood the magistrate's house, for which Jefferson favored the ideal geometry set by one of the greatest modern buildings, Palladio's Villa Rotunda. Still further down came the private house, where Jefferson permitted greatest latitude of design. Last, he mentioned on more than one occasion an enduring love of the aesthetic of what he called "light and airy."[6]

In his *Notes,* Jefferson opened his discussion of architecture by stating the masonry principle: "the private buildings are very rarely constructed of stone or brick" in Virginia; most consisted "of scantling [small pieces of lumber] and boards, plastered with lime. It is impossible to devise things more ugly, uncomfortable, and happily more perishable." Jefferson saw no architectural value, aesthetic or otherwise, in the manner by which Virginians constructed their houses. His attack on domestic architecture alludes also to the lack of training among builders as well as their apparent indifference toward aesthetics. After this condemnation, Jefferson commented neutrally that "two or three plans" governed "most of the houses," hinting at his preference for using existing floor plans and vernacular interior room arrangements within a temple-form exterior.[7]

Jefferson then turned to his second major topic, public buildings. Here he focused on what he knew from firsthand experience in Williamsburg. He lamented the town's architecture, saying that four of its structures were "the only public buildings worthy [of] mention." Jefferson began with what he described as "the most pleasing piece of architecture we have," the second Williamsburg capitol building (1751–53). Jefferson described it as "light and airy." This favorite phrase most likely referred only to the two-story Palladian portico. As such, Jefferson evaluated nothing but the orders and completely avoided describing the interior room arrangement. Jefferson focused on one of his two architectural principles by criticizing the orders of the Williamsburg capitol's portico in great detail. He stated that the lower Doric order was "tolerably just in its proportions and ornaments," while the upper row of Ionic columns was "much too small" and "not proper to the order."[8]

The Governor's Palace served as Jefferson's second example. "Not handsome" externally, Jefferson nonetheless regarded it as commodious, well

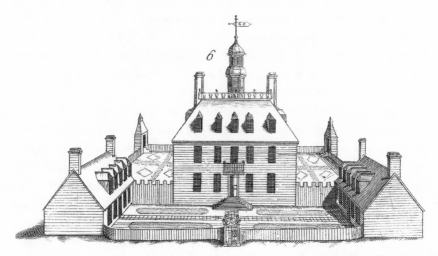

Detail of Governor's Palace from the Bodleian Plate, ca. 1740. (The Colonial Williamsburg Foundation, accession #R1980-103, image #78-655)

sited, and "capable of being made an elegant seat." To make the palace "elegant," Jefferson drew up a plan transforming the building with a monumental display of the orders. He proposed turning the building into a powerful temple-form edifice with a mighty and deep octastyle—or eight-column—portico in front, a grand but shallower octastyle portico in back, and colonnaded wings at its sides. Jefferson's reform clad the exterior with the orders but accepted the existing room arrangements within the interior.[9]

Jefferson's third and fourth examples of public buildings were the College of William and Mary and the Public Hospital. Here he was particularly harsh, describing them as "rude, misshapen piles, which, but they had roofs, would be taken for brick-kilns." Like the Governor's Palace, the College and Hospital lacked porticos or any other architectural reference to the orders. Williamsburg contained "no other public buildings but churches and courthouses," and in these "no attempts are made at elegance. Indeed it would not be easy to execute such an attempt, as a workman could scarcely be found here capable of drawing an order." In this restatement of his belief that elegance in architecture meant the display of the orders, he hinted at both the cause and solution to this architectural problem: the education of workmen.[10]

Jefferson lamented the expensive private buildings that not only lacked "symmetry and taste" but also were burdened with "barbarous ornaments" that fell outside of the proper proportional system that Jefferson had gleaned from Palladio. In Williamsburg, Jefferson bemoaned that "the first principles of the art are unknown and there exists scarcely a model among us sufficiently chaste to give an idea of them." Jefferson voiced the hope that the revised curriculum at William and Mary would produce the necessary reformers, but he would remain dissatisfied.[11]

While Jefferson's discussion focused on Virginia, his descriptions and criticisms could easily fit many towns in the American colonies, where steeples, lanterns, cupolas, and spires rather than porticos generally served to mark important public edifices. Without the benefit of trained architects and builders, the buildings of colonial America were oftentimes muddled translations of English architecture. As in Virginia, the vernacular style, which was dictated by trial and error, was the predominant mode of architectural expression. This is not to say that early American public architecture was not memorable. The fact is that English-inspired houses of government and worship served as the only examples of architecture to which Americans could look for inspiration.[12]

In addition to criticizing the Virginia builders' apparent ignorance of the orders, Jefferson also challenged the overwhelmingly dominant Virginia tradition of constructing with wood. In his *Notes* he made a methodical attempt to counter the prejudice that masonry houses suffered from condensation problems. Condensation could easily be prevented or ameliorated, he argued, and it offered important practical advantages over wooden structures. Equally important, Jefferson thought, was that "when buildings are of durable materials, every new edifice is an actual and permanent acquisition to the state, adding to its value as well as to its ornament."[13]

When taken in its entirety, Jefferson's discussion in *Notes* reveals that two overriding principles constitute the foundation of his plan to reform Virginia architecture: builders should erect public and private houses with masonry and they should adorn public buildings with the orders. In addition, Jefferson revealed the three principal techniques by which his architectural reform would be accomplished: by setting models (particularly of the orders), by training workmen, and by educating leaders to appreciate architecture.

Jefferson's understanding of the power of imitation could be considered his most successful architectural accomplishment. He may not have been the first to notice that architecture had didactic uses, but he perfected the use of didactic architecture. From one end of his career to the other, Jefferson created models for use as the principal means by which to inspire a new American architectural aesthetic. Even a brief chronological sampling of Jefferson's diverse applications of the principle of imitation demonstrates how fundamental the principle of setting models was to him. This tradition reveals a rich play of ideas gained from European sources as well as his American surroundings. The practice of looking to existing buildings as a source for new ones was common in America during the colonial period, before the standardization of formalized architectural education.[14]

It is unclear under what circumstances Jefferson first realized the benefits of setting models, but what we do know is that he used the practice to successfully initiate a broad reform without the benefit of educational institutions pushing his agenda. He made it abundantly clear that he despised most of the architecture around him, stating that "English architecture is in the most wretched style I ever saw, not meaning to except America, where it is bad, nor even Virginia, where it is worse than in any other part of America." More than any other American architect of his day, Jefferson saw the vast potential of infusing classical models, specifically the orders in the temple form, with existing architectural customs. This mixing of building traditions was probably his second-greatest architectural accomplishment because it afforded him the perfect opportunity to introduce to Virginia a set of models based on the orders of Palladio. These models have been described as "Museums of the Orders" that exposed individuals to examples of correct proportion and enlightened taste.[15]

Jefferson favored the orders of Palladio, a modern practitioner of the Italian Renaissance, over those of the Greeks and Romans. One can see how Jefferson envisioned a museum of the orders based on Palladio by looking to his first conception of Monticello and his list of "Orders of the Rooms." The most formal parts of the house were to provide the sequence of Palladio's Doric, Ionic, and Corinthian in quick succession: a portico with the Doric of Palladio downstairs and the Ionic of Palladio upstairs with an adjacent parlor adorned with Palladio's Corinthian entablature. Jefferson planned to use Palladio's Tuscan on two outbuildings. Jefferson's hierarchy of design linked order with function and location.[16]

Jefferson did not finish building Monticello as first conceived, and he seems to have failed to execute much if any of his internal museum of the orders. His most ambitious attempt to set such a model was his planned five-story Observation Tower at Monticello. It was to display a full set of five orders, one on each level. Although never built, the tower illustrates how Jefferson's architectural thought process integrated classical forms within vernacular custom. Jefferson became a designer because he had no other way of getting good architecture for his own house. He advanced into civic design because he saw no other way of getting good architecture for public buildings or educating the masses about proper forms.[17]

For Jefferson, Palladio's handling of the orders was the best in history, and he continued to return to Palladio again and again. Jefferson owned multiple versions of Palladio's *Four Books,* which he referred to as his architectural "bible." In this treatise, Palladio gave the orders favorable attention at the expense of other building matters. There is, however, a problem with Jefferson's interpretation of Palladio's orders, for he took as his authoritative version a highly corrupted edition altered by the Florentine Renaissance architect Giacomo Leoni. These editions suffered from an unreliable text and plates that Leoni had pervasively altered to serve as advertisements for his own architectural practice. Although Jefferson thought that he was using the orders of Palladio, he was really using Palladio's orders as reworked by Leoni.[18]

In 1777, Jefferson laid the groundwork for his architectural reformation, advocating the abandonment of Williamsburg in favor of Richmond as Virginia's new capital. By 1779, the year Jefferson was elected governor of Virginia, his master plan for the creation of a new capital in Richmond had been approved by the State Legislature. In Richmond, in 1785, seven years before a plan had been approved for the U.S. Capitol, Jefferson established a very important and influential architectural model: the Virginia State Capitol (1786–98). The result would be a national preference for classically inspired temple-form buildings over the established architectural styles transplanted from England.[19]

At the State Capitol in Richmond he developed a prototype of the standard American civic temple. He stated in his autobiography that "it [was] a favorable opportunity of introducing into the State an example of architecture, in the classic style of antiquity." Regarding the idea of classically inspired prototypes, Jefferson further stated that his design for the Virginia State Capitol was based on "the Temples of Erectheus at Athens, of Balbec, and of the Maison quarrée . . . all of which are nearly the same form and proportions, and are considered as the most perfect examples of cubic architecture,

"The Virginia State Capitol," 1801, drawing by Lawrence Scully, engraved by Alexander Lawson. (The Library of Virginia)

as the Pantheon of Rome is of the spherical." Based on these sources, a conclusion can be made that Jefferson found ancient architecture authoritative because of its embodiment of a precise proportional system based on the cube and the sphere. These basic elements of ideal proportions would guide Jeffersonian architectural principles involving public space, memorial space, and interaction within space well into the twentieth century.[20]

As Jefferson stipulated, the use of masonry construction was a guiding principle of design. In actuality, the Virginia State Capitol is a red brick building covered with stucco. Jefferson adapted this technique in part from Palladio, who used it frequently. It appears that Jefferson, at the outset of his career in civic architecture, intended a wholesale application of this practice. This custom, however, proved too problematic for American workmen. The stucco concealing the Capitol's red brick exterior failed; there ensued a constant battle of repairs to keep up the Palladian covering. Jefferson would later undergo a significant evolution from Palladian stucco to the more practical Virginia custom of using exposed red brick with lightly colored trim. His acceptance of the contrasting red brick and light trim is a milestone. He integrated one of the most recognizable of architectural "Americanisms" into his Palladian reform program of permanent construction and decoration with the orders.[21]

The use of the orders as ornament, the second component of Jefferson's architectural reformation, characterized not only his first design for Monticello but also his plan for the Virginia Capitol. The clearest evidence of his intent comes from the penultimate design phase of the Capitol, when Jefferson prepared a set of specifications, "Notes explicatives des plans du Capitole pour l'etat de la Virginie" (1785), for the French artisan Charles-Louis Clérisseau. Jefferson stipulated a generous collection of Palladian orders. Externally, the portico is composed of the Ionic order. The internal culmination, as part of the interior hall around the Jean-Antoine Houdon statue of George Washington, was to have the Leoni-Palladio Ionic colonnade downstairs under a Leoni-Palladio Corinthian colonnade upstairs. As to the Tuscan, Jefferson reserved entablatures in this order for lesser rooms and did not identify which of Palladio's alternatives he wanted. In the Capitol's rebuilding and enlargement (1904–6), a redecoration significantly altered Jefferson's intentions for the orders.[22]

Last, it is important to note Jefferson's precedent of accepting the customary interior room arrangements of Virginia buildings. His Virginia Capitol affords us an excellent opportunity to witness this practice. Architectural historian Marc R. Wenger has shown that Jefferson's room layout for the Capitol in Richmond parallels the floor plan of the second Williamsburg Capitol (1751–53). In both Jefferson's design for Richmond and that of the capitol at Williamsburg, the main entry, or "ceremonial entry," opened into the side of a courtroom. A central space used for both formal and informal gatherings is positioned next to the courtroom. In both capitols these central rooms feature statues of important leaders. Richard Hayward's statue of Lord Botetourt was in Williamsburg and Houdon's George Washington is in Richmond. Just beyond the center room, in both capitols, is a space for the lower house of legislature to convene.[23]

The sequel to Jefferson's Richmond capitol came in Washington, D.C., with the United States Capitol building. The problems surrounding the design and construction of the U.S. Capitol are well documented. Pierre Charles L'Enfant planned the federal city but failed ever to produce designs for public buildings. Washington dismissed him in 1792 and an open competition was held in which architects, all amateurs, submitted an array of capitol designs. When the submissions failed to win approval, President Washington informed Jefferson, his secretary of state, that the Capitol "ought to be upon a scale far superior to any thing in this Country." Clearly, Jefferson and

Washington did not favor the "Congress Hall" or "Federal Hall" concept that most submitted designs were based upon. In fact, they most likely had in mind an idealized national temple concept related to the Temple of Jupiter Optimus Maximus Capitalinus, which had stood upon the Capitaline Hill in ancient Rome.[24]

Several factors illustrate Jefferson's influence on the U.S. Capitol. First, the evidence overwhelmingly shows that he was one of the architects of the building, oftentimes becoming so involved in the design process that he found himself at odds with his friend B. Henry Latrobe, the supervising architect of the project. Second, he established his Virginia State Capitol as a basic prototype, both in form and layout, from which the United States Capitol followed. Third, as secretary of state in Washington's administration, Jefferson headed the commission charged with building the Capitol. He later helped to disband the committee, retaining control of the design process for himself. Furthermore, it was Jefferson who persuaded President Washington to solicit entries from a public design competition. Finally, as the nation's third president, he had direct oversight of the design and construction of the national Capitol for eight years. This included appointing Latrobe, the first professionally trained architect to work in the United States, to lead the project.[25]

In his design for the Virginia State Capitol, Jefferson replicated the "cubic" temple and placed it on Shockhoe Hill, the highest hill in Richmond. At some point he turned to his thoughts of "spherical" architecture, based on the Pantheon of Rome, for the basis of a design for a circular national Capitol. Jefferson wanted Congress housed in a replica of an ancient temple, and because he established the "cubic" form in Richmond, he wanted the "spherical" or Pantheon version in Washington. He got his wish, for a classically inspired design echoing the Pantheon was eventually selected. Well after the close of the competition, a plan by William Thornton was presented to Washington and the committee. This was the second plan submitted by Thornton. The first was a rejected design consisting of nothing more than an overgrown English house, complete with lantern. Jefferson dismissed architectural features such as cupolas and lanterns as being unclassical and regarded them as "most offensive" and among "the degeneracies of modern architecture."[26]

Thornton's second submission omitted the architectural features reminiscent of Williamsburg and completely reworked the center pavilion into a dome and portico derived from the Roman Pantheon. Circumstantial evidence suggests that Jefferson helped to influence Thornton's second design. Jefferson, while an amateur, was more than likely the most accomplished of any of the officials or entrants involved in the design competition. He had already proven his ability in Richmond with the Virginia State Capitol. President Washington, moreover, was closely associated with Jefferson's wish to erect a classically inspired building. The origin and circumstances surrounding Thornton's second submission, however, remain unclear.[27]

Jefferson strove diligently to see ancient and modern exemplars set in the new federal city. In a letter to L'Enfant, Jefferson advised that "whenever it is proposed to prepare plans for the Capitol, I should prefer the adoption of some one of the models of antiquity which have had the approbation of thousands of years; and for the President's house I should prefer the celebrated fronts of Modern buildings which have already received the approbation of all good judges." Jefferson's hierarchy seems to have called for the greatest new buildings, such as the Capitol, to imitate the form of the greatest ancient buildings, which normally meant temples. On the same day, Jefferson suggested to Washington a means of providing modern domestic models that might "decide the taste of the new town." Jefferson proposed engraving copies of European prints that he had collected of "a dozen or two of the handsomest fronts of private buildings" and giving the copies away. Nothing came of Jefferson's suggestion; however, his plan to house the Capitol within a huge temple based on the Pantheon, or spherical form temple, succeeded. As Jefferson wished, Thornton reworked his design to include a Capitol rotunda, a survival of Jefferson's idea of modeling the entire building on the Pantheon in Rome.[28]

Regardless of the circumstances, Jefferson's two principles of architectural reform, masonry construction and the use of the orders as ornament, are abundantly evident in the U.S. Capitol. A massive hulk of brick and stone, the building dominated the new capital city. George Munger's "The Capitol in Ruins," which illustrates the burned-out shell of the Capitol shortly after it was torched by the British during the War of 1812, reveals its masonry construction.

The use of the orders as ornament for the Capitol was an unprecedented feat of American architectural expression. Just as Jefferson had intended for Monticello, and as he had successfully executed at the Virginia Capitol, in the new U.S. Capitol he had constructed a museum of the orders. With Latrobe

"University of VA From the South," 1826, drawing by Ennion Williams, engraved by Benjamin Tanner. (The Library of Virginia)

serving as architect of the Capitol, his idea for the orders materialized as the three greatest neoclassical interiors in the nation: the Doric courtroom, the Ionic senate chamber (now the Old Senate Chamber), and the Corinthian Hall of Representatives (now Statuary Hall). Jefferson's imitative practices also manifest themselves through the magnificent East Portico, for which he sent Latrobe the model of a reconstruction of a reputed "Portico of Diocletian." These instances are only part of the story of how Jefferson's models shaped the Capitol.[29]

At the University of Virginia in Charlottesville, Jefferson, together with Latrobe, established one of the strongest precedents for temple-form public structures built with masonry construction and using the orders as ornament. At the university, however, there are two other developments that helped propel Jefferson's architectural reform. First, Jefferson not only attracted brick masons to Charlottesville for the purpose of erecting the multitude of buildings, but he also took part in their training. Second, Jefferson educated those same builders in subjects such as Palladio and his treatment of the orders.[30]

One of the most prolific craftsmen to be trained at the university was Dabney Cosby. Cosby, a Virginia brickmason who had a large practice in Staunton, went on from the university to erect numerous buildings in Virginia and North Carolina. Directly involved with some of the finest Jeffersonian courthouses in Virginia, his 1862 obituary notes his status as one of the early practitioners of Jefferson's architectural reforms: "More than sixty [*sic*] years ago Mr. Cosby, when a young man, worked on the University of Virginia, under the direction and superintendence of Mr. Jefferson. We have often heard him speak of his conversations with that illustrious man, and of the information he received from him in architecture and the art of making brick." This gives us direct evidence that Cosby received, followed, and preached Jefferson's instructions for building with permanent materials and using the orders as ornament.[31]

Others also benefited from Jefferson's tutelage. As recently as 2002, evidence uncovered by the Virginia Historical Society and architectural historian Bryan Clark Green showed that a young Virginia carpenter named Thomas Blackburn became a major Virginia Palladian architect by way of lessons that he learned at the university. The three volumes of Blackburn's architectural drawings contain evidence suggesting that Jefferson had a direct hand in training workmen at the university. These books contain a series of painstaking copies of the orders as illustrated in the Leoni edition of Palladio, copies most plausibly made from Jefferson's copy while Blackburn worked at the university. As the volumes show, Blackburn subsequently left the university and designed a series of Jeffersonian Palladian villas executed for Jefferson's associates. Blackburn's case, like Cosby's, is most likely not unique.[32]

As the university supplied the nation with trained builders and architectural models, craftsmen went on to build structure after structure in fine red brickwork, fulfilling a key theme of Jefferson's reform agenda by fashioning buildings of permanent materials. The contrast of red brick along the colonnades and through the pavilion porticoes is one of Jefferson's masterful elements of architectural reform. He merged the common Virginia practice of exposed red brick with light trim into his Palladian reform program of permanent construction and decoration with the orders. Of course, his acceptance of exposed brick is at least in part due to the tremendous failure of the exterior stucco at his Virginia State Capitol.[33]

When Jefferson set out to design the university buildings he desired that the upper stories of the two-story pavilions present "models of taste and correct architecture" as well as "a variety of appearance, no two alike, so as to serve as specimens of the orders for the architectural lectures." Latrobe then convinced Jefferson that the pavilions, rather than having two-tier porticos, take the form of temples with unified porticos of gigantic orders. The

Latrobe-Jefferson correspondence even establishes that Latrobe's sheet of drawings, now lost, featured the orders of Palladio to suit Jefferson, rather than the Greek orders that Latrobe preferred. Yet again Jefferson established a museum of the orders to help cultivate a new American architectural aesthetic.[34]

Another important novelty, one later repeated in Jeffersonian courthouses, is the incorporation of lunette windows into the pediments of various university pavilions. Lunettes in pediments have nothing to do with ancient temples of Greece and Rome, nor do they appear in the works of Palladio or the designs of Latrobe. Such windows originated with the Romans as wall openings fitted under the curves of vaulted ceilings found in structures such as baths but never placed within the pediments of temples. Jefferson, who no doubt appreciated the practicality of the pediment lunette as a means of lighting and ventilating an attic, must also have admired the way that it constituted a semicircle within a pediment's triangle. This, after all, echoed the geometry of the university's focal point, the Rotunda, a building that he envisioned as a sphere inscribed within a cube. The lunette, which first appeared in his final design for Monticello, would migrate from the university to the Jeffersonian courthouse and beyond.[35]

With the enormous group of buildings at the university, Jefferson's lifelong habit of setting up examples of durable construction and the orders as ornament reached its zenith. Partly by assembling craftsmen and partly by educating them, Jefferson created the workforce to disseminate his models' qualities throughout Virginia. Moreover, by responding to ideas from Latrobe, Jefferson set up even greater models than he could ever imagine. Latrobe gave Jefferson the idea of erecting monumental temple façades with porticos composed of giant orders. In turn, Jefferson gave those temple façades a beautiful, unique intimacy by bringing their pavements down to the ground. Shortly thereafter, the porticoes of giant orders, along with the fine masonry, the red brick walls, the stuccoed columns, and the light trim would make their way from the university to the Virginia courthouse.

Not until recently have scholars appreciated the degree to which Jefferson and his architectural reform program shaped Virginia courthouses.[36] Courthouses built after Jefferson's Virginia State Capitol and University of Virginia pavilions exemplify his success at employing classical forms, using permanent building materials, and creating structures worthy of emulation. Perhaps most Jeffersonian of all, in these post-Revolutionary courthouses American citizens, through elections and court days, exercised their republican rights and responsibilities.

During the colonial period, Virginia courthouses had evolved from buildings of perishable construction into an array of durable and recognizable public buildings. As a result, Virginia courthouses had acquired a range of plans and a tradition of solid construction. In his *Notes on the State of Virginia,* Jefferson's only criticism against courthouses was that, in their designs, "no attempts are made at elegance." The courthouses, in other words, lacked the orders as ornament.[37]

The courthouse design that Jefferson inherited and used as the basis for his reforms was a simple oblong or longitudinal hall with an apse at the bench and jury rooms in the gallery at the opposite end. This plan, referred to by architectural historians as the "Virginia basilica," constituted the perfect platform from which Jefferson could extend his campaign to elevate architecture as a source of enlightenment, a model of proper taste, and a tangible representation of democratic principles—light and liberty expressed in masonry form.

Four elements possessed major significance in Jefferson's plans: apse, porch, orders, and cupola. These same elements appeared in various forms throughout the American temple-revival period, an architectural movement in which Jefferson's designs assumed a leading role. The courthouse apse, of Roman basilica origins, embraced a curved bench where the magistrates sat. Even before Jefferson's involvement in courthouse architecture, the basilica plan had become the universal plan in Virginia. It can be seen, for example, at the general court in the first Capitol in Williamsburg (1701–5).[38] The second of the four elements, the porch, holds great importance for Virginia courthouses. No later than the 1730s arcaded "piazzas" across courthouse façades entered into popularity. These entry markers accentuated buildings and served as outdoor rooms offering shelter from the sun and rain. The third element is the orders, and in Jeffersonian designs the porch and orders went hand-in-hand. Jefferson, of course, accepted nothing less than the full temple porticos recommended by Palladio.[39] The fourth and final element, the cupola, related to the lantern; it held a bell used to alert the public. Cupolas and lanterns somewhat haphazardly marked buildings of civic importance as they were added in after-thought fashion to the roofs of a wide variety of public houses. Jefferson regarded the cupola as "most offensive"

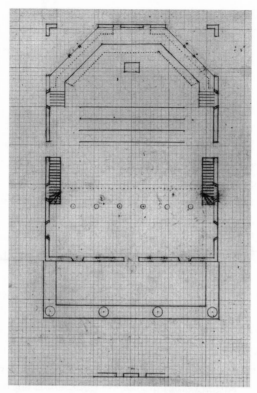

Marysville: Court House (plan), 1 page, 1821, by Thomas Jefferson. N23; K214; 29.3cm x 21.9cm (11⁹⁄₁₆″ x 8⅝″). (Courtesy of the Massachusetts Historical Society, Coolidge Collection of Thomas Jefferson Manuscripts)

and "one of the degeneracies of modern architecture." By rejecting bell cupolas as unclassical, Jefferson entangled himself in a design problem that he never solved. Instead, he left the problem of where to house the courthouse bell to the local builder and county officials.[40]

The most obvious evidence to consider when studying Jeffersonian courthouses is Jefferson's own generic model for a Virginia courthouse, a design most likely used as the plan for the Buckingham County Courthouse. This plan, which survives, served as the template for the designs of many Virginia courthouses during and after the first quarter of the nineteenth century. Jefferson's drawing, which he neither labeled nor dated, consists of a plan on a printed grid with some written specifications. It showed even the most inexperienced workman how to insert a blend of customary features from the

Virginia courthouse inside a container shaped along the lines of a temple with a tetrastyle portico.[41] For the four-column portico, Jefferson specified "the Order Tuscan," in Palladian tradition, with "columns of brick plaistered / caps and bases stone." This front area, while a temple portico, occupied the same space and served the same purposes as the eighteenth-century courthouse "piazza," or public "outdoor room."[42]

Inside the courtroom Jefferson preferred the oblong space entered endwise, running from under raised jury rooms to a Virginia basilican apse. A pair of staircases led to the gallery from the courtroom floor. These staircases, survivors of the old broadwise entries, started at lateral entrances and provided access to the gallery-level jury rooms. Jefferson, who did not render in detail the furnishings of the courtroom, nonetheless drew lines to denote the bar, an area restricted to participants in the trial such as counsel and clients. Jefferson also denoted placement of the bench, the sheriff, the clerk's desk, the jury, and the public.[43]

Just beyond the lines that probably indicated the bar, a polygonal apse enfolded the bench. Here, dotted lines signified a lower set of seats for the jury and an upper set of seats for the magistrates and other court officials, with the chief magistrate's chair placed at the apex of the apse. A similar arrangement of seating minus the apse can be seen in a painting entitled *Patrick Henry Arguing the Parson's Cause at Hanover Courthouse.* The painting, attributed to George Cooke and possibly painted in the 1830s (certainly later than the actual 1763 event), shows one of Henry's famous orations at the Hanover County Courthouse. The interior arrangement, which fails to match the architecture of the actual building, nonetheless suggests the generic elements of a traditional Virginia courtroom.[44]

Jefferson's specifications, which noted that "the windows embrac'g the judge's chair give light & air there," reaffirmed his comments in the *Notes on the State of Virginia* about the value of buildings that are "light and the airy." His treatment of the apse, which he presented as a continuation of the oblong body of the building, also served to promote natural light and ventilation. "To give light & air thro' the windows of the court," Jefferson tucked his three-sided apse within corners connected by arches. While Jefferson's apse-within-corners design never caught on, his architectural disciples incorporated into their works other major elements of his influential courthouse plan, including the importance of light within these temples dedicated to liberty and democracy.[45]

Patrick Henry Arguing the Parson's Cause at Hanover Courthouse by George Cooke (attrib.). (Virginia Historical Society [1965.2])

The success of Jefferson's campaign to reform architecture through the establishment of models is suggested by the connections between Jeffersonian courthouses constructed in Buckingham, Charlotte, Lunenburg, Mecklenburg, and Goochland counties. Henry Carrington, a commissioner for the new Charlotte Courthouse (1822–23), liked the Buckingham courthouse design so much that he acquired Jefferson's drawing. The Charlotte commissioners wished to execute Jefferson's Buckingham County design faithfully. As built, the interior followed Jefferson's plan to a very significant degree. The pediment's lunette, a feature of specifically Jeffersonian Palladianism, points directly to the University of Virginia's pavilions. Jefferson's reliance on the imitation of standing models paid rich rewards in Charlotte, producing, as at Buckingham, a courtroom approved by custom within a four-column temple casing of solid brick walls and the ornamentation of the orders.[46]

Just as Jefferson's courthouse plan inspired the Buckingham Courthouse, and just as the Buckingham design inspired builders in Charlotte County, the Charlotte Courthouse would spark imitation as well. In 1823 the Lunenburg Court directed that its new building "be built after the plan of the new courthouse in charlotte [*sic*] County." The commissioners employed two men who stood among Jefferson's most dedicated practitioners. The first, Dabney Cosby, was probably in charge at Buckingham, a position held after

Lunenburg Courthouse. (Courtesy of Janette Kreuzen Wright)

Jefferson had schooled him in design and brickwork during his employment as a workman at the University of Virginia. The other man, William A. Howard, was not associated directly with Jefferson but had contracted for the woodwork and made the drawings for Buckingham.[47]

Using the Charlotte Courthouse as a starting point, the two erected a Temple Revival building with a tetrastyle portico that is exceptional for its order. Instead of the Tuscan, which Jefferson had specified in his Buckingham design, Lunenburg uses the Doric order, illustrating that, within the Jeffersonian movement room existed for negotiation. Underscoring a key point of Jeffersonian architectural reform, a tetrastyle Doric portico marks the entrance. The ornamentation represented a slight modification of the Doric of Palladio, which is very distinctive and was Jefferson's favorite. He had preferred it for the exterior of Monticello and for the portico of the Pavilion I at the University of Virginia. Once again a lunette appears in the pediment via Jefferson's precedents at the university and Monticello. Inside, Cosby and Howard provided the standard courtroom, a gallery with side stairs, and an apse. The apse, curved and not encased within the corners of the building, mounted to the only significant interior departure from the Charlotte design until decades later, when the replacement of the gallery with a full second floor prompted the movement of the stairs. Nonetheless, the original configuration possessed all of the specifications of Jeffersonian design: a plan based on an existing model, masonry construction, and a standard courtroom within a temple-form exterior complete with the orders. The Lunenburg Courthouse even boasted a Jefferson-trained craftsman.[48] Jefferson's original "generic" courthouse plan inspired the Buckingham Courthouse. Its design enticed the Charlotte commissioners to build a similar courthouse, which the Lunenburg Commissioners then took as their example.

The third Goochland County Courthouse (1826–27), by Dabney Cosby and Valentine Parrish, stands next in line and marks one of the high points of Jeffersonian reform. It constitutes not only a clear continuation of the Buckingham plan, but also a more mature handling of Jefferson's original scheme. Its connection to Jefferson and the lineage of Jeffersonian court-houses is clear. Jefferson, of course, helped to train Cosby, and Valentine Parrish had most likely contracted with William A. Howard for the wood-work of the Buckingham County Courthouse. The Goochland specifications cite the Buckingham Courthouse's handling of jury rooms; originally, they even had a plan of the Buckingham Courthouse attached.[49]

The county commissioners erected a Temple Revival structure that, like the Jeffersonian courthouses preceding it, employed masonry construction and ornamental orders. A tetrastyle Tuscan portico fronts the Goochland building, while the interior embraces the standard Jeffersonian arrangement: apse (here a shallow one), columnar gallery with jury rooms, and paired side staircases. The gallery is designated as Tuscan in the specifications. Again the apse frames the bench, the semicircular jury box around which the bench wrapped, and a semicircular clerk's table.

The next county to follow suit was Mecklenburg, where Lunenburg's William A. Howard and his partner James T. Whitice constructed yet another Jeffersonian courthouse (1838–42). The essential elements remained in place: durable construction and a display of the orders with an interior arrange-ment that featured a longitudinal courtroom with a gallery at one end and an apse at the other.[50]

Howard and Whitice made some of the first major attempts at improving on Jefferson's original plan. To better serve proper flow to and from the gal-lery, they planned a stairway outside of the courtroom, placing it just inside the front vestibule. This gave easy access to and from the gallery and a di-rect path from the gallery to the portico without disrupting court proceed-ings. On the exterior, Howard was able to build an imposing hexastyle—or six-column—Ionic portico with wooden angle-volute capitals derived not

Mecklenburg Courthouse. (Courtesy of Janette Kreuzen Wright)

from Palladio's Ionic but from the Ionic of Palladio's successor Vincenzo Scamozzi. This handling of the orders, while always reminiscent of Jefferson's Virginia State Capitol, has seemed downright derivative of that building since the 1950s, when workers first applied a coat of white paint to the Mecklenburg Courthouse's exterior. Unlike the Virginia State Capitol, the designers of this courthouse never intended to cover its exterior brickwork in a white shell. The Mecklenburg Courthouse possessed a wholly different persona in its original red brick and white trim. Modeled not after Jefferson's Virginia Capitol, its inspiration came from a long succession of Jeffersonian courthouses that trace their lineage back to Jefferson's original design for a courthouse.[51]

The success of Jefferson's strategy—his provision of models of good architecture for others to emulate and further propagate—appears clear. Over and over, county commissioners erected new courthouses in accordance with examples set forth by Jefferson. They established a chain of models, one influencing the next. Their interpretations varied, but they never strayed from the core principles that Jefferson laid out in his *Notes on the State of Virginia:* the use of permanent materials and the orders as ornament.

Alongside the many examples of Jeffersonian courthouses stands an equally instructive counterexample, the Cumberland County Courthouse (1818–21). Lacking many of the characteristics of the previously discussed chain of models, it nonetheless falls within the larger family of Jeffersonian courthouses. Cumberland officials hired William A. Howard, the carpenter-builder of Buckingham, Lunenburg, and Mecklenburg Counties, to supervise the project. A single-level oblong rectangular structure, with a simple court-room and entrance located on the long side, the courthouse featured a four-column Tuscan portico. The portico struck the county officials as especially important, for the building contract specifically mandates that Howard execute "the external front of the building" in "the Tuscan order, according to Palladio." What a testimonial to the success of Jefferson's reformation. Not only did builders adhere to one of the most important of Jefferson's princi-ples, but so also did elected officials. How the county commissioners decided to adopt Palladio's Tuscan order may never be known, but surely it had some relation to Jefferson's establishment of architectural models and quite pos-sibly the specifications laid down in his generic courthouse plan first used in Buckingham County.[52]

Jefferson spent a lifetime reforming the architecture that surrounded him. In this endeavor he enjoyed great success. At the root of his reform lay the long-established practice of erecting buildings based on existing ones. He recog-nized that, in the absence of formal institutions to train Americans in the architectural arts, setting forth models for imitation remained the most prac-tical manner in which to educate the amateur builders and civic leaders of the new American nation. In part, he convinced Virginians to accept his archi-tectural reforms by conjoining vernacular custom with classical models. In part, he provided them with representations, rendered in bricks and mortar, of an enlightened republic governed by a liberty-loving people.

The principal themes of Jefferson's reform included the construction of buildings with permanent materials and the use of the orders, specifically those of Palladio, as the buildings' ornament. He clearly stated these prin-ciples in his book, *Notes on the State of Virginia.* As Jefferson embarked on his reformation, he established a number of architectural models, as well as museums of the orders. Look no further than Jefferson's own words to understand the foundation of his program of architectural reform. As he stated in 1785, "how is a taste in this beautiful art to be formed in our countrymen, unless we avail ourselves of every occasion when public build-ings are to be erected, of presenting . . . models for . . . study and imitation?"[53]

Notes

1. TJ, *Notes on the State of Virginia*, in *The Portable Thomas Jefferson*, ed. Merrill D. Peterson (New York, 1975), 203 (hereafter cited as *Notes*).

2. TJ to James Madison, 20 September 1785, *TJP*, 8:535.

3. TJ to Roger C. Weightman, 24 June 1826, *TJW*, 1517.

4. See *Notes*, 23–232. Jefferson's discussion of Virginia architecture is found in "Query XV: Colleges, Buildings, and Roads," 200–205.

5. TJ to James Madison, 20 September 1785, *TJP*, 8:534–37; TJ to Edmund Randolph, 20 September 1785, ibid., 537–39; TJ to James Buchanan and William Hay, 26 January 1786, ibid., 9:220–23. I would like to thank Charles Brownell for his discussions with me about the republican misinterpretation.

6. See Charles Brownell in Brownell, Calder Loth, William M. S. Rasmussen, and Richard Guy Wilson, *The Making of Virginia Architecture* (Richmond, 1992), 46–53. For Palladio's handling of the orders, which Jefferson had studied, see *The Architecture of A. Palladio; in Four Books*, trans. Nicholas Dubois and ed. Giacomo Leoni, 2nd ed. (London, 1721).

7. *Notes*, 202.

8. Ibid., 203.

9. Ibid. Jefferson's design for the Governor's Palace is drawing no. K98 (also numbered N425) in the Massachusetts Historical Society, Boston, Mass.

10. *Notes*, 203.

11. Ibid. See *The Architecture of A. Palladio*, especially Book I, for Palladio's treatment of the orders.

12. For a discussion of English architectural forms, see Brownell et al., *Making of Virginia Architecture*, 1–34.

13. *Notes*, 205.

14. I am indebted to Charles Brownell for helping me to work out the importance of new buildings imitating extant ones, especially Jefferson's reliance on this practice. For examples of the custom of new Virginia buildings being based on existing examples, see Carl R. Lounsbury, ed., *An Illustrated Glossary of Early Southern Architecture and Landscape* (New York, 1994), under "Model," and Lounsbury, *The Courthouses of Early Virginia: An Architectural History* (Charlottesville, Va., 2005), 181–83. See also Marcus Whiffen, "The Early County Courthouses of Virginia," *Journal of the Society of Architectural Historians* 18 (March 1959): 2–10.

15. TJ to John Page, 4 May 1786, *TJP*, 9:445. For the "Museum of the Orders" interpretation see Brownell et al., *Making of Virginia Architecture*, 49, 52, 210, 212, 220, and 248–52.

16. For the Museum of the Orders concept as it relates to the first house at Monticello, see Brownell, "Thomas Jefferson's Architectural Models and the United States Capitol," in *A Republic for the Ages: The United States Capitol and the Political Culture of the Early Republic*, ed. Donald R. Kennon (Charlottesville, Va., 1999), 331–37. This essay includes an annotated transcription of Jefferson's "Orders of the Rooms" from a problematic notebook apparently dating largely from the mid-1770s or after. See also Brownell et al., *Making of Virginia Architecture*, Survey No. 8 (Monticello, First House) and No. 7 (Monticello, Observation Tower).

17. Brownell et al., *Making of Virginia Architecture*, Survey No. 7 (Monticello, Observation Tower).

18. Jefferson's reference to Palladio's architectural treatise as "the Bible" appears in the report that Colonel Isaac A. Coles wrote to General John Hartwell Cocke on his conference with

Jefferson concerning architecture; see Coles to Cocke, 23 February 1816, Cocke Papers, No. 640 etc., Box 21, in the Albert and Shirley Small Special Collections Library, University of Virginia Library. The basic discussion of Leoni's editions of Palladio in Eileen Harris, assisted by Nicholas Savage, *British Architectural Books and Writers, 1556–1785* (Cambridge, Eng., 1990), 355–59, understates how profoundly Leoni altered Palladio's illustrations.

19. For the current state of study of the Virginia State Capitol, see Brownell, "Introduction to the 2002 Edition," in Fiske Kimball, *The Capitol of Virginia: A Landmark of American Architecture,* ed. Jon Kukla, with Martha C. Vick and Sarah Shields Driggs, revised and expanded edition, with a new introduction by Charles Brownell and an essay on the Capitol model by F. Carey Howlett (Richmond, 2002).

20. TJ to Madison and Randolph, 20 September 1785, *TJP,* 8:534–39.

21. See Justin Gunther, "Jefferson, Palladio, and the Capitol of Virginia," Graduate Seminar Report, James Branch Cabell Library, Special Collections, Virginia Commonwealth University, Richmond. For Latrobe's opinion of the Virginia Capitol stucco, see his letter to John Wickham, 16 March 1811, in *The Papers of Benjamin Henry Latrobe,* microfiche edition, ed. Thomas E. Jeffrey (Clifton, N.J., 1976), 84/E14, 3:42–44.

22. Jefferson's "Notes explicatives" (N271) are MS 9374 in the collections of the Huntington Library, San Marino, Calif. For details on the Museum of the Orders scheme, see Brownell, "Jefferson's Architectural Models," 338–41, and Brien J. Poffenberger, "Jefferson's Design of the Capitol of Virginia" (Master of Architectural History thesis, University of Virginia, 1991).

23. For Wenger's interpretation of Jefferson's use of the Williamsburg plan for Richmond, see Brownell, "Introduction to the 2002 Edition," in Fiske Kimball, *The Capitol of Virginia,* xxiii; Brownell, "Jefferson's Architectural Models," 322–23, n. 5.

24. The authority to establish Washington, D.C., and to build public buildings was provided by the Residence Act of 1790. For additional information on it and the committee charged with overseeing the Capitol's construction, see William C. Allen, *The Dome of the United States Capitol: An Architectural History* (Washington, D.C., 1992), 1–2; and Allen's *History of the United States Capitol: A Chronicle of Design, Construction, and Politics* (Washington, D.C., 2001), 3–49. For Washington's quote, see Allen, *The Dome,* 2.

25. No one has recounted the full story of Jefferson's unending involvement in the design and construction of the national Capitol, but see Brownell et al., *Making of Virginia Architecture,* 35–81; Brownell, "Jefferson's Architectural Models," 338–41; and Allen, *History of the United States Capitol,* 49–96. For Jefferson's work with the building commission, see Allen, *History of the United States Capitol,* 1–48. For Jefferson as president and his work with Latrobe on the Capitol, see Brownell et al., *Making of Virginia Architecture,* 35–81; Allen, *History of the United States Capitol,* 49–96; and Jeffrey A. Cohen and Charles Brownell, eds., *The Architectural Drawings of Benjamin Henry Latrobe,* 2 vols. (New Haven, Conn., 1994), 2:327–423, 577–636.

26. For Jefferson on cupolas and lanterns, see TJ to Latrobe, 22 April 1807, *Papers of Benjamin Henry Latrobe,* microfiche ed., 190/B5. Jefferson may well have owed some of his thinking about cupolas to Palladio's remarks on cupolas as a difference between temples and churches; see *The Architecture of A. Palladio,* Book 4, chap. 5, p. 53. For Thornton's plans, see Allen, *History of the United States Capitol,* 20–21. Also see C. M. Harris, ed., *Papers of William Thornton,* 1 vol. to date (Charlottesville, Va., 1995), vol. 1.

27. For Thornton's plans, see Allen, *History of the United States Capitol,* 20–21. See also Harris, ed., *Papers of William Thornton,* vol. 1.

28. See Brownell, "Jefferson's Architectural Models"; TJ to L'Enfant, 10 April 1791, *TJP,* 20:86; TJ to Washington, 10 April 1791, *TJP,* 20:87–88. Jefferson's 10 April 1791 letter to Wash-

ington also appears in *The Papers of George Washington, Presidential Series*, 15 vols. to date, ed. W. W. Abbot et al. (Charlottesville, Va., 1987–), 8:77–80, where it varies insignificantly in the transcription. The editors (p. 80, n. 6) agree that Jefferson's suggestion bore no fruit.

29. For some of the evidence regarding Jefferson's influence on the national Capitol, see Brownell, "Jefferson's Architectural Models."

30. For Jefferson's use of models at the University of Virginia and the training of builders, see Brownell et al., *Making of Virginia Architecture;* Brownell, "Jefferson's Architectural Models"; Richard Charles Cote, "The Architectural Workmen of Thomas Jefferson in Virginia," 2 vols. (Ph.D. diss., Boston University, 1986); K. Edward Lay, *The Architecture of Jefferson Country: Charlottesville and Albemarle County, Virginia* (Charlottesville, Va., 2000); and Richard Guy Wilson, *Thomas Jefferson's Academical Village: The Creation of an Architectural Masterpiece* (Charlottesville, Va., 1993).

31. Dabney Cosby's obituary appears in the *North Carolina Standard* (Raleigh), 12 July 1862, 3:1. See also Sara Moline, "Dabney Cosby (1779–1862), Early Nineteenth-Century Architectural Master," Graduate Seminar Report, Virginia Commonwealth University, Special Collections, 2002; and Lay, *Architecture of Jefferson Country*, 103–4, and Frank Edgar Grizzard Jr., "Documentary History of the Construction of the Buildings of the University of Virginia" (Ph.D. diss., University of Virginia, 1996), now available online as "Documentary History of the Construction of the Buildings of the University of Virginia, 1817–1828," http://etext.virginia.edu/jefferson/grizzard/ chaps. 3 and 7.

32. Bryan Clark Green, *In Jefferson's Shadow: The Architecture of Thomas R. Blackburn* (New York, 2006), augmenting Green's "In the Shadow of Thomas Jefferson: The Architectural Career of Thomas R. Blackburn, with a Catalog of Architectural Drawings," (Ph.D. diss., University of Virginia, 2004).

33. I am indebted to Charles Brownell who pointed out to me Jefferson's unfamiliarity with the practical applications of exterior stucco, his failures at the Virginia State Capitol, and his ultimate acceptance of exposed red brick against white trim at Monticello and the University of Virginia.

34. See Fiske Kimball, *Thomas Jefferson, Architect: Original Designs in the Collection of Thomas Jefferson Coolidge, Junior* (1916; repr., with an introduction by Frederick Doveton Nichols, New York, 1968); Brownell et al., *Making of Virginia Architecture*, 52–53, 68–71, Survey Nos. 26–28. For Jefferson's letter to Latrobe, see Latrobe, *Papers*, microfiche edition, 232/F3.

35. On the pedimental windows, see Heather A. Foster, "Jefferson, Wren, Philadelphia, and the Portico with Lunette," in *The Classical Tradition: From Andrea Palladio to John Russell Pope: New Findings from Virginia Commonwealth University, Abstracts of the Sixth Annual Architectural History Symposium, 1998*, ed. Charles Brownell (Richmond, 1998), 10–11.

36. The final result of the courthouse study is Brownell, with Craig A. Reynolds, Erika S. A. Moore, and the Members of Virginia Commonwealth University Graduate Seminar ARTH 789 (2003) "The World of Jefferson and Latrobe," "The Jeffersonian Courthouse in Virginia, 1810–1850: NHL Thematic Nomination Project" (Richmond, 2006), now available online, http://www.dhr.virginia.gov/registers/Counties/MultipleCounty/JEFFERSONIAN_COURTHOUSE _IN_VIRGIN IA_MPS_2006_NHL.pdf.

37. See Carl R. Lounsbury, *The Courthouses of Early Virginia: An Architectural History*, Colonial Williamsburg Studies in Chesapeake History and Culture (Charlottesville, Va., 2005), and John O. Peters and Margaret T. Peters, *Virginia's Historic Courthouses* (Charlottesville, Va., 1995), chaps. 1–2.

38. In three places on p. 139, Lounsbury, *Courthouses*, discusses the curved bench, a deriva-

tive from the Roman basilican plan, as a standard late seventeenth-century feature of English courtrooms; cp. figs. 40–41 and p. 140.

39. For the arcaded porch, or piazza, see Lounsbury, *Courthouses,* 42–45, and 100–117.

40. For Jefferson's quote on cupolas and lanterns, see his letter to Latrobe of 22 April 1807, Latrobe, *Papers,* microfiche ed., 190/B5.

41. While publishing the Coolidge collection of Jefferson's architectural drawings in 1916, Fiske Kimball introduced the pages and catalogued them as 214–215. The front of the pair (K214) bears Jefferson's only plan for a courthouse, drawn on a printed grid; the back (K215) has Jefferson's specifications for the design, written on plain paper. Both sheets contain evident second thoughts, are unfinished, offer no functional analysis, and exemplify how maddeningly unclear Jefferson's self-taught conventions for drawing can be. Frederick Doveton Nichols renumbered K214-K215 as 23–24 (that is, N23-N24, as usually cited). See his *Thomas Jefferson's Architectural Drawings, with Commentary and a Check List,* 5th ed. (Charlottesville, Va., 1984). The Massachusetts Historical Society numbers K214-K215 as 227. The basic scholarship on K214-K215 is Kimball, *Thomas Jefferson, Architect: Original Designs in the Collection of Thomas Jefferson Coolidge, Junior;* Delos Hughes, "The Charlotte County Courthouse: Attribution and Misattribution in Jefferson Studies," *Arris* 4 (1993): 8–18; and Bryan Clark Green, "Thomas Jefferson's Design for the Buckingham County Courthouse," Graduate Research Report, ARTH 700 (Brownell), University of Virginia, 1989.

42. Quoted from Jefferson's courthouse specifications; see K214–K215.

43. I am grateful to John O. Peters and Charles Brownell for helping me to understand the functional needs of a courtroom. See also Lounsbury, *Courthouses,* 128–67.

44. For "Patrick Henry Arguing the Parson's Cause," see Virginius Cornick Hall Jr., comp., *Portraits in the Collection of the Virginia Historical Society: A Catalogue* (Charlottesville, Va., 1981), 114–15. See also Lounsbury, *Courthouses,* 151–59.

45. See K214-K215. Again, I am grateful to Charles Brownell for his shared interpretation of the Virginia basilica. See also Lounsbury, *Courthouses,* 138–51.

46. See William H. Cabell to Jefferson, 28 December 1821, Thomas Jefferson Papers, Coolidge Collection, Massachusetts Historical Society, Boston. See also Hughes, "Charlotte County Courthouse," and Hughes, "Courthouses of Buckingham County: Jefferson and Beyond," *Arris* 15 (2004): 1–25.

47. Quoted from County of Lunenburg, Order Book 24, p. 408 (10 November 1823). See also Craig A. Reynolds, "William A. Howard, Dabney Cosby, and the Jeffersonian Palladian Courthouse," paper for the conference "Classics and Exotics: New Findings from Virginia Commonwealth University," Eleventh Annual Symposium in Architectural History and the Decorative Arts, Virginia Commonwealth University/Virginia Historical Society/Center for Palladian Studies in America/and other cosponsors, November 2003, VCU Special Collections; and Reynolds, "William A. Howard, Southside Virginia Carpenter and Jeffersonian Builder (ca. 1787–1854/1860)," Graduate Student Report, ARTH 789 (Brownell), Virginia Commonwealth University, 2003, VCU Special Collections; Lounsbury, *Courthouses,* 365–66; and Commonwealth of Virginia, Virginia Landmarks Registry, File No. 55–14 and File No. 55–105 (Lunenburg County Courthouse).

48. See Reynolds, "William A. Howard, Dabney Cosby, and the Courthouse," and Reynolds, "William A. Howard."

49. Lounsbury, *Courthouses,* 319–20, and Muriel B. Rogers, "John Hartwell Cocke (1780–1866) and Philip St. George Cocke (1809–1861): From Jeffersonian Palladianism to Romantic Colonial Revivalism in Antebellum Virginia" (Ph.D. diss., Virginia Commonwealth Univer-

sity, 2003), 77–86 and Appendix B, 343–48, which includes a reproduction of the Goochland specifications.

50. On the Mecklenburg County Courthouse, see Reynolds, "William A. Howard, Dabney Cosby, and the Courthouse"; Reynolds, "William A. Howard"; and Virginia Landmarks Register, File No. 173–06 (Mecklenburg County Courthouse); and Lounsbury, *Courthouses,* 366.

51. See Reynolds, "William A. Howard, Dabney Cosby, and the Courthouse"; Reynolds, "William A. Howard"; and Virginia Landmarks Register, File No. 173–06. Of specific relevance is a photocopy of the lost plan, unidentified as to source, which is located in Virginia Landmarks Register File No. 173–06. According to Charles Brownell, the combination of the Scamozzi Ionic capital and Palladio's Ionic cornice probably originated with Inigo Jones.

52. Quoted from the contract between Cumberland County Commissioners and William A. Howard, 23 November 1818, which is located in a display case at the Cumberland County Clerk's Office, Cumberland, Va. See also Reynolds, "William A. Howard, Dabney Cosby, and the Courthouse," and Reynolds, "William A. Howard."

53. TJ to Madison, 20 September 1785, *TJP,* 8:535.

Recording History

The Thomas Sully Portrait of Thomas Jefferson

GAYE WILSON

I N EARLY FEBRUARY 1821 THOMAS JEFFERSON RECEIVED A LETTER POSTED
from the United States Military Academy at West Point. The letter, penned
by mathematics professor Jared Mansfield, was written on behalf of the
academy's officers, cadets, and faculty and requested that Jefferson pose for a
portrait that would be displayed in the academic library. His image would
hang beside that of the "great" Washington and that of Colonel Jonathan
Williams, the school's first superintendent, and would serve posterity as an
"appropriate memorial of your person." Feeling confident of Jefferson's consent, they had commissioned Thomas Sully, one of America's leading portrait
artists. The letter noted the former president's services to the nation and his
patronage of the academy, which he signed into law on March 16, 1802.
Professor Mansfield concluded by suggesting that he supply dates on which it
would be convenient for Mr. Sully to call upon him at his Virginia home.[1]

When Jefferson read this letter he must have realized the potential such a
portrait offered as a lasting visual contribution to his legacy. Not only would
it be executed by an accomplished artist, it would hang in the academy's
library and so be available to visiting public as well as West Point cadets and
faculty. He demurred only slightly by responding that Sully's fine pencil
would be "illy bestowed on an ottamy of 78" but then suggested convenient
dates for the artist's visit. The following month Sully spent over a week at

Monticello taking a bust portrait from life and making studies for the full-length that would be installed at West Point the next year.[2]

The request from West Point came at a time when the aging Jefferson felt anxious about the future of the American republic, the great "experiment" in which he had invested so much of his life. In the previous year he had become extremely agitated by the Missouri question, as he received accounts of the highly charged congressional debates that surrounded Missouri's petition to enter the union as a slave state. For Jefferson this became a "fire bell in the night" that roused him in his retirement at Monticello. In the geographical lines being drawn between the slave and nonslave holding states, he saw what could become the death knell of the Union and caused him to question whether a state should not have the right to enter the nation on a parity with the existing states without federal restrictions. The alarm had been "hushed" by a tenuous compromise, but Jefferson feared this was only a temporary reprieve. Were the sacrifices of "the generation of 1776" to be thrown away by "the unwise and unworthy passions of their sons"?[3]

Jefferson's fears for the future of the republic connected directly with his insistence that its history be correctly remembered and recorded. He believed that a true understanding of the events of the Revolution and the principles on which the American republic was founded would influence the future direction of the nation and ultimately the destiny of representative government throughout the world. It was important that subsequent generations fully comprehend the character of the founders, their motives, their actions, and their concept of republican virtue. The future was irrevocably linked to the past; a correct understanding of history was, therefore, imperative.[4]

Jefferson's fears had been aroused by contemporary histories that cast doubts upon his own role in the American Revolution and early formation of the nation. The first edition of John Marshall's five-volume *The Life of George Washington* had been completed in 1807. This work extended beyond just a biography of Washington and outlined American history from colonial settlement through the Revolution and the founding of the republic. The final volume dealt with the rise of the partisan politics of the 1790s and unfavorably compared Jefferson and his political allies, the Jeffersonian Republicans, with the Federalists and their initial leader, Alexander Hamilton. Jefferson's perceived pro-French sympathies were questioned as well. Equally unsettling was an 1812 publication by fellow Virginian Henry Lee III. In his *Memoirs of the War in the Southern Department,* Lee criticized Jefferson as an incompetent wartime governor who reacted with cowardice during the British invasion of Virginia.[5]

To Jefferson these histories were dangerous, not just to his own reputation but also to American republicanism in general. Their retelling of early American history gave a more favorable impression of those who supported the Federalists and their ambitions for a more powerful, more centralized government. Even though the Federalists had been in decline since his election to the presidency in 1801, Jefferson continued to fear his old enemies' monarchial leanings and the influence of their ideas on future generations of Americans.

Early in his political career Jefferson had stated that "the first object of my heart is my own country. In that is embarked my family, my fortune, & my own existence." Now, in January 1821, at seventy-eight years of age, he not only faced ever-increasing debts that could leave his family destitute but also felt ever-increasing anxiety that the experiment in representative government to which he had devoted so much of his life was headed toward irrevocable scission. Succeeding generations would need to understand the character and the aims of the founders and their concept of republican virtue. Thus the West Point commission arrived at a time when Jefferson's thoughts revolved around preserving his own legacy in order to exemplify the virtue and character that could strengthen the republic. As a gentleman he could not be seen promoting his own reputation without compromising the selflessness on which it was based. He could, however, support the efforts of a talented artist and collaborate on a portrait that could potentially capture for posterity a sense of character that suggested civic virtue and an enlightened worldview, a character befitting a founder of the new republican nation. He could justify this portrait as not just a contribution to his own legacy but as a record of early American history as well.[6]

Jefferson understood the power of art to capture history and to educate the populace. "I am an enthusiast on the subject of the arts," he informed his good friend and colleague, James Madison, in no small part because art possessed the potential "to improve the taste of my countrymen, to increase their reputation, to reconcile to them the respect of the world & procure them its praise." For Jefferson there was a purpose to art beyond just enjoyment of the art itself. It could be a means of informing and cultivating the public taste, perhaps eventually removing the stigma of provincialism in the view of Europe.[7]

Over his lifetime Jefferson collected art in its many forms, including an impressive number of portraits, both painted and sculpted. The subjects of these portraits were men who had in some way contributed to the culture and formation of the United States, whether through politics, philosophy, or exploration. He described his "Collection of American Worthies" as "public records" worthy of study, duplication, and preservation.[8]

He was following a long tradition, as portraits had been used in western art and culture for several centuries as a testament to those who were notable in history. Since classical times, sculpted or painted works of art aimed to instruct or inspire the viewer. During the seventeenth and eighteenth centuries, Europe's pantheons of worthies began to expand beyond the traditional portraits of aristocratic rulers and military leaders to include those who had made intellectual or moral contributions to society. With the Revolution, American collections of worthies began to appear that honored the idea of a natural aristocracy of virtuous and capable leaders of the new United States. Their purpose was not only to praise specific individuals but also to inspire virtue within contemporary society.[9]

As he prepared to join Benjamin Franklin and John Adams in Paris in 1784, Jefferson began his own collection of "Worthies" with a hurriedly commissioned portrait of George Washington by the American artist Joseph Wright. Once in Europe, he quickly began to add images of other notable Americans such as Franklin, Adams, and John Paul Jones. His own portrait, taken by young American artist Mather Brown during a trip to London in 1786, may have joined the growing collection at his Paris residence, the Hôtel de Langeac. While in France, he continued to expand the parameter of his collection with both painted and sculptured portraits of Europeans favorable to the American cause, such as the French nobles Turgot and Lafayette. From the Uffizi in Florence he requested copies of explorers who had first opened the New World: Columbus, Americus Vespucius, Cortez, and Magellan, and then added the noted English explorer Sir Walter Raleigh. When he commissioned copies of the portraits of Francis Bacon, Isaac Newton, and John Locke that hung in the Royal Society in London, he reasoned that "I consider them the three greatest men who had ever lived, without any exception." Jefferson's collection was semiprivate, available first to those who had business at the American ministry in Paris, and then after his return to the United States to those who might be invited to his residences at the seats of the government in New York, Philadelphia, and Washington. After his retirement, his collection was on display at Monticello.[10]

The West Point portrait, however, was intended for a public space, the library at the academy. As far back as the fifteenth century, European libraries had been selected to display portraits of notables, especially writers and scholars. The intended placement of the West Point commission should have pleased Jefferson, as a library would be an appropriate location for a portrait of a statesman-scholar and principal author of the Declaration of Independence. It was significant that it was to hang alongside the portrait of George Washington, already the most identifiable of the founders and described in Jared Mansfield's letter as "the great Washington" and the "Founder of the Republic."[11]

Jefferson had not met Sully personally prior to the artist's visit to Monticello in March 1821, but certainly Jefferson knew of his reputation as one of the country's leading portrait artists and proponents of the fine arts in the United States. In a May 1811 letter, Benjamin Henry Latrobe, a Philadelphia and Washington architect who had worked with Jefferson on the Capitol and the President's House, gave the retired president an assessment of the current art scene and noted that "a Young artist, Tho[mas] Sully, is certainly the first on the list of our portrait painters."[12]

Shortly after Latrobe's report, Sully and Jefferson had a brief, formal correspondence when Jefferson was elected an honorary member of the newly formed Society of Artists of the United States and Sully was acting as secretary of the organization. Jefferson must have agreed with the stated purpose of this new organization, as it echoed closely what he had written to Madison many years before. Sully's letter proposed that the society would have "a tendency to form a correct taste in this Country" and that, "by calling into Action Native genius, many prejudices will be removed with respect to foreign productions." Sully began his letter stating "your love for the arts and sciences, and your long & unremitted exertions to promote the Independence & prosperity of our Country are known to the world."[13]

Needless to say, Jefferson's response was positive. He had just sent his letter of thanks for the offer of honorary membership, which expressed his good wishes for the society, when he received a second letter from Sully announcing that he had been elected president of the organization. Sully's letter was candid in the hope that the infant society might benefit from its association with Jefferson's name. Jefferson graciously declined the appointment, expressing "uneasiness of unmerited distinction." However, as the society included architecture along with painting, sculpture, and engraving, Jefferson's inclusion was not totally "unmerited" even though it would be several years before his finest public buildings for the University of Virginia would be realized.[14]

Sully had some knowledge of Jefferson's architectural work; in his "Recollections of an Old Painter," he wrote of visiting the Virginia Capitol building in Richmond. He had admired Jefferson's model, on view in the Capitol's library, but found many faults in the execution of the building itself. Even so, he maintained that "Mr. Jefferson was a very good judge of architecture." Jefferson was aware of the shortcomings of the Capitol and that the plan he had sent from Paris in 1786 had been executed "with some variations, not for the better."[15]

Perhaps this contributed to his eagerness to have the artist view his latest architectural designs for the University of Virginia, at that time under construction in the neighboring village of Charlottesville. Jefferson made arrangements for Sully to tour the building site but did not accompany him due to the unusually cold weather and instead sent a note stating, "The bearer Mr. Sully, a celebrated Portrait painter of Philadelphia calls to see the University, and as he is a judge, and will be questioned about it on his return, I will request you to shew it to him advantageously."[16]

Conversations about architecture must have ensued. Upon Sully's return to Baltimore, where he was maintaining a studio at the time, he apologized for his inability to locate a copy of a book he had promised to send his host, a French architectural work by J. N. L. Durand titled "Recueil et parallèle des édifices de tout genre, anciens et modernes." Jefferson assured Sully not to worry; he would add this title to a book order that he was preparing to send to Paris. He must have approved of Sully's recommendation, for he included Durand's study in his list of books for the library at the University of Virginia.[17]

Jefferson may have had some idea of the merits of Sully's abilities as a portrait artist other than Latrobe's recommendation. Sully had painted a small, full-length portrait of James Madison in 1809, during his first year as president, specifically for reproduction by engraver David Edwin. Though Jefferson would not have the advantage of seeing Sully's original, as the intent of this commission was a print of the new president intended for public sale, it is possible he could have seen one of the resulting prints. James and Dolley Madison visited Monticello regularly, and if they did not have a print in-hand, some mention might have been made of Madison's experience with the well-known artist. For sure, Jefferson had another reassurance of Sully's merits prior to his arrival at Monticello from good friend, John Vaughn. He had "learnt with pleasure that the Establishment of West Point is to possess a full length portrait of yourself executed by Mr. Sully . . . I am gratified that it has fallen to Mr. Sullys lot to be the artist employed and beg leave to recommend him."[18]

Given their mutual interest in the arts in America as well as their respect for each other's work, it is not unreasonable to speculate that artist and subject worked closely in creating the portrait for West Point. The reputation of each would be invested in the portrait's success. It was up to Sully to capture a truthful likeness that suggested an elevated character. Jefferson could make recommendations as the artist considered the appropriate pose, the choice of props and clothing, and the background that would surround the figure. All elements working together should reflect Jefferson's role as a founder of both the nation and the military academy.

In the final painting, Sully's "Jefferson" stands erect, confident, and with an air of composure. In the pose of the figure, the portrait adheres to some elements of the traditional grand manner style with the head turned to the right and the gaze directed into the distance and away from the viewer; the stance adheres to the requirement that the weight of the body rest on the right foot with the left foot slightly advanced. But rather than portray the right hand extended in the usual oratorical gesture or as an alternative, resting in the waistcoat, Sully leaves the arms at the sides with a document in the left hand. This rolled piece of paper serves as the only prop within the painting. As such it becomes notable, especially with Sully's subtle placement of light along the leading edge of the paper. A close examination of the document gives no clue as to its identity. The absence of visible writing leaves open the possibility that it could represent the bill signed by Jefferson in 1802 creating the military academy.[19]

The positioning of Jefferson between two columns with the arms relaxed alongside the body gives a very linear aspect to the figure that is enhanced by the long, unbroken line of the handsome fur-lined greatcoat. Such a coat with fur lining was often referred to as a "pelisse." The coat could be presumed to have come from Jefferson's wardrobe or at least to have been a part

Thomas Jefferson by Thomas Sully, 1822, oil on canvas, 102¼″ x 66″. (West Point Museum Art Collection, United States Military Academy, West Point, New York)

of the original study, as Sully preferred to sketch in drapery at the first sitting and advised beginning painters that "if it is a large picture where more of the person is seen, the drapery must be painted from an exact study made from the person." Possibly this garment was encouraged by Sully as it adds compositionally and makes the figure far more substantial than it would have appeared otherwise.[20]

Aside from its artistic contributions, there is a tradition attached to the coat that could imply its choice came from reasons of provenance as well. There has been some thought that this must be the coat presented to Jefferson by Thaddeus Kosciuszko, the Polish patriot and American Revolutionary War hero. Considering the commission, a link with Kosciuszko would be appropriate. After he joined the American cause in 1776, Kosciuszko served in the Continental Army as a military engineer and was responsible for the enhanced fortification of West Point, important to the defense of the Hudson River. His name remained a part of West Point tradition.

A friendship developed between Kosciuszko and Jefferson upon Kosciuszko's return to the United States in 1797 following his liberation from a Russian prison where he had been incarcerated since his failed attempt at the liberation of his native Poland. His stay was brief. When he returned to Europe in the spring of 1798, he gave Jefferson his power of attorney to manage his business affairs, and as a parting gift he requested, "Give me leave to present you a Fur." His note did not specify the type of fur or whether it was a pelt or a garment, but over the years Jefferson, family members, and friends mentioned a "pelisse" or "cloak," and some references connected this garment to General Kosciuszko.[21]

The term "pelisse" was used throughout the eighteenth and into the nineteenth century to identify an outer garment that could be cut as a coat or simply as a cloak, worn by either men or women, with a fur lining usually the distinguishing characteristic. This was especially true for a man's pelisse, and the term often appeared in reference to European military uniforms.

Jefferson first mentioned his pelisse in December 1798, several months after Kosciuszko's departure from the United States. He reported to his daughter Martha that the weather was extremely cold on his return to Philadelphia from Monticello, yet he assured her that he stayed as comfortable as if he had been in a "warm bed"—"thanks to my pelisse." Years later, well into his retirement, he made another reference to his pelisse. He had suffered from the cold on the three-day trip from Monticello to his retreat home, Poplar Forest, in southern Virginia. He requested that Martha send "my wolf-skin pelisse and fur-boots." She would find the items in the closet over his bed, and he was specific as to how the items should be packed. "The pelisse had better be sowed up in a striped blanket to keep it clean and uninjured," he suggested, but it would suffice to package "the boots in any course wrapper." Jefferson obviously regarded the wolf-skin pelisse as valuable.[22]

The following year he loaned his fur to his grandchildren, Ellen and Jeff, as well as Jeff's wife, Jane, for a trip to Richmond. Ellen informed her mother that "we found Grand Papa's fur delightful. I do not know what we should have done without it, for we were out until past eight Wednesday evening,

and off again an hour before day the next morning." If the three had benefited from the fur, then it is probable that this pelisse was in the form of a
cloak rather than cut as a coat.[23]

It was an anecdote written by a family friend that defined Jefferson's fur as
a "cloak" and linked it to Kosciuszko. "The Fur Cloak, A Reminesence,"
written by Margaret Bayard Smith, began on a winter evening in 1805 when
she was a dinner guest at the President's House in Washington. Following
dinner, she began to feel ill with chills and a fever. Smith, whose husband,
Samuel Harrison Smith, edited the Jeffersonian Republican *National Intelligencer*, described how Jefferson wrapped her in his fur cloak as protection
from the winter air. On her way home she reflected on the legend she knew
attached to this cloak and thought, "Strange! . . . that I, an obscure individual
in America, should be wrapped in the same mantle that once enveloped the
Czar of Russia—that was afterwards long worn by the Palust Hero, of Poland,
and now belongs to one of the greatest men alive!" As a young woman, she
had met Kosciuszko and had listened to his account of his release from a Russian prison. Czar Paul had taken off his own cloak and impulsively wrapped it
around Kosciuszko as he left his cell. Her "Reminesence" concluded with
Kosciuszko's final departure from the United States when "Kosciuszko, left
his cloak, with his revered friend Jefferson."[24]

This still does not establish that the fur Jefferson referred to as "my wolf
skin pelisse" was the cloak that Smith described as descending from Czar Paul
I to Kosciuszko and then to Jefferson. But the cloak that she viewed with such
awe came into her care again after Jefferson's death. In January 1837, as his
grandchildren took an inventory of furniture items, probably in relation to
their mother's death the previous October, it was mentioned that "Mary says
Kosciusko's wolf skin pelisse is at Mrs. H[arrison] Smith's who suggested it
would be well to give it to some society which she named (but Mary had
forgotten). She thought they would go to the expense of having a glass case
made for it to preserve it from the moths." Was this idea carried forward? At
this point it is not known what happened to the Kosciuszko-Jefferson wolf
skin pelisse, but obviously friends and family members believed it possessed
enough historical importance to merit preservation.[25]

Since the evidence points toward the conclusion that the fur presented to
Jefferson by Kosciuszko upon his departure was wolf-skin and shaped into a
cloak, it is obviously not the coat worn by Jefferson in Sully's portrait. More
likely this Kosciuszko fur is the one in which Jefferson wrapped himself for

the 1805 presidential portrait by Rembrandt Peale. Yet there exists one other possible connection between Kosciuszko and the coat that Jefferson wore for the portrait commissioned by West Point.

After he sailed from America another of Kosciuszko's furs came into Jefferson's possession. Jefferson inventoried the items that Kosciuszko had left behind when he returned to Europe. He listed among them "a pelisse of fine fur." Due to its value, he decided to store it at his own apartments rather than placing it in the warehouse with the remainder of his friend's property. Jefferson reported to Kosciuszko that "your fur was valued by an honest furrier here at 25 Doll. according to the price of Martins [*sic*] here." The marten, the North American equivalent of the Russian sable, was considered a very fine fur, and thus Jefferson thought that the pelisse should be sold privately rather than at auction. No additional information about this marten-skin pelisse appears in the known Kosciuszko-Jefferson correspondence.[26]

Many years later, in May 1907, one of Jefferson's great-granddaughters was making a written inventory of "Monticello relics" that had remained within the family. Among these was listed "the splendid 'Golden Sables' over coat, very large & long, which 'Kosiosko' [*sic*] wore during his 'Russian Campaign', this garment was cut up into *Muffs & Tippets*."[27]

Did the fine pelisse left behind by Kosciuszko remain with Jefferson, and if so, was this the coat selected for Sully's portrait? Certainly Sully's rendering implies a fur such as marten or sable, and as the commission came from West Point, it could have brought up recollections of Kosciuszko's fortification of that Hudson River stronghold during the War for American Independence. Jefferson was revisiting that time in American history and his own history as well; he had begun the writing of his autobiography two months prior to Sully's March visit to Monticello. This review of the past together with the anxieties provoked by the Missouri Crisis and the Republic's future could have generated thoughts of the Poland that Kosciuszko had defended. On the eve of another crisis, the War of 1812, Jefferson contemplated the hard lesson that Poland provided: "a lesson which all our countrymen should study; the example of a country erased from the map of the world by the dissensions of its own citizens."[28]

A garment with a Kosciuszko connection would seem a logical choice for the West Point commission. Yet Sully did not choose the cloak that can be given a convincing provenance as the parting gift to Jefferson, perhaps because it had been used earlier by artist Rembrandt Peale. If another Kos-

ciuszko garment remained in Jefferson's closet, certainly it could have cap-
tured the artist's attention. In his *Register of Portraits* Sully does not elaborate
upon any of his paintings of Jefferson that came from the initial study taken
at Monticello but simply lists them with dates and the amounts paid for each.
Some mystery still surrounds the elegant fur-lined topcoat but the family
tradition referenced by a great-granddaughter makes a possible connection
between Jefferson, Kosciuszko, and the West Point portrait.[29]

The other garments and accessories selected for the portrait reflect Jefferson's years as president. Beneath the topcoat Jefferson wears a three-piece
black suit that Sully's skillful rendering implies to be velvet. There are references to Jefferson in a black suit during his presidency. After attending a
dinner at the Executive Mansion, Federalist Senator William Plummer noted
in his journal that his host had worn "a new suit of black—silk hose—shoes—
clean linen and his hair highly powdered." On the day of Jefferson's second
inauguration another observer described him "in high spirits, dressed in
black and even in black silk stockings."[30]

Jefferson was not unique in his preference for black, which by the beginning of the nineteenth century was becoming a frequent choice in a gentleman's wardrobe. Black had represented modesty, stability, and sobriety in
western clothing for hundreds of years. It had moved from medieval clergy
and Renaissance scholars to the professional and commercial classes. Before
Jefferson left Paris in the fall of 1789, he would have seen the black suit at the
center of the crisis that would evolve into revolution.[31]

On May 5, 1789, he attended the opening of the assembly of the Estates
General at Versailles and continued to go frequently to hear the debates.
There he could have observed the clothing prescribed by the Grand-Master
of Ceremonies, the Marquis de Brezé, for the delegates representing the three
estates: the First Estate, the clergy, was to wear ecclesiastical dress appropriate
to their position in the church; the Second Estate, the aristocracy, was expected to appear in black silk suits with lavish gold trim, white stockings, lace
jabots, hats with plumes and dress swords; the Third Estate, one-half the
delegates representing the middle to lower classes, was instructed to wear
simple suits of black wool, black stockings, plain muslin cravats, and untrimmed hats. As they were not representing members of the aristocracy,
they were not to carry a gentleman's dress sword. Through these dictates of
attire, the plain, untrimmed black suit came to signal an empathy with the

Third Estate, the deputies of the people, and for a short while, became an emblem of political position.[32]

Outside the dramatic events in Paris, the popularity of the black suit steadily advanced during the final quarter of the eighteenth century. Black clothing for men served as the great leveler. Associated with democracy, first in France during its revolution but then even more pervasively in nineteenth-century America, black came to signify simplification and uniformity in men's dress. It gained such currency that some lamented the passing of more colorful and individualistic attire and derided the continual appearance of men in their "black uniforms."[33]

Black would remain the color of choice among well-dressed men, both in Europe and the United States, even though the cut of the suit would change. In Sully's portrait Jefferson wears a suit coat with long sloping sides over a waistcoat cut in a wide "V." This paired with knee-breeches definitely ties the suit to the beginning of the century and a style fashionable during Jefferson's presidency. As comparison, the more fashionable cut for the 1820s is well illustrated in another of Sully's portraits, that of Revolutionary War hero the Marquis de Lafayette, taken just four years after that of Jefferson. During Lafayette's celebratory return visit to the United States in 1824–25, a committee from Philadelphia commissioned a portrait of the Marquis to be presented to the city. Sully details Lafayette's fashionable suit coat with its high rolled collar joining the "M-Notch" lapel and the higher, rounded waist of the coat revealing a small portion of the horizontal line of the waistcoat. Knee breeches have been replaced with ankle-length pantaloons. Obviously the clothing choices for Jefferson's portrait were intended to place him in an earlier time. His suit, even though in the prevailing black, is recognizable as a style fashionable during his presidential years.

The shoes that Jefferson wears in the portrait identify him with his presidential years as well. A number of contemporaries noted that rather than displaying elegant buckles, Jefferson wore shoes that laced. Often infused with a tone of sarcasm when made by a member of the political opposition, one Federalist remarked that Jefferson's shoes "closed tight round his ankles, laced up with neat leather strings and absolutely without buckles." For this viewer Jefferson's footwear made the statement that buckles were "superfluous and anti-republican especially when he has strings." Another Federalist attributed this style preference to Jefferson's deliberate attempt at

Gaye Wilson

The Marquis de Lafayette by Thomas Sully. (Independence National Historical Park)

"singularity." A brief editorial in the *New York Commercial Advertiser* in 1802 claimed that "in every age of the world, rulers and philosophers have made themselves remarkable for the affectation of some singularity." The writer also speculated that "our philosophic president chooses to have his singularities as well as European kings—He prefers shoestrings, when other folks wear buckles."[34]

Jefferson may have bristled at being compared to a European king, especially since shoes laced with strings were considered by many as another sign of republican leveling and became popular especially during the French Revolution. In his *Memoirs* Sir William Wraxall reflected that dress totally "fell" in the "era of Jacobinism and equality in 1793 and 1794." In Wraxall's eyes "it was then that pantaloons, cropped hair, and shoe-strings, as well as the total abolition of buckles and ruffles, together with the disuse of hair-powder, characterized the men."[35]

Apparently Jefferson continued to wear laced, ankle-high boots whether due to ideological leanings, practicality, or simply comfort. When Congressman Daniel Webster visited Monticello in 1824, he described Jefferson as wearing "shoes of the kind that bear his name." Although they may have remained his favored footwear, in Sully's portrait the shoes recall a fashion that distinguished him as president.[36]

In the final portrait Sully creates a setting for the figure that reflects western portrait traditions and yet is unique. Through his skilled use of light he guides the eye across the space within the painting and creates an impression that Jefferson has just stepped before his audience, the viewer. The face is illuminated as though by a spotlight, and the slight dash of red provided by the collar of Jefferson's under-waistcoat draws further focus to the face. Sully followed his own advice offered in his *Hints to Young Painters and the Process of Portrait Painting* that "in a portrait every part may be exactly rendered, but should be kept subordinate in regard to the face."[37]

The setting of the figure, just like the pose, also borrows some elements of the grand manner style. Jefferson is flanked by impressive columns and backed by a swag of red drapery, but to this tradition that is often found in European state portraits, Sully added detail that makes the space specific to the United States. From the face the lighting guides the eye downward, tipping the rolled document in Jefferson's hand but then strongly illuminating the lower shaft of the column to the right in the painting. The lower shaft and base of the column catch almost as much light as the face and become a secondary area of focus. Sully's careful rendering of the base's carved water leaf design and his painterly indication that the shaft is breccia marble identify the column as belonging in the Hall of the House of Representatives (known, after 1857, as National Statuary Hall). When Capitol architect Benjamin Henry Latrobe rebuilt the House chamber after the Capitol was burned during the War of 1812, he replaced the sandstone columns with the breccia marble and added the unique water leaf pattern to the base. William Allen, architectural historian for the Washington Capitol has explained that the unpredictable nature of breccia marble made it problematic to attempt a cincture at the bottom of the shaft. To compensate for the lack of a cincture, Latrobe devised the water leaf design, resulting in the unique and

Thomas Jefferson by Thomas Sully. (Yale University Art Gallery, Leila A. and John Hill Morgan, B.A. 1893, LL.B. 1896, M.A. [Hon.] 1929, Collection)

identifiable base. He created a very grand room, the pride of the country at the time, but one that Jefferson never saw.[38]

A small study for the portrait indicates that at some point Sully had thoughts of placing Jefferson in a more complex setting with a background narrative, not unlike what he created for his *Lafayette*. The study is very loosely painted, but the figure of Jefferson is recognizable and comparable to the final West Point version. The pose is similar, and the long coat, although closed, is essentially the same. Here a sheaf of papers replaces the rolled document, and they are moved from the left to the right hand. The most notable difference is the setting, busy with other figures. Men stand behind Jefferson, and a crowd is gathered in front of what appears to be an outdoor portico. It seems likely that this may have been Sully's initial idea for the composition, perhaps executed at Monticello but then rejected.

How Sully came to select the House chamber as the appropriate setting can only be surmised. Certainly many links existed between Jefferson's presidency and the House of Representatives, including the vote for the funding of the United States Military Academy in 1802. The new Hall of the House of Representatives had been reopened in 1819, and at the time Sully was completing his *Jefferson* in 1822, interest was being generated in the new House chamber by the work of a fellow artist, Samuel F. B. Morse. It was the subject of a large and complex painting by Morse that depicted a nighttime session of the House and included miniature but recognizable portraits of many of the congressmen. Morse had been given studio space in the Capitol itself; he wrote to his wife in January 1822 that "I find the picture becoming the subject of much conversation, and every day gives me greater encouragement to believe that it will be more popular than any picture heretofore exhibited." A few weeks later, Samuel Harrison Smith's *National Intelligencer* described Morse's rendering of the chamber interior "mathematically correct."[39]

It is probable that Sully would have been aware of the attention being given Morse's work. This could have influenced his decision to use the new House chamber as the setting for his commission, or it is equally possible that he and Jefferson discussed various settings. The two men seem to have enjoyed discussions about architecture during Sully's stay at Monticello, and the newly completed House chamber would have been of interest to Jefferson. Sully's obvious familiarity with the detail and placement of the columns and the drapery of the room suggest that he had visited the site. The final portrait, with its simplified composition and classical setting, became a much stronger work. The focus rests completely upon Jefferson.

Jefferson never saw the completed full-length portrait. Sully finished the West Point commission in May 1822, but the earliest known engraving was not produced until 1834. Would it have fulfilled Jefferson's hopes for an appropriate and enduring likeness? He never mentioned the portrait, but his granddaughter Ellen expressed her views in a letter to her cousin shortly after Sully left Monticello. She believed that he had "succeeded admirably." The area around Jefferson's mouth and chin constituted the only shortcoming, "but the painter seems to be aware of this defect, and will endeavor to correct it." She predicted that the finished full-length portrait "will probably be the best representation existing of one to whom future ages must look back with gratitude and admiration."[40]

Approximately 120 people paid to see the completed full-length portrait during the ten days that Sully displayed it in his Philadelphia gallery. In his journal he noted that he made about $30 from the showing, and as the usual price of admission to the gallery was twenty-five cents per person, over one hundred Philadelphians must have had the means and the desire to see the portrait of the former president. Sully's matter-of-fact records give no indication whether he considered the showing successful, but on May 20, 1822, he packaged portrait and frame for the trip to West Point.[41]

The reaction of one contemporary viewer provides a better gauge of the success of the Sully-Jefferson collaboration. In 1823, when James Fenimore Cooper visited West Point, this son of a staunch Federalist opponent of Jefferson's was not particularly eager to see the newly installed painting. "I would have gone twice as far," Cooper wrote, "to see the picture of almost any other man." Nevertheless, he was assured by men whom he respected that the merits of the painting made a visit to the West Point library worthwhile. A member of Cooper's traveling party, British theatre comedian Charles Matthews, described the painting as "one of the finest portraits he had ever beheld." While the assessment of Matthews, an avid art collector, focused on the execution of the work, Cooper reacted more to the image of Jefferson and his memories of bitter partisan politics. For him the name of Jefferson had always been associated with "political heresy," but after viewing the portrait he conceded to a change of opinion. Cooper admitted, "I saw nothing but Jefferson, standing before me . . . a gentleman, appearing in all republican simplicity, with a grace and ease on the canvas, that to me seemed unrivalled." The Sully-Jefferson collaboration proved in at least this one instance to have overcome political biases and presented a figure appropriate to the legacy of a founder of the American republic. In Cooper's assessment, Jefferson had been positioned for posterity "appearing in all republican simplicity."[42]

Notes

1. Jared Mansfield to TJ, 26 January 1821, Special Collections, U.S. Military Academy Library, West Point, N.Y.

2. TJ to Mansfield, 26 January 1821, ibid.

3. TJ to John Holmes, 22 April 1820, ibid. See also TJ to Albert Gallatin, 26 December 1820, *TJW*, 1447–50; TJ to James Breckinridge, 15 February 1821, ibid., 1452–54; Peter S. Onuf, *Jefferson's Empire: The Language of American Nationhood* (Charlottesville, Va., 2000), esp. chap. 4.

4. For an excellent discussion of Jefferson's views on history and his personal legacy, see Frank D. Cogliano, *Thomas Jefferson: Reputation and Legacy* (Charlottesville, Va., 2006).

5. Cogliano, *Thomas Jefferson*, 50–52; John Marshall, *The Life of George Washington*, ed. Robert Faulkner and Paul Carrese (Indianapolis, Ind., 2000), xii, xv, 366; Henry Lee III, *Memoirs of the War in the Southern Department*, 2 vols. (Philadelphia, 1812), as cited in Cogliano, *Thomas Jefferson*, 62.

6. TJ to Elbridge Gerry, 26 January 1799, *TJP*, 30:647.

7. TJ to James Madison, 20 September 1787, ibid., 8:535.

8. TJ to Joseph Delaplaine, 3 May 1814, TJ Papers, Lib. Cong.

9. Brandon Brame Fortune, "Portraits of Virtue and Genius: Pantheons of Worthies and Public Portraiture in the Early American Republic, 1780–1820" (Ph.D diss., University of North Carolina at Chapel Hill, 1987), 1–14, 34; David Hackett Fischer, *Liberty and Freedom: A Visual History of America's Founding Ideas* (New York, 2005), 178.

10. Susan R. Stein, *The Worlds of Thomas Jefferson at Monticello* (New York, 1993), 122–37 and 221–23; TJ to John Trumbull, 15 February 1788, *TJP*, 14:561.

11. Fortune, "Portraits of Virtue and Genius," 15.

12. Benjamin Henry Latrobe to TJ, 19 May 1811, *TJP:RS*, 3:625.

13. Thomas Sully (for the Society of Artists of the United States) to TJ, 22 December 1811, ibid., 4:355–56.

14. TJ to Thomas Sully, 8 January 1812, ibid., 407; Thomas Sully to TJ, 6 January 1812, ibid., 398–400; TJ to Thomas Sully, 25 January 1812, ibid., 459–60.

15. Thomas Sully, "Recollections of an Old Painter," in *Hours at Home: A Popular Monthly of Instruction and Recreation*, No. 10 (November 1869): 69–74; Thomas Jefferson, *Autobiography*, 1821, *TJW*, 41.

16. TJ to Arthur Brockenbrough, 28 March 1821, TJ Papers, Special Collections, University of Virginia Library.

17. Sully to TJ, 6 April 1821, TJ Papers, Lib. Cong.; TJ to Sully, 17 April 1821, ibid.; William B. O'Neal, *Jefferson's Fine Arts Library: His Selections for the University of Virginia Together with His Own Architectural Books* (Charlottesville, Va., 1976), 106–8.

18. Thomas Sully, *A Register of Portraits Painted by Thomas Sully, 1801–1871*, ed. Charles Henry Hart (Philadelphia, 1909), 114; John Vaughn to TJ, 14 March 1821, TJ Papers, Massachusetts Historical Society, Boston.

19. F. Nivelon, "Rudiments of Genteel Behavior" (1737), as quoted in Robin Simon, *The Portrait in Britain and America* (Oxford, England, 1987), 76.

20. Thomas Sully, *Hints to Young Painters and the Process of Portrait Painting* (Philadelphia, 1873; reprint, New York, 1965), 15.

21. T. Kosciuszko to TJ, before 5 May 1798, *TJP*, 30:331.

22. TJ to Martha Jefferson Randolph, 27 December 1798, ibid., 605; TJ to Martha Jefferson Randolph, 4 November 1815, *Family Letters of Thomas Jefferson*, eds. Edwin M. Betts and James A. Bear Jr. (Charlottesville, 1986), 411.

23. Ellen Wayles Randolph to Martha Jefferson Randolph, 5 January 1816, Ellen Wayles Randolph Coolidge Correspondence, Special Collections, University of Virginia Library.

24. Margaret Bayard Smith, "The Fur Cloak, A Reminesence," Margaret Bayard Smith Papers, Lib. Cong.

25. Jane Hollins Randolph to Thomas Jefferson Randolph, [?] January 1837, Edgehill-Randolph Papers, Special Collections, University of Virginia Library.

26. TJ to Kosciuszko, 21 February 1799, *TJP*, 31:52.

27. Martha Burke, *List of Monticello Relics, 1907–08*, Trist-Burke Family Papers 1825–1936, Special Collections, University of Virginia Library.

28. TJ to William Duane, 25 July 1811, *TJP:RS*, 4:56.

29. Thomas Sully, *A Register of Portraits*, 91–92.

30. William Plumer, *William Plumer's Proceedings in the United States Senate, 1803–1807*, ed. Everett Somerville Brown (New York, 1923), 211; Augustus John Foster, *Jeffersonian America*, ed. Richard Beale Davis (San Marino, Calif., 1954), 15.

31. For the history of the color black in men's clothing see John Harvey, *Men in Black* (Chicago, 1995), 41–71, and Diane de Marly, *Fashion for Men: An Illustrated History* (New York, 1985), 49–53, 77–91.

32. Aileen Ribeiro, *Fashion in the French Revolution* (London, 1988), 45–46.

33. Harvey, *Men in Black*, 26–28; reference to men in their "black uniforms" is from William Irving, James Kirke Paulding, and Washington Irving, *Salmagundi*, No. 1, 24 January 1807 (printed as a collection, New York, 1860), 28.

34. Bernard Mayo, "A Peppercorn for Mr. Jefferson," *Virginia Quarterly Review* (Spring 1943): 224; *Commercial Advertiser* (New York), 21 July 1802.

35. Nathaniel William Wraxall, *Memoirs of Sir Nathaniel William Wraxall*, ed. Henry B. Wheatley, 5 vols. (London, 1884), 1:99.

36. Daniel Webster, "Memorandum of Mr. Jefferson's Conversations," in *Private Correspondence of Daniel Webster*, ed. Fletcher Webster (Boston, 1857), 1:364–66, reprinted in *Visitors to Monticello*, ed. Merrill D. Peterson (Charlottesville, Va., 1989), 97–99.

37. Sully, *Hints to Young Painters*, 31.

38. Verification of the column as from the Hall of the House of Representatives obtained from the Architect of the Capitol, William Allen, 5 July 2006. For further discussion of Latrobe's design of the Capitol, see William C. Allen, *History of the United States Capitol: A Chronicle of Design, Construction, and Politics* (Washington, D.C., 2001).

39. Samuel F. B. Morse to Lucretia Pickering Walker Morse, 5 January 1822, Samuel F. B. Morse Papers, Lib. Cong., Bound Vol. 24 January 1821–8 December 1823, 129–31; *National Intelligencer*, 16 February 1822, as quoted in William Kloss, *Samuel F.B. Morse* (New York, 1988), 69–70.

40. Ellen Wayles Randolph to Francis Eppes, 5 April 1821, Eppes Collection, Special Collections, University of Virginia Library.

41. Thomas Sully, "Thomas Sully's Journal," microfilm copy of the transcription held at the New York Public Library.

42. James Fenimore Cooper to Charles Kitchel Gardner, c. 24 April–17 June 1823, in *The Letters and Journals of James Fenimore Cooper*, ed. James Franklin Beard, 6 vols. (Cambridge, Mass., 1960–68), 1:95–97.

Afterword

Light, Liberty, and Slavery

JOYCE APPLEBY

R EADING THIS CLUSTER OF FINE ESSAYS MADE ME AWARE THAT A NEW generation of Jefferson scholars has arrived. It has fascinated me to see how they are taking possession of this most interesting forebear of ours. People are always saying something is a great pleasure, but I want to begin by stressing that it really is a great pleasure to learn that there is a fresh group of historians studying Jefferson and bringing to bear on his career questions that their generation—and their generation alone—can ask.

I was amused years ago when I read a quip from Millicent Sowerby, one of Jefferson's great bibliographers. Noting the practical indebtedness of scholars to Jefferson, she wrote that "one of the really outstanding achievements & contributions to humanity, is the number of people, including of course myself, whom Jefferson has helped to support since his death."[1] Evidently he is still doing it.

When people ask why we need a new history of Jefferson or the Monroe Doctrine or the Depression, I explain that history is not just about the past— it is a conversation between the past and present because the people in the present bring a fresh set of questions to the past. All historical scholarship begins with people's questions. And those questions are generated out of their experiences, unique to their time and to the years in which they matured and the state of knowledge when they became historians.

Because my comments focus on this notion of a new cohort of Jefferson scholars I want to repeat the point. Vast numbers of things happen in the past—as they do in the present, which is about to become the past. We are only curious about a subset of those events and developments. Because we have been studying founding fathers for seven or eight generations, which means introducing the questions of seven or eight successive groups of scholars, we know a lot about them, but the studies will go on, marked by the curiosity of each cohort.

I find in these essays two consistent features and one surprise. As befits historians doing graduate work in the past decade and a half, the authors are more interested in culture than politics, economics, or diplomacy. In truth, historians have not been interested in diplomacy for fifty years. Although this collection is subtitled "the power of knowledge," the essays reveal more an interest in Jeffersonian rhetoric than in his knowledge per se. By that I mean Jefferson's splendid use of words to convey the beauty, dignity, and hope that he invested in learning and teaching.

What captures the authors' imagination is Jefferson's imagination—his vision for the new nation and its westward expansion, his understanding of learning, of architecture, of human nature, and his passion for books, his thoughts on the American people and democracy, upon religion and morality, and the source and importance of human talents. This is a great place to start studying Jefferson, but this weft in the nation's cultural fabric needs the warp of politics to be complete.

The second consistency I see is a reaction to the group of Jefferson scholars of the previous period—those who did their graduate work in the 1970s and 1980s. It was their lot to reconcile the nation to the founding fathers' deep immersion in slavery and the problems created when the Mason-Dixon line went from surveyors' boundary to one between free and slave labor in the new United States after northern laws abolished slavery. Their work signaled a critical shift in American history—one not always welcome to a public used to avoiding the subject of slaves. Jefferson, the slaveholder, appears in the shadows of these essays, even when his rhetorical flourishes inadvertently bring to the reader's mind the incongruity between what he is saying and his status as the holder of people as slaves. I do not think Jeffersonian scholarship needs to be like a stuck needle on a record (for those who remember phonograph records) but rather that it should be noted when a contradiction occurs between what Jefferson says and does and his experience as the owner, at any given time, of over 200 men, women, and children.

Christine and Rob McDonald have convincingly offered a new interpretation of why Jefferson was interested in establishing West Point. They offer an important corrective to the standard interpretation. Jefferson got beaten up before and after the Civil War for his advocacy of state's rights, but Jefferson was actually one of the great nationalists in American history. His was both a generous and a limited nationalism: generous in promoting an expansive, peaceful development of the continent; limited in his marked preference for the white race. Nowhere is this more evident than in the letter that Virginia Governor Jefferson wrote to the revolutionary frontier leader, George Rogers Clark: "If we are to wage a campaign against these Indians the end proposed should be their extermination, or their removal beyond the lakes of the Illinois River. The same world will scarcely do for them and us."[2] Jefferson claimed to oppose fiercely the mixing of races, which makes his probable fathering of children by Sally Hemings more puzzling.

Jefferson took a pretty strong line on nature, as many of these essays detail. Just as Newton's laws were based upon the uniform reactions of matter, social laws for Jefferson rested upon a universal human nature. This premise encouraged a critical attitude toward difference. In Jefferson's thinking, women were naturally different, blacks were naturally different, and native America suffered from attachment to a backward way of life. He chose nature over nurture to explain the apparently different behavior of women, blacks, and American Indians. And their differences placed these groups outside the liberal thrust of Jefferson's "empire of liberty."

Frank Shuffelton gives us Jefferson the "colporteur," a human link in the chain of book-learning. Like the McDonalds, Shuffelton emphasizes the importance of the future. This signals a rejection of the idea of Jefferson, popular among historians twenty-five years ago, as the carrier of the classical republican tradition. Edmund Randolph noted, Shuffelton reminds us, that "it constituted a part of Mr. Jefferson's pride to run before the times in which he lived," adding that "he had been ambitious to collect a library, not merely amassing a number of books, but distinguishing them in subordination to every art and science . . . to present to genius the scaffolding, upon which its future eminence might be built, and to approve the restless appetite which is too apt to seize the mere gatherer of books." Jefferson's success as a lawyer was based on extensive reading in the law. Comparing Jefferson to sometime rival Patrick Henry, Randolph observed that "Mr. Jefferson drew copiously from the depths of the law, Mr. Henry from the recesses of the human heart." Maybe that explains Jefferson's contempt for Henry.

Shuffelton does an excellent job of exploring Jefferson's imagery about knowledge—variously described as "a machine oriented toward the future" and "the world that progress might bring to us." I was interested in Jefferson's negative attitude toward American youth going to Europe, whatever the nation. He conceded that they might "learn to speak the language, but put this in the scale against the other things he will learn and evils he is sure to acquire and it will be found too light." "I have always disapproved of a European education for our youth from theory," Jefferson wrote, "I now do it from inspection." The Europe that Jefferson found attractive, Shuffelton notes, was suitable only for fully formed republicans. I think that this is coded language discussing sex. The looseness of sexual morals among the European aristocracy shocked both Jefferson and John Adams. European travel was not so much for fully formed republicans as mature men who had passed through the stormy years of young manhood—unless they happened to be John Quincy Adams.

Brian Steele's "The Yeomanry of the United States Are Not the *Canaille* of Paris" has undertaken a comprehensive examination of the special qualities that Jefferson thought Americans had that made them fit for self-rule as well as the powerful undercurrent of skepticism about the capacity of people to wisely govern themselves and an ambivalence about the relationship of democratic majorities to dissenting minorities and individual liberty. It is important to remember, however, that the popular distrust of democracy antedates the French Revolution and was deeply embedded in the thinking of eighteenth-century men and women.

Steele might overstate Jefferson's reservations about the French and their revolution. As late as 1793, he excoriated William Short for losing faith in the French Revolution when he had written Jefferson from Paris of his distress at the violent direction it was taking. Jefferson reminded him that "the liberty of the whole earth was depending on the issue of the contest." Better to see "half the earth desolated" than to witness the French Revolution fail. "Were there but an Adam and an Eve left in every country, and left free," he wrote, "it would be better than as it now is."[3] At that time, Jacobins had not yet begun to desolate their enemies. The Federalists' supercilious attitude toward the French probably prevented Jefferson from being more critical.

What comes across in Steele's essay is how much Jefferson reflected the prejudices of his age and class. His strictures against the suitability of Latin Americans and French for self-government came straight from Protestant prejudices against Catholics. What Jefferson said about the "ignorance & bigotry of the mass" of the people and his doubt of "their capacity to understand and to support a free government" would have been repeated by almost all Americans then, as would references to the "degrading ignorance into which their priests and kings have sunk them" and their disqualification from "the maintenance or even knowledge of their rights."

When Steele moves to Jefferson's observations about Romans, bells ring in my head. Listen to Jefferson: Romans "were so demoralized and depraved as to be incapable of exercising a wholesome controul" over their government. "Steeped in corruption vice and venality as the whole nation was," he asked, "what could even Cicero, Cato, Brutus have done, had it been referred to them to establish a good government for their country?" The people needed deep training to understand "what is right and what wrong" as well as long inculcation "in habits of virtue" to "render" them "a sure basis for the structure of order and good government." I think Jefferson's real subjects here were the slaves that his French friends thought should be freed and incorporated into the American polity.

Jefferson lived on the tightrope of hope and despair. If you hope much you open yourself to disappointment. John Adams, George Washington, and James Madison don't get on that tightrope. Not having raised our expectations with affirmations of natural rights, these other leaders have not disappointed us. Jefferson's buying, selling, and owning of enslaved men and women has disturbed the pages of our history as no other's has. We want founding fathers who summon us to a civic calling higher than going to the polls and paying taxes. Jefferson did that; his words continue to soar above the banalities of daily life, acting as both inspiration and goad. But he has elevated us and let us down at the same time. That Jefferson carries the odium of slavery for his generation is a wry tribute to the voice for America's better self.

Cameron Addis in "The Jefferson Gospel" does a splendid job of following the tortuous route Jefferson traveled in his quest for religious toleration. Even bolder was his promotion of secular education. Jefferson suffered as many old people do in being overtaken by unexpected developments launched by a younger generation with different concerns and sensibilities. As he was pursuing a curriculum of ethics rather than Christian dogma in the first two decades of the nineteenth century, major evangelical awakenings erupted on the campuses of Yale, Williams, Middlebury, Princeton, and Dartmouth. The *North American Review* may have noted favorably the revolutionary character of the Rockfish Gap Report in 1820, but the University of Virginia's outline of a curriculum devoid of denominational content definitely went against the spirit of the times.

Considering that major universities throughout the United States and Europe maintained their religious foundations well into the nineteenth century, Jefferson's plan represented a dramatic departure. Edward Everett, writing in the *Review,* told the journal's readers that they would be gratified to view portions of the report since this was the "first instance, *in the world,* of a university without any such [orthodox religious] provision." Others had implemented nondenominational curriculums before but, as Addis tells us, like the founders' experiment in representative democracy, Jefferson had few successful precedents to build on in erecting an Enlightenment college.

After Thomas Paine died in 1809, younger college administrators focused their attention on Jefferson, the infidel they considered Paine's heir apparent. Their new mission was to stamp out all but the most watered-down versions of Enlightenment philosophy on America's campuses. The venerable Sage of Monticello emerged as the foremost public symbol of discredited radicalism. Never one to back away from a fight—with words—Jefferson claimed that these men were "pant[ing] to reestablish the Holy Inquisition" by challenging his plans for the University of Virginia. Following Franklin, who believed that if you sifted out all the particularities of the major religions you would be left with "a universal constellation of values that 'all sects could agree on,'" Jefferson zeroed in on the discrepancies in dogma and superfluous details.

It is interesting to consider that Jefferson also argued the proof of God from intelligent design. Addis obviously approves of Jefferson's crusade for a religious education that transcended the doctrinaire and expanded the mind. But what are we to make of Jefferson's intolerance of the Christian faith of his fellow Americans? Successive groups of historians have shared Jefferson's preferences, and this has prevented them from looking at the underside of Jefferson's campaign for supplanting religious teachings with ethical ones. At the very least, it reveals the limits of Jefferson's famous tolerance.

Craig Reynolds's " 'Presenting to Them Models for Their Imitation': Thomas Jefferson's Reformation of American Architecture" is such a model of clarity that I shall long remember his learned discussion of Jefferson as a lover of classical buildings and his insistence upon using materials for permanent construction of these models. His careful analysis of Jefferson's scattered writings on architecture and his building plans has enabled him to dispel several myths about Jefferson and the building styles he favored and promoted, such as his supposed desire to return to architecture's origins or adopt the French avant-garde's forms, or even create a totally new American style. Reynolds draws attention to Virginia's courthouses, upon which Jefferson bestowed great interest and hope. From this close study, he concludes that Jefferson's political and social goals harmonized with the principles of architecture itself.

Richard Samuelson argues in his essay on "Natural Aristocracy and the Problem of Knowledge" that the key to understanding Jefferson's thoughts on these subjects is his belief that men could achieve a great deal of certainty about nature and that clarity and certainty were the keys to Jefferson's hopes for the future, nowhere more so than in his hopes for natural aristocracy. Samuelson carefully explains how Jefferson understood Bacon, Newton, and Locke to be "the three greatest men that have ever lived" and how, as Bacon understood, promotion of the scientific method had political implications.

Jefferson, according to Samuelson, "never entirely escaped from the eugenic implications of his belief in natural aristocracy"—an idea Jefferson evoked with the rather frightening image of finding worthy students "raked from the rubbish." Jefferson returned to this theme in his famous final letter. "The general spread of the light of science," he wrote, "has already laid open to every view the palpable truth, that the mass of mankind has not been born with saddles on their backs, nor a favored few booted and spurred, ready to ride them legitimately, by the grace of God." Think what a remarkable statement that is from an old man who has owned enslaved men and women most of his life. Samuelson concludes that Jefferson's solution to the problem of reconciling natural rights with natural aristocracy was to trivialize politics.

I would interpret that differently. Jefferson lived at a time when the concept of society had just begun to take hold. In the thinking of Thomas Hobbes and John Locke there were two human situations: the state of nature and a political order. Throughout the eighteenth century, the voluntary realm of civic associations and market transactions had stirred an awareness of a third situation: society. Thomas Paine opened *Common Sense* noting that people often confound society and government when they are very different, one being created by our wants, the other through our wickedness. Civil society provided new options to men who wished to be engaged in public affairs, but not in politics. After all, Jefferson had to ask four or five men before he could get someone to accept the post of secretary of the navy.

Johann Neem, in "To Diffuse Knowledge More Generally through the Mass of the People," deals with similar themes. He calls upon contemporary theorists like the late Pierre Bourdieu, Amartya Sen, and Martha Nussbaum in his subtle account of Jefferson's effort to plumb the depths of human desire and purpose. Using the concepts of cultural and social capital, Neem, like others, has accepted at face value Jefferson's desire "to guarantee each citizen access to cultural capital." Perhaps the key word here is citizen, but this Jeffersonian goal needs examination in the context of his connection with slavery. We may never know how Jefferson reconciled his various positions about human beings, but to ignore the subject is to slip back into the long tradition of avoiding the unpleasant task of explaining how a slaveholding nation was founded on promises of liberty.

West Point commissioned the Sully portrait of Thomas Jefferson that now hangs in its new library building, Thomas Jefferson Hall. The Thomas Jefferson Foundation, which owns and interprets Monticello, gave the academy a replica of the furniture in Jefferson's study to honor the building's opening, so it was especially satisfying to learn from Gaye Wilson in "Recording History: The Thomas Sully Portrait of Thomas Jefferson" how quickly Jefferson seized the opportunity to influence history through art once the academy had asked him to pose for Sully. The invitation, we learn, came in 1821 at a time of heightened anxiety in part because of his debts, but also because of the publication of pro-Federalist accounts of the nation's first decade and the angry debates about slavery occasioned by the entrance of the first state carved from his "Empire of Liberty."

Wilson's close reading of the portrait certainly pleases as does her account of Sully's week at Monticello working on the portrait. Jefferson's choice of footwear with shoe strings instead of buckles denoted him as an egalitarian with affinities to the spirit of the French Revolution. Jefferson was the first president to abandon buckles as he was also the first to trade in the courtly bow for a handshake. In many ways the consummate statesman, Jefferson never seems to have missed an opportunity to promote the political ideals that have turned his name into a term of reference for rights and democracy. Having aroused our curiosity about how the Sully portrait mitigated Jefferson's anxieties by giving him yet another means of instilling his principles, Wilson points not only toward details such as Sully's rendering of Jefferson's shoes but also to the color of his suit, the document in his hand, and the column next to which he stands—all of which placed him on the side of common people rather than their self-proclaimed social superiors.

I note that "yeoman" is still evoked as a resonating concept for Jefferson. This comes as a personal disappointment since I have written—convincingly, I thought—an article that demonstrated that "yeoman" was not a term in Jefferson's vocabulary. He referred to individuals, husbandmen, persons, and citizens, but never yeomen. "Yeomanry" enjoyed usage, but not yeoman, as Noah Webster himself noted. Referring to yeomen came into historical literature with the republican revisionism of the 1960s and 1970s.

I mentioned at the outset that I found in these excellent essays two common features and one surprise. The features are the salience of culture in the topics chosen to pursue and the neglect of Jefferson's deep involvement practically and intellectually in slavery. The surprise for me was the alloyed favor the authors found with Jefferson and his ideas. I do not mean that the essays are not sophisticated. They are. Instead, I mean that they give unstinting admiration to their subject.

Jefferson was not a profound thinker, and his lapses deserve inspection. I offer one example. For Jefferson, almost every moral question contained a scientific solution, at the very least a scientific-sounding solution. Reflecting on the population pressures from which his contemporary, Thomas Robert Malthus, had drawn such grim conclusions, he claimed with some hyperbole that American crops grew exponentially. He envisioned great benefits from the fact that Europe was running out of food. Indeed the fortuitous fertility of America's farm acreage enabled him to square the circle of self-interest and community welfare. "So invariably do the laws of nature create our duties and interests," he wrote the French economist, J. B. Say, "that when they seem to be at variance, we ought to suspect some fallacy in our reasonings."[4]

Two possible explanations for the approach taken to Jefferson in this collection occur to me. Perhaps this cohort is reacting to the harsh treatment of Jefferson from older writers' studies, such as Conor Cruise O'Brien's *The Long Affair* and Garry Wills's *The Negro President*. Perhaps the trashing Jefferson has suffered recently has led to a preference for developing his ideas rather than speculating about hidden agendas in them. The other possibility is the impact that 9/11 and the Iraq War may have had upon younger scholars. Perhaps there is a subtle pressure to circle the wagons of American history when our country is taking such a beating in the world court of opinion.

Let me end with a puzzle about Jefferson that I hope some scholar will take up. There have been few men, entrusted by their peers with positions of responsibility, who have seriously entertained as many subversive ideas as Thomas Jefferson. How did he manage this? What does it tell us about the Virginia gentry or Jefferson's personality? Douglass Adair used to tell his students that James Madison almost had a nervous breakdown living among fellow planters whose principal pursuits were cock fighting, horseback riding, and dancing. Why did Jefferson appeal to such men?

It occurs to me that during the colonial period members of the local elite had to protect themselves vigilantly from imperial authority and so concluded that political talent was too valuable to waste. Perhaps, but maybe not. I do not have an answer, which is why I am calling it a puzzle. We have studies of Jefferson's books and buildings, writings and women, positions and politics. Why not a study of the many elections for high office that he won?

Notes

1. "Thomas Jefferson and His Library," *Papers of the Bibliographical Society of America* 50 (1956): 213.

2. TJ to George Rogers Clark, 1 January 1780, *TJP*, 3:259.

3. TJ to William Short, 3 January 1793, ibid., 25:14.

4. TJ to Jean Baptiste Say, 1 February 1804, *TJW*, 1144.

Contributors

CAMERON ADDIS is Professor of History at Austin Community College. He taught previously as a Visiting Professor at Texas A & M University. His first book, *Jefferson's Vision for Education* (2003), covers the founding of the University of Virginia, a subject on which he has also written for the forthcoming *Companion to Thomas Jefferson*. He received his Ph.D. from the University of Texas in 2000.

JOYCE APPLEBY, Professor Emerita, University of California, Los Angeles, studies the changing social theories about human nature, politics, and economic development that accompanied the modern transformation of Europe and America. She is past president of the American Historical Association, the Organization of American Historians, and the Society for Historians of the Early American Republic. Her most recent publications are *Inheriting the Revolution: The First Generation of Americans* (2000), *Thomas Jefferson* (2003), *A Restless Past: History and the American Public* (2004), and *The Relentless Revolution: A History of Capitalism* (2010).

CHRISTINE COALWELL MCDONALD is History Coordinator at the Tuxedo Park School in Tuxedo Park, New York. A former research associate at Monticello's Robert H. Smith International Center for Jefferson Studies, she is a graduate of the American University and St. John's College in Annapolis, Maryland. She is coauthor (with Jennings L. Wagoner Jr.) of "Mr. Jefferson's Academy: An Educational Interpretation," which appeared in *Thomas Jefferson's Military Academy: Founding West Point* (2004).

Robert M. S. McDonald is Associate Professor of History at the United States Military Academy in West Point, New York. Editor of *Thomas Jefferson's Military Academy: Founding West Point* (2004), he is completing a book to be titled *Confounding Father: Thomas Jefferson and the Politics of Personality.*

Johann N. Neem is Associate Professor of History at Western Washington University in Bellingham, Washington. He is the author of *Creating a Nation of Joiners: Democracy and Civil Society in Early National Massachusetts* (2008). His work has appeared in *History and Theory,* the *Journal of Interdisciplinary History,* and the *Journal of the Early Republic.*

Andrew Jackson O'Shaughnessy is Saunders Director of the Robert H. Smith International Center for Jefferson Studies at Monticello and Professor of History at the University of Virginia. He taught at Eton College in England before becoming Visiting Professor at Southern Methodist University and then Professor of History at the University of Wisconsin–Oshkosh. He is the author of *An Empire Divided: The American Revolution and the British Caribbean* (2000) and coeditor of *Old World, New World: America and Europe in the Age of Jefferson* (2010).

Craig A. Reynolds is an art history Ph.D. student at Virginia Commonwealth University. He has held research grants from the Thomas Jefferson Library, Monticello, and the Virginia Department of Historic Resources, and has presented at the Virginia Historical Society, the Savannah College of Art and Design, the United States Military Academy, and the University of Virginia.

Richard A. Samuelson is Assistant Professor of History at California State University, San Bernardino. He is currently completing a study of John Adams's constitutional thought to be titled *John Adams and the Republic of Law.* He has published several essays on various members of the Adams family, on the politics and political thought of revolutionary America, and on John Adams and Thomas Jefferson.

Frank Shuffelton was Professor Emeritus of English at the University of Rochester. The author of *Thomas Hooker, 1586–1647* (1977), *Thomas Jefferson:*

A Comprehensive, Annotated Bibliography of Writings about Him (1826–1980) (1983), and *Thomas Jefferson, 1981–1990: An Annotated Bibliography* (1992), he published editions of Jefferson's *Notes on the State of Virginia* (1999) and *The Letters of John and Abigail Adams* (2004) and edited *A Mixed Race: Ethnicity in Early America* (1993) and *The Cambridge Companion to Thomas Jefferson* (2008). He served as president of the Northeast American Society for Eighteenth Century Studies and was winner of the Modern Language Association's Distinguished Scholar of Early American Literature Award.

BRIAN STEELE is Assistant Professor of History at the University of Alabama at Birmingham. He is the author of "Thomas Jefferson's Gender Frontier" (*Journal of American History*, June 2008) and is completing a book on the problem of nationhood in Jefferson's thought and politics.

GAYE WILSON is a historian at the Robert H. Smith International Center for Jefferson Studies at Monticello. She holds an M.F.A. from the University of Texas at Austin and is currently pursuing a Ph.D. from the University of Edinburgh. The author of several publications and conference presentations, her current research focuses on the image of Thomas Jefferson as preserved in his life portraits and how these images reflect his personal and political ambitions.

INDEX

The abbreviations "TJ" and "USMA" stand for Thomas Jefferson and United States Military Academy, respectively. Italicized page numbers refer to illustrations.

RECENT BOOKS IN THE JEFFERSONIAN AMERICA SERIES

Douglas Bradburn
The Citizenship Revolution: Politics and the Creation of the American Union, 1774–1804

Clarence E. Walker
Mongrel Nation: The America Begotten by Thomas Jefferson and Sally Hemings

Timothy Mason Roberts
Distant Revolutions: 1848 and the Challenge to American Exceptionalism

Peter J. Kastor and François Weil, editors
Empires of the Imagination: Transatlantic Histories of the Louisiana Purchase

Eran Shalev
Rome Reborn on Western Shores: Historical Imagination and the Creation of the American Republic

Leonard J. Sadosky
Revolutionary Negotiations: Indians, Empires, and Diplomats in the Founding of America

Philipp Ziesche
Cosmopolitan Patriots: Americans in Paris in the Age of Revolution

Leonard J. Sadosky, Peter Nicolaisen, Peter S. Onuf, and Andrew J. O'Shaughnessy, editors
Old World, New World: America and Europe in the Age of Jefferson

Sam W. Haynes
Unfinished Revolution: The American Republic in a British World, 1815–1850

Michal Jan Rozbicki
Culture and Liberty in the Age of the American Revolution

Ellen Holmes Pearson
Remaking Custom: Law and Identity in the Early American Republic

Seth Cotlar
Tom Paine's America: The Rise and Fall of Transatlantic Radicalism

John Craig Hammond and Matthew Mason, editors
Contesting Slavery: The Politics of Bondage and Freedom in the New American Nation

Ruma Chopra
Unnatural Rebellion: Loyalists in New York City during the Revolution

Maurizio Valsania
The Limits of Optimism: Thomas Jefferson's Dualistic Enlightenment

Peter S. Onuf and Nicholas P. Cole, editors
Thomas Jefferson, the Classical World, and Early America

Hannah Spahn
Thomas Jefferson, Time, and History

Lucia Stanton
"Those Who Labor for My Happiness": Slavery at Thomas Jefferson's Monticello

Robert M. S. McDonald, editor
Light and Liberty: Thomas Jefferson and the Power of Knowledge